CATO MAIOR DE SENECTUTE

M. Tulli Ciceronis

CATO MAIOR DE SENECTUTE

WITH INTRODUCTION AND NOTES

By JAMES S. REID, M.L.

FELLOW OF GONVILLE AND CAIUS COLLEGE, CAMBRIDGE, UNIVERSITY LECTURER
IN ROMAN HISTORY

American Edition Revised

By FRANCIS W. KELSEY

UNIVERSITY OF MICHIGAN

Boston

ALLYN AND BACON

1896

UNIVERSITY PRESS:
JOHN WILSON AND SON, CAMBRIDGE.

PREFACE.

THREE years ago Mr. James S. Reid, of Gonville and Caius
College, Cambridge, prepared for the Syndics of the University Press editions of Cicero's *Cato Maior de Senectute*
and *Laelius de Amicitia.* The thorough and accurate
scholarship displayed, especially in the elucidation of the
Latinity, immediately won for the books a cordial reception ;
and since then they have gained a permanent place in the
esteem of English scholars.

The present volume has the full authorization of Mr.
Reid, and was prepared with the design of presenting to
American students, in a form best adapted to their use,
the results of his work. The Text remains substantially
that of Mr. Reid ; while mention is made in the notes of
the most important variations in readings and orthography
from other editions. The Introductions have been recast,
with some enlargement ; the analyses of the subject-
matter in particular have been entirely remodelled. The
Notes have been in some instances reduced, in others
amplified, — especially by the addition of references to the
standard treatises on grammar, history, and philosophy.
It was at first the intention of the American editor to

indicate by some mark the matter due to himself; but as this could hardly be done without marring the appearance of the page, and thus introducing a source of confusion to the student, it was not attempted. In the work of revision free use of the principal German and English editions has been made.

To some the notes of the present edition may appear too copious. The aim throughout, however, has been not simply to give aid on difficult points, but to call attention to the finer usages of the Latin, and to add also whatever explanation seemed necessary to a clear understanding of the subject-matter. Latin scholarship which shall be at the same time broad and accurate, including not only a mastery of the language but also a comprehensive view of the various phases of Roman life and thought, will, it is believed, be best assured by the slow and careful reading of some portions of the literature and by the rapid survey of others. Certainly of the shorter Latin classics few would more fully repay close and careful study of both language and thought than these charming colloquies on Old Age and Friendship. While almost faultless in expression, they embody in a remarkable degree that universal element which characterizes the literary masterpiece, and makes it the valued possession not merely of an age or a nation, but of all time.

FRANCIS W. KELSEY.

LAKE FOREST, ILL., May, 1882.

INTRODUCTION.

———•◦•———

I. CICERO AS A WRITER ON PHILOSOPHY.

(i.) STATE OF PHILOSOPHY IN CICERO'S TIME.

IN Philosophy the Romans originated nothing. Their energies in the earlier years of the state were wholly absorbed in organization and conquest. Resting in a stern and simple creed, they had little speculative interest in matters outside the hard routine of their daily life. But with the close of the Period of Conquest came a change. The influx of wealth from conquered provinces, the formation of large landed estates, the excessive employment of slave labor, and the consequent rise of a new aristocracy, prepared the way for a great revolution. The old religion lost its hold on the higher classes ; something was needed to take its place. With wealth and luxury came opportunity and desire for culture. Greece, with Art, Literature, and Philosophy fully developed and highly perfected, stood ready to instruct her rude conqueror.[1]

In Cicero's time the productive era of Greek Philosophy had well-nigh passed. Its tendency was less speculative, more ethical and practical than in the earlier time. There were four prominent schools, the New Academy, the Peripatetic, the Stoic, and the Epicurean. The supporters of the last-named advocated in Science the doctrine of the atom, in Ethics the pursuit of pleasure, in Religion the complete inactivity of the gods.

---

[1] Horace, Ep. 2, 1, 156 :—

> *Graecia capta ferum victorem cepit, et artes*
> *Intulit agresti Latio.*

The Stoics and Peripatetics were divided by comparatively un-important differences. In Ethics, considered by them as almost the whole of Philosophy, which was itself defined as 'the art of living', the main question between the two schools was the amount of importance to be attributed to Virtue, — the Stoics declaring that in comparison with Virtue all other things sink into absolute insignificance, while the Peripatetics maintained that these have a certain though infinitesimally small signifi-cance. The New Academy taught at this time no complete philosophical system. It simply proclaimed the view that in the field of knowledge certainty is unattainable, and that all the inquirer has to do is to balance probabilities one against the other. The New Academic, therefore, was free to accept any opinions which seemed to him to have the weight of probability on their side, but he was bound to be ready to abandon them when any-thing appeared which altered his views of the probabilities. He not only might be, but he could not help being, *eclectic;* that is, he chose such views promulgated by other schools as seemed to him at the moment to be most reasonable or probable. Cicero called himself an adherent of this school. On most points how-ever, although eclectic, he agreed with the Peripatetics, but with a decided leaning toward the Stoic ethical system. The Stoic opinion that it is the duty of the wise man to abstain from public life, which the Peripatetics contested, Cicero decisively rejected. With the Epicureans he had absolutely no sympathy. Up to this time these schools and their teachings were known to the Romans only through the medium of the Greek. The only Latin philosophical literature was Epicurean, and, excepting the poem of Lucretius (*De Rerum Natura*), scarcely famous as yet, consisted entirely of books rudely written, although considerably read.

(ii.) THE MISSION OF CICERO IN PHILOSOPHY.

Cicero made no claim to originality as a philosopher, nor even to complete acquaintance with every detail of the Greek systems.[1]

---

[1] De Off. i, 1, 2 : *philosophandi scientiam concedens multis* etc.

In early life he had studied with enthusiasm and success all the learning of the Greeks, but especially in the two departments of Rhetoric and Philosophy, then closely connected, or rather hardly distinguished. He not only sought the society of learned Greeks, but spent considerable time in study at Rhodes and Athens, which had become not merely the 'school of Greece', as Thucydides makes Pericles call her, but the school of the civilized world.[1] When, by reason of political troubles, he was forced to retire to private life, he began to carry out a great plan for interpreting the best philosophical writings of the Greeks to his fellow-countrymen. For this work his liberal views as a New Academic peculiarly fitted him. His usual method was to take one or two leading Greek works on the subject with which he was dealing, and to represent freely in his own language their subject-matter, introducing episodes and illustrations of his own. He thus presented to the Romans in their own tongue the most significant portions of the Greek Philosophy ; and in his writings there has come down to us much, especially of the Post-Aristo-telian Philosophy, that was doomed to oblivion in the original Greek. But further than this, to Cicero more than to any other Roman is due the formation of a Latin philosophical vocabulary, by which the language was enriched and fitted for the part it has since taken as the Language of the Learned. While on many points Cicero's own views can hardly be determined with perfect exactness, the exalted sentiments and the exquisite liter-ary finish of his philosophical writings have always won admira-tion ; and through them he has exerted no small influence on the literature and life of modern times.[2]

[1] To judge rightly of Cicero it must be remembered that he was a politician only by accident: his whole natural bent was towards literature.

[2] To see the truth of this it is only necessary to refer for ex-ample to the weight given to the opinions of Cicero in the heated political discussions of the six-teenth and seventeenth centuries.

(iii.) The Philosophical Writings of Cicero

During the whole of an exceptionally busy public life Cicero devoted his spare moments to reading and to the society of the learned. After his exile in 58 and 57 B. C. his political career, except for a brief period just before his death, was over, and it is at this time that his period of great literary activity begins. In 55 he produced the work *De Oratore*, in 54 the *De Re Publica*, and in 52 the *De Legibus*, all three works, according to ancient ideas, entitled to rank as philosophical.[1]

From 51 to 46 B. C., owing first to his absence in Cilicia, then to the civil troubles, Cicero almost ceased to write. But in the latter year he was reconciled with Caesar, and as the Senate and law courts were closed against him on his refusal to compromise his political principles, he betook himself with greater devotion than ever to literature. The first work written in 46 was the *Hortensius*, or *De Philosophia*, now lost. It was founded on a lost dialogue of Aristotle, and set forth the advantages of studying Philosophy. During the same year Cicero completed several oratorical works, the *Partitiones Oratoriae*, the *Brutus*, or *De Claris Oratoribus*, and the *Orator*, all of which are extant.

Early in 45 Cicero lost his beloved daughter Tullia. He passed the whole year in retirement, trying to soothe his grief by incessant writing. In quick succession appeared

De Consolatione, an attempt to apply philosophy to the mitigation of his own sorrow and that of others ;

Academica, an exposition of the New Academic Philosophy, advocating probability rather than certainty as the foundation of philosophy ;

De Finibus Bonorum et Malorum, a work criticising the most prominent views entertained concerning Ethics ;

Disputationes Tusculanae, treating of certain conditions essential to morality and happiness ;

---

[1] Almost every branch of learning was ranked under the head of Philosophy. Strabo even claimed that one branch of Philosophy was Geography.

INTRODUCTION.

De Natura Deorum, an examination of the principal theories
  regarding the nature and power of the gods;
Cato Maior, on old age; *Laelius*, on friendship;
De Fato, discussing Fate and Free Will;
Paradoxa, a book setting forth certain remarkable views of the
  Stoics;
De Officiis, a treatise on practical ethics, the application of
  moral principles to the questions and difficulties of ordinary
  life.

These works, written mostly in 45 and 44, are, except the *De
Cons.*, still extant. To the list may be added also other works of
a rhetorical nature, such as the *Topica* and *De Optimo Genere
Dicendi*, and some lost philosophical books, such as *De Gloria*.

Even though allowance be made for the fact that Cicero was
giving in Latin the substance of Greek books with which he had
been familiar from boyhood, the mental vigor and literary power
exhibited by this series of works appear prodigious when we
consider their great compass and variety and the generally high
finish of their style.

References. — For a fuller account of Cicero's philosophical
views and writings consult Ritter, 'History of Ancient Philosophy', Vol. 4, Ch. 2; Maurice, 'Moral and Metaphysical Philosophy', Ch. 7, § 5; Tennemann and Morell, 'History of
Philosophy', Ch. 3 Ueberweg, 'History of Philosophy', Vol
1, § 61; J. B. Mayor, 'Sketch of Ancient Philosophy', pp. 223–
244; Teuffel, 'History of Roman Literature', Vol. 1, § 172 *et
seq.*; Cruttwell, 'History of Roman Literature', Bk. II. Part 1,
Ch. 2; 'Cicero', by Collins, in Ancient Classics for English
Readers, Ch. 10, *et seq.*; also the Introduction to Reid's edition
of the *Academica*, and the account of Cicero by Prof. Ramsay
in Smith's Dictionary of Biography and Mythology. The most
attractive biography of Cicero in English is that by Forsyth.
That by Trollope is able but quite partisan. On the philosophy,
consult also Zeller's 'Eclectics.'

II. THE CATO MAIOR.

(i.) ORIGIN AND SCOPE.

1. *Date and Circumstances of Composition.*

The date at which the Cato Maior was written can be determined with almost perfect exactness. A mention in Cicero's
work entitled *De Divinatione*[1] shows that the Cato Maior pre-
ceded that work by a short time. The *De Divinatione* was
written after the assassination of Caesar, that is, after the 15th
of March in the year 44.[2] Again, the Cato Maior is mentioned
as a recent work in three letters addressed by Cicero to Atticus.[3]
The earliest of these letters was written on or about the 12th
of May, 44.[4] We shall hardly err, therefore, if we assume that
Cicero composed the Cato Maior in April of the year 44.[5] This
agrees also with slight indications in the work itself. In the
dedicatory introduction Cicero speaks of troubles weighing
heavily on himself and Atticus.[6] Any one who reads the letters to Atticus despatched in April, 44, will have little doubt
that the troubles hinted at are the apprehensions as to the
course of Antonius, from whom Cicero had personally something to fear. Atticus was using all the influence he could
bring to bear on Antonius in order to secure Cicero's safety;

---

[1] 2, 3 *interiectus est nuper liber
is quem ad nostrum Atticum de
senectute misimus.* No argument
can be founded on the words *interiectus est,* over which the editors have wasted much ingenuity.
They simply mean 'there was inserted in the series of my works'.

[2] See 2, 23.

[3] 14, 21, 3; 16, 3, 1; 16, 11, 3.

[4] See Att. 14, 21, 1.

[5] It was certainly not written,

as Sommerbrodt assumes, in the
intervals of composing the De
Divinatione. The words in 2, 7
of that work — *quoniam de re publica consuli coepti sumus* etc. —
point to the end of September or
beginning of October, 44, when
Cicero returned to Rome and
began to compose his Philippic
orations.

[6] § 1.

hence Cicero's care to avoid in the dedication all but the vaguest possible allusions to politics. Had that introduction been written before Caesar's death, we should have had plain allusions (as in the prooemia of the *Academica*, the *De Finibus*, the *Tusculan Disputations*, and the *De Natura Deorum*) to Caesar's dictatorship.[1]

The time was one of desperate gloom for Cicero. The downfall of the old constitution had overwhelmed him with sorrow, and his brief outburst of joy over Caesar's death had been quickly succeeded by disgust and alarm at the proceedings of Antonius. The deep wound caused by his daughter's death[2] was still unhealed. It is easy to catch in the Cato Maior some echoes of his grief for her. When it is said that of all Cato's titles to admiration none is higher than the fortitude he showed in bearing the death of his son,[3] the writer is thinking of the struggle he himself had been waging against a like sorrow for more than a year past; and when Cato expresses his firm conviction that he will meet his child beyond the grave,[4] we can see Cicero's own yearning for reunion with his deeply loved Tullia.

2. *Greek Sources.*

All Cicero's philosophical and rhetorical writings were confessedly founded more or less on Greek originals.[5] The stores from which he principally drew in writing the Cato Maior are clearly indicated in several parts of the work. Passages from Xenophon's *Oeconomicus* are translated in Chapters 17 and 22. In Chapters 2 and 3 there is a close imitation of the conversation between Socrates and Cephalus at the beginning of Plato's *Republic*, while in Chapter 21 is reproduced one of the most

---

[1] It is perhaps not a mere accident that the prowess of L. Brutus *in liberanda patria* is mentioned in § 75. There may be a reference to the latest Brutus who had freed his country.

[2] In March, 45.

[3] § 12.

[4] § 84.

[5] See p. iii. above.

striking portions of the *Phaedo*, 72 E–73 B, 78–80.[1] The view of the divine origin and destiny of the human soul contained in the passage from the *Phaedo* is rendered by Cicero in many of his works,[2] and was held by him with quite a religious fervor and sincerity.

Besides these instances of special indebtedness Cicero, in composing the Cato Maior, was no doubt under obligations of a more general kind to the Greeks. The form of the dialogue is Greek, and Aristotelian rather than Platonic.[3] But further, it is highly probable that Cicero owed to some particular Greek dialogue on Old Age the general outline of the arguments he there brings forward. Many of the Greek illustrative allusions may have had the same origin, though in many cases Roman illustrations must have been substituted for Greek. Whether the dialogue by Aristo Cius, cursorily mentioned in the Cato Maior,[4] was at all used by Cicero or not it is impossible to determine.[5]

3. *Purpose.*

The Cato Maior is a popular essay in Ethics, applying the principles of philosophy to the alleviation of one of life's chief burdens, old age. In ancient times, when philosophy formed the real and only religion of the educated class, themes like this were deemed to afford a worthy employment for the pens even of the greatest philosophers. Such essays formed the only substitute the ancients had for our Sermons. There can be no doubt of Cicero's sincerity when he says that the arguments he sets

[1] In the notes exact references will be given to the places in the original where the other passages mentioned may be found.

[2] Particularly the first book of the *Tusculan Disputations*, the *De Republica*, and the *Laelius*.

[3] See 4, below.

[4] § 3.

[5] Works on Old Age are said to have been written by Theophrastus and Demetrius Phalereus, either or both of which Cicero might have used. One passage in § 67, *facilius in morbos ... tristius curantur*, is supposed by many to have been imitated from Hippocrates; but the resemblance is probably accidental. Cf. De Off. I, 24, 83.

forth in the treatise had given him real comfort,[1] and the opening words of the dedication show that he meant and hoped to administer the same comfort to his friend Atticus, who indeed acknowledged the benefit he derived from the work.[2] When Cicero wrote the treatise he was himself sixty-two years of age, while his friend was three years older. He speaks, therefore, rather euphemistically when he says that his purpose is to lighten the trouble of an old age which is already close at hand, or at all events approaching.[3]

But in addition to the main ethical purpose, there was, as in many of Cicero's works, a distinct political purpose. He desired to stimulate in his readers an admiration for what he regarded as the golden age of Roman politics, the era of the Punic wars, and to do this by making the contrast between that age and his own appear as striking as possible. A like double purpose is apparent throughout the *De Re Publica*, where Africanus the younger is the chief personage, and in the treatise on Friendship, where Laelius is the central figure. For the dialogue on Old Age M. Porcius Cato the Censor is selected as the principal speaker for two reasons: first, because he was renowned for the vigor of mind and body he displayed in advanced life;[4] and secondly, because in him were conspicuously exhibited the serious simplicity, the unswerving adherence to principle, and the self-sacrificing patriotism which were the ideal Roman virtues, and which Cicero could not find among the politicians of his time.

4. *Form and Language.*

The Cato Maior, like most of Cicero's philosophical writings, is cast in the form of a dialogue. Among the ancients the dia-

---

[1] See § 2.

[2] See Att. 16, 11, 3; 16, 3, 1; 14, 21, 3.

[3] § 2.

[4] As Cicero's intention was to set old age in a favorable light, he slights Aristo Cius for giving to Tithonus the chief part in a dialogue on old age. See § 3; cf. also Laelius, § 4.

logue was a common rhetorical device, especially in the presen-
tation of abstruse subjects. The introduction of characters to
conduct the discussion gave vividness and clearness to the un-
folding of the argument, as well as a kind of dramatic interest to
the production. In the Cato Maior [1] and the Laelius, as generally, Cicero followed the plan of Aristotle's dialogues (now lost)
rather than that of the dialogues of Plato. In the former there
was more of exposition and less of discussion than in the latter;
one person stated his views on some question, and the company
in attendance only made occasional remarks without attempting
to debate the question. In the latter, although one person, Socrates, is everywhere prominent, others are continually drawn
into the discussions, and there is a quick interchange of question and answer. The Aristotelian form was better adapted to
Cicero's purposes than the Platonic; the progress of the argument was less interrupted, and thus better opportunity for a
symmetrical development of the theme was afforded. Then,
too, the former was more popular. The style of Aristotle [2] had
been imitated by Theophrastus and many other writers down
to Cicero's time, while that of Plato had found hardly any
imitators.

The editors of the Cato Maior have generally assumed that
Cicero attempted to give an antique coloring to the diction of
the dialogue in order to remind readers of Cato's own style. It
is only necessary to read a page or two of Cato's *De Re Rustica*
to have this illusion dispelled. The only things actually alleged
to be archaisms are (1) the use of deponent participles as passives in §§ 4, 59, 74, a thing common enough in Cicero; (2) the
occurrence of *quasi = quem ad modum* in § 71; (3) of *audaciter
= audacter* in § 72; (4) of *tuerentur* for *intuerentur* in § 77;
(5) of *neutiquam* in § 42; (6) of the nominative of the gerundive governing an accusative case in § 6. In every instance the

---

[1] See below (ii.), 1.

[2] On the whole subject of Aristotle's dialogues see Bernays'
monograph, *Die Dialoge des Aris-
toteles.*

notes will supply a refutation of the allegation. That Cicero should attempt to write in any style but his own is exceedingly improbable.

5. *Personages*.

The conversation is supposed to take place between Cato, Scipio Africanus the younger, and Laelius, in the year before Cato's death, *i. e.* 150 B. C., when he was in his eighty-fourth year,[1] Scipio being about 35 and Laelius a few years older.

(1.) *Cato.* M. Porcius Cato was born in 234 B. C.[2] at the ancient Latin town of Tusculum. Little is known of his family except that it was plebeian, and possessed a small patrimony in the territory of the Sabines, close to the farm of M'. Curius Dentatus, one of Cato's great heroes and models. The heads of the family, so far as memory extended, had distinguished themselves as tough warriors and hardy farmers. Among the Sabines, who even down to the times of the Empire were famed for simplicity of manners and the practice of all the sterner virtues, Cato passed those portions of his life which were not occupied with business of state. From his earliest days he toiled in his own fields, and contented himself with the hardest rustic life.[3] Yet even in his boyhood Cato must have passed intervals at Rome, and seen something of the great statesmen and generals of the time.[4] He seems to have received when young as thorough an education as was possible without learning Greek, such an education as was to be obtained only in the capital. He grew up to manhood in the comparatively quiet

---

[1] § 32 *quartum ago annum et octogesimum*. Cf. Lael. 11 *memini Catonem ante quam est mortuus mecum et cum Scipione disserere* etc.

[2] Cicero always indicates this date; cf. § 14. Some other writers, as Livy, give, probably wrongly, an earlier date.

[3] He himself says (Festus, p. 281) *ego iam a principio in parsimonia atque in duritia atque industria omnem adulescentiam, abstinui agro colendo, saxis Sabinis silicibus repastinandis atque conserendis.* Cf. Gell. *Noct. Att.* 13, 23.

[4] See Cat. M. 44.

period between the first and the second Punic wars ; the most exciting event of his younger years must have been the destruction at Clastidium of the vast hordes of Celts who had swept over the northern half of Italy, almost within reach of Rome.

Cato was of the age for military service about the time of the battle of Lake Trasimenus, and entered the army then as a common soldier.[1] The first expedition in which he is definitely said to have taken part is that of Q. Fabius Maximus Cunctator against Hannibal in Campania, in 214.[2] This Roman commander was a man entirely after Cato's heart, and became one of his models in public life.

Before and during the early years of his soldier's life, Cato succeeded in winning some reputation as an orator, having practised first in the provincial courts near his home, and afterwards at Rome.[3] This reputation as well as his great force of character procured for him a powerful life-long friend and patron, M. Valerius Flaccus, a statesman of the old Roman conservative-democratic school of politics, the leader of which was Fabius Cunctator. Through the influence of Flaccus, possibly with the aid of Fabius, Cato became military tribune, and served with that rank under Marcellus in Sicily, under Fabius again at the capture of Tarentum in 209,[4] and under C. Claudius Nero at the battle of the Metaurus, where he contributed materially to that great victory.

In 204 Cato began his political career with the quaestorship.[5] As he was a *novus homo* and a man of small private means, it was no small distinction that he had forced his way to office in

---

[1] Plut. c. 1 ; Cat. M. §§ 18, 32 : Cato himself ap. Fest. s. v. *ordinarius* says *quid mihi fieret si non ego stipendia in ordine omnia ordinarius meruissem semper ?*

[2] § 10.

[3] If Plutarch may be trusted, Cato at the age of 30 had won for himself the title of 'the Roman Demosthenes'.

[4] § 10.

[5] In § 10 Cicero makes the quaestorship fall in 205, but he refers to the election, not to the actual year of office.

his thirtieth year. The lot assigned him as quaestor to Scipio, then in Sicily and about to cross over into Africa. The chance was most unfortunate, if for no other reason, because Cato was intimately connected with the party in the senate opposed to Scipio, which had been attempting to bring him to trial for the atrocities committed by the Roman army in southern Italy. But in addition the two men were so utterly different that there was no possibility of the quaestor standing in that filial relation to his consul, which old Roman custom required. As financial officer, Cato complained of the luxury and extravagance which Scipio allowed not only to himself but to his army. Yet the complaint was made not so much on economic as on moral grounds ; it seemed to Cato that the old Roman discipline and power to endure hardships were being swept away. The dispute was ended by Scipio allowing Cato to return to Rome, some authorities say from Sicily, others from Africa. According to one writer,[1] he came home by way of Sardinia and brought thence with him Ennius the poet.[2]

In 199 Cato was plebeian aedile, and exercised with severity the police jurisdiction pertaining to that office, yet so as to win popular approval, since he was chosen praetor for 198 without the usual interval. The province of Sardinia was entrusted to him, and he strained every nerve to make his government present as strong a contrast as possible with the lax and corrupt administration of the nobles who took Scipio for their pattern. The troops were sternly disciplined, and law-breakers of every kind severely dealt with ; in money matters the strictest economy prevailed ; all gifts from provincials to Roman officers were forbidden. The praetor, the great representative of Roman power, passed from town to town attended by a single servant.

In 196 Cato was occupied with his canvass for the consulship

---

[1] Nepos (or pseudo-Nepos), Cat. 1.

[2] Cato afterwards made it a charge against M. Fulvius Nobilior that he had taken Ennius with him on a campaign (Tusc. 1, 3). But Cato used Ennius as soldier while Nobilior employed him as poet.

of the year 195, to which he was elected in company with his friend Flaccus. Cato was the first *novus homo* elected since C. Flaminius, the consul of 217. It is probable, though not certain, that he paved the way to his election by carrying the first of the *leges Porciae*, restricting the right of punishing Roman citizens. During the whole of his career Cato showed a high sense of the importance of the individual *civis Romanus*.

One of the first official acts of the new consul was to deliver a set speech to the people against a proposal to repeal the Oppian law, passed twenty years before, the object of which was to prevent lavish expenditure on dress and adornments, particularly by women. We have a lively report of Cato's speech from Livy's pen, partly founded on the speech as published by Cato himself.[1] The earnest pleading in favor of simple manners and economy failed, after having almost caused an open insurrection on the part of the women.[2]

The two new provinces in Spain, Hispania Citerior and Ulterior, were still in a very unsettled state. The nearer province was made a consular province and assigned to Cato ; the praetor who governed the farther province was also placed under Cato's jurisdiction. Before leaving Rome Cato carried a law for protecting the provincials from extortion. During the whole of his year of office he practised with the utmost exactness his principles of purity, simplicity, and economy in public affairs. He is said to have started from his house on the journey to Spain with only three servants, but when he got as far as the forum, it struck him that such an attendance was scarcely worthy of a Roman consul, so he purchased two more slaves on the spot ! In the same spirit, before returning he sold his horse that the state might not be at the expense of transporting it to Italy. Cato was no less careful of the revenue than of the expenditure. He largely increased the productiveness of the mines and other

---

[1] It is difficult, however, to fix the date of this enactment. Some authorities place it after Cato's return from Spain.

[2] Livy 34, cc. 1–8.

property belonging to the state, and all goods captured from the enemy were sold for the benefit of the exchequer. On leaving the province Cato made an unusually large gift to each soldier, saying that it was better for all to bring home silver than for a few to bring home gold. The provincials were thoroughly content with their ruler and ever after looked on him as their best friend. The army was kept in the strictest discipline. Some disorderly conduct of the *equites* was rebuked by Cato in a bitter harangue which he afterwards published. Partly by craft, partly by good leadership in the field, Cato broke the strength of the turbulent natives and returned to enjoy a well-earned triumph.[1] In the same year (194) a brilliant triumph was celebrated by Flamininus.

Scipio, probably uneasy at the great reputations quickly won by Flamininus and Cato, secured his second consulship for the year 194, but failed to achieve anything remarkable. Cato probably spent the three years after his return for the most part at his Sabine farm. When the war against Antiochus broke out, he took service along with his friend Flaccus on the staff of the consul Glabrio,[2] and by a difficult march over the mountains broke in on the king's rear, and so was chiefly instrumental in winning the great battle of Thermopylae, by which Antiochus was driven out of Greece. Immediately after the battle Cato returned home with despatches. We have dim and uncertain information that he took the field once or twice again, but his career as a soldier was practically ended.

From this time to his death, forty years later, Cato was the leading figure on the stage of Roman politics. In season and out of season he attacked abuses or innovations in speeches addressed to the senate, the people, or the courts. Soon after his return from Thessaly he struck a heavy blow at the unrepublican honor-hunting among the magistrates, of which the example

---

[1] See Livy, 34, 18.

[2] *i. e.* he was *legatus consularis.* It was at the time a common thing for ex-consuls to take service under their successors. So Liv. 36, 17, 1, but Cic. Cat. M. c 10 says *tribunus militaris.*

had been set by P. Scipio Africanus. Most provincial governors drove their subjects into war, sent lying despatches home about their victories, and claimed a triumph. In 190 Cato attacked with success the proposal to grant a triumph to Q. Minucius Thermus, who had already triumphed over the Spaniards as praetor, and after his consulship in 193 had fought against the Ligurians. Cato's next victim was his former commander M'. Acilius Glabrio, who came forward at the same time with Cato, Marcellus (a son of the captor of Syracuse), L. Cornelius Scipio Nasica, T. Quinctius Flamininus (the conqueror of Macedonia) and Cato's friend L. Valerius Flaccus, as candidate for the censorship of 189. Cato by his violent speeches procured the trial of Glabrio for appropriating the plunder captured in Thessaly, and himself gave evidence concerning some property which had disappeared. Glabrio denounced Cato as a perjurer, but yet retired from his candidature. On this occasion Cato and Flaccus failed, Marcellus being elected as plebeian and Flamininus as patrician censor.

In the next year (188) Cato acted in the senate with the party which tried unsuccessfully to refuse the triumph to the two consuls of 189, M. Fulvius Nobilior and Cn. Manlius Vulso, the former of whom had gained none but trifling advantages over the Aetolians, while the latter had disgraced the Roman name by making war without authorization upon the Gauls of Asia Minor, and had also suffered a humiliating defeat from some Thracian robber bands on his homeward march. Not disheartened by ill success, Cato and his friends determined to strike at higher game. L. Scipio Asiaticus (or Asiagenus), the brother of Africanus, was asserted in the senate to have appropriated 3000 talents of public money when in command against Antiochus. Legal proceedings were taken not only against Asiaticus, but against Africanus, who behaved with great violence and arrogance. In the end Africanus withdrew to his country estate, while his brother was condemned to pay a heavy fine. A death-stroke had been given to the almost kingly authority of Africanus, who never again showed his face in Rome. The proceedings against the Scipios seem to have begun in 187 and not to have been completed before 185.

Nearly twenty years had passed since the conflict between Cato and Scipio began, and now it had ended in a complete triumph for Cato.[1] But the new modes of which Scipio was the chief patron were too strong to be conquered, and Cato spent the rest of his life in fighting a hopeless battle against them, though he fought for a time with the strongest weapons that the constitution supplied. In 184 he was censor along with Flaccus, who seems to have allowed his colleague full liberty of action. Every portion of the censor's duty was carried out on the most severe and 'old Roman' principles. Seven senators were degraded, among them L. Flamininus, an ex-consul and brother of the 'liberator of the Hellenes,' for serious misconduct,[2] also Manilius, an ex-praetor, for no worse offence than that of having kissed his wife in presence of his daughter. M. Furius Purpurio, who had actually competed with Cato for the censorship, was punished for diverting a public aqueduct for his private advantage. Flaccus was named leader of the senate in the place of Scipio Africanus, now dead.

On reviewing the *equites*, Cato removed from that body L. Scipio and many others on various charges : this one had allowed himself to grow too fat for horsemanship ; that had failed to groom his horse properly ; another had neglected his farm ; another again had made an untimely jest on the occasion of the review itself. With the ordinary citizens Cato dealt just as harshly. In his censorian edict he sharply reproved the extravagance prevalent at private feasts. All articles of luxury, such as slaves purchased at fancy prices, luxurious clothing, carriages, statues, and pictures were rendered liable to heavy taxation. In this way Cato revenged himself for the repeal of the Oppian law.

---

[1] Cicero's statements throughout the treatise concerning the relations between Cato and Africanus the elder, particularly in § 77 where Cato calls his enemy *amicissimus*, are audaciously inexact.

[2] See Cato M. § 42.

In looking after the property and income of the state Cato followed the same principles he had acted on in Spain. He reduced the expenditure on public works as far as possible, and took care to sell at the full price the right to collect the revenue. Encroachments on the property of the nation were severely punished.

Not by acts only, but by constant speeches, full at once of grimness and humor, did Cato struggle against the degeneracy of his time.[1] He concluded his period of office with a self-laudatory harangue, and assumed the title *Censorius*, while his statue was placed in the temple of the goddess Salus with an inscription affirming that he had reformed the Roman nation.

But in a very brief time all trace of Cato's activity as censor was swept away, except that afforded by the numerous life-long quarrels in which he had involved himself.[2] In less than two years one of his victims, Purpurio, was employed by the senate on a high political mission, while another, L. Flamininus, sat among the senators at the games in defiance of Cato's sentence. Yet Cato remained by far the most powerful member of the senate. Titus Flamininus, his only important rival, quickly passed out of notice. So far as there was any democratic opposition to the senatorial oligarchy, Cato was the leader of that opposition for the remainder of his life. But at that period no great political movements agitated the state within; nearly the whole interest of the time was centred in the foreign relations of Rome. On matters of foreign policy Cato offered but little opposition to the prevailing tendencies of the age, though on particular occasions he exercised great influence. But his voice was at all times loudly heard on all questions of morality and public order. He supported the *lex Furia* and the *lex Voconia*, the object of which was to prevent the dissipation of family property, and the *lex Orchia*, directed against extravagant expendi-

---

[1] We possess the titles of 26 speeches delivered during or concerning his censorship.

[2] He is said to have undergone 44 prosecutions, and to have been prosecutor as often.

ture on feasts, also the *lex Baebia de ambitu*, the first serious attempt to check bribery. We hear also that Cato bitterly attacked Lepidus, censor in 180, for erecting a permanent theatre in place of the movable booths before used. The building was actually pulled down. We are told that from time to time he denounced the misdoings of provincial governors. In 171 he was one of a commission of five for bringing to justice three ex-praetors who had practised all manner of corruption in Spain. Almost the last act of his life was to prosecute Galba for cruel misgovernment of the Lusitanians. The titles of Cato's speeches show that he played a great part in the deliberations of the senate concerning foreign affairs, but as his fighting days were over and he was unfitted for diplomacy, we have little explicit evidence of his activity in this direction. At the end of the third Macedonian war he successfully opposed the annexation of Macedonia. He also saved from destruction the Rhodians, who during the war had plainly desired the victory of Perseus, and in the early days, when the Roman commanders had ill success, had deeply wounded the whole Roman nation by an offer to mediate between them and the king of Macedon.

Cato had all his life retained his feeling of enmity to the Carthaginians, whom Scipio, he thought, had treated too tenderly. In 150 he was one of an embassy sent to Carthage, and came back filled with alarm at the prosperity of the city. It is said that whatever was the subject on which he was asked for his opinion in the senate, he always ended his speech with ' *ceterum censeo delendam esse Carthaginem* '. P. Scipio Nasica, the son-in-law of Africanus, and the representative of his policy, always shouted out the opposite opinion, thinking that the fear of Carthage had a salutary effect on the Roman populace at large. But the ideas of Cato prevailed, and a cruel policy, carried out with needless brutality, led to the extinction of Rome's greatest rival. Cato did not live to see the conclusion of the war ; he died in 149, at the age of 84 or 85 years, having retained his mental and physical vigor to the last. He had two sons, one by his first wife, and one by his second wife, born when Cato was 80 years of age. The elder son, to whom many of Cato's works were addressed, died as praetor-elect, before his father[1]. The other was grandfather of Cato Uticensis.

The literary activity of the old censor was great, though his leisure was small.[2] In Cicero's time a collection of 150 speeches was still extant. The titles of about 90 are still known to us, and of some we possess a few fragments. Cato's greatest work, however, was his *Origines*, the first real historical work written in Latin. His predecessors had been merely compilers of chronicles. The work was founded on laborious investigations, and comprised the history of Rome from the earliest times perhaps down to 150 B.C.[3], as well as notices of the history of other important Italian states. Further, Cato wrote of Agriculture, to which he was enthusiastically devoted. We still have his *De Re Rustica*, a collection of maxims loosely strung together. He also composed works on law ; a sort of educational encyclopædia for his son ; and a collection of witty sayings, Ἀποφθέγματα, drawn from Greek as well as from Roman sources.

Plutarch seems to have known a collected edition of the pungent and proverbial utterances for which the censor was famous, and for which (not for any knowledge of philosophy[4]) he received the title of *sapiens* ('shrewd') which he bore at the end of his life. This edition, however, was not compiled by Cato himself.

In view of Cicero's treatise, the Cato Maior, it is necessary to say something of Cato's relations with the Greeks and Greek literature. The ancients give us merely vague statements that he only began to learn Greek 'in his old age.' The expression must be liberally interpreted if, as seems clear, the whole of his writings showed the influence of Greek literature. It is certain, however, that he thoroughly detested the Greek nation. This hatred was shown in acts more than once. No doubt Cato was

---

[1] See Lael. 9; Cat. M. 12 and 84.

[2] Cf. Livy, 39, 40.

[3] The common view is that Cato said nothing of Roman history from 509-266 B. C.

[4] Cf. Cic pro Arch. 7, 16.

at least a consenting party to the expulsion from Rome of Greek teachers in 161 B.C. When in 155 the famous embassy came from Athens consisting of Carneades the Academic, Critolaus the Peripatetic and Diogenes the Stoic, Cato was a prime mover of the decree by which they were removed from the city. Socrates was one of Cato's favorite marks for jests. And this is the man into whose mouth Cicero puts the utterances, but slightly veiled, of Greek wisdom !

(2.) *Scipio.* P. Cornelius Scipio Africanus, the younger, was no blood relation of the conqueror of Hannibal, but the adopted son of his son. It must be remembered, however, that adoption was much more formal and binding, and produced much closer ties in ancient than in modern times.[1] The elder Africanus was unfortunate in his sons. The younger of these attained to the praetorship in 174, but was immediately driven from the senate by the censors of that year on account of his disreputable life. The elder was an invalid, who never held any office except that of augur, and died at an early age. He adopted the son of L. Aemilius Paulus, the victor of Pydna ; the adopted son bore the name Aemilianus in memory of his origin. Cato's son married a daughter of Paulus, so that the censor was brought into relationship with the Cornelii, whose most illustrious representative he had hated and attacked.

The young Scipio was born about 185, and when scarce 17 years old fought with daring bravery at Pydna. While still very young he showed a great devotion to study, which he retained through life. He was a thorough partisan of the new Greek learning, and grouped around him in friendship all the leaders of the Hellenistic movement. Among his dearest friends were Polybius, the Greek statesman and historian, and later Panætius, the Stoic. In 151 B.C. when the consuls found it difficult to enlist officers and men for service in Spain, where great defeats had been suffered, Scipio volunteered, and served with great distinction as military tribune. When the war with Carthage broke out he

---

[1] See Coulanges, 'Ancient City', Bk. II. Ch. 4.

held the same rank, and shone by comparison with his blundering superior officers. Coming to Rome in 148 he stood for the ædileship, but was elected consul for the year 147, and again for 146, when he finished the war. He is said to have grieved over the fate of Carthage, and to have dreaded any further increase of the Roman territory. In 142 Scipio was censor, and acted with almost Catonian severity. In 134, though not a candidate, he was elected to the consulship and put in command of the Roman army then besieging the city of Numantia in Spain. The war, of which this siege formed a part, had been going on for some years most disastrously for the Romans, but Scipio speedily brought it to a conclusion in 133. While before Numantia he received news of the murder of Ti. Gracchus, whose sister he had married and whose cousin he had become by adoption, but whose policy he had on the whole opposed, though he had occasionally coquetted with the democrats. This course cost him the favor of the people, and when in 131 he desired to conduct the war against Aristonicus, only two of the thirty-five tribes voted for his appointment. In 129, after a violent scene in the senate, where he had opposed the carrying out of Ti. Gracchus' agrarian law, he was triumphantly escorted home by a crowd, composed chiefly of Italians whose interests had been threatened by the law. Next morning he was found dead in his bed. Opinion as to the cause of his death was divided at the time and so remained. In the *Laelius* the death is assumed to have been from natural causes.[1] Elsewhere, however, Cicero adopts the view of many of Scipio's friends that he was murdered by Carbo.[2] Carbo afterwards lent color to the suspicions by putting himself to death, in order, as was supposed, to avoid a direct prosecution. In ancient times even C. Gracchus was suspected of having thus avenged his brother's death, but no modern scholar of any rank has countenanced the suspicion.

Whether the degree of intimacy between Cato and Scipio, which Cicero assumes, ever existed or not, cannot be determined.[3]

---

[1] See §§ 12, 41 etc.

[2] De Or. 2, 170; Fam 9, 21, 3; Qu. Fr. 2, 3, 3.

[3] In *De Re Publica* 2, 1 Cicero makes Scipio talk extravagantly of Cato.

There was much in Scipio that would attract Cato.   Unlike
the elder Africanus, he was severe and simple in his outward life,
and though a lover of Greek and Greeks, yet attached to all that
was best in the old Roman character and polity.   Though an
opponent of revolution, he was far from being a partisan of the
oligarchy.   Altogether, of all Romans, he most nearly deserved
the description, ' ἀνὴρ τετράγωνος ἄνευ ψόγου,' ' a man four-square
without reproach.'   In his *De Re Publica*, Cicero points to
Scipio as the ideal statesman, and often elsewhere eulogizes
him as an almost perfect Roman.

(3.) *Laelius.*   Gaius Laelius, born about 186, was Scipio's most
distinguished officer before Carthage, and his most intimate
friend throughout life.   The friendship of the two was one of
the most famous in antiquity, and is celebrated in the *Laelius*.
Laelius was an able speaker, writer and soldier, and devoted to
Greek learning, particularly to the Stoic philosophy.   He is with
Cicero the type of a man of culture.[1]   He, too, is one of the
interlocutors in the *De Re Publica*.

(ii.) SUBJECT-MATTER.

1. *General View.*

The Cato Maior falls naturally into three parts : —

> Preliminary, dedication to Atticus, §§ 1–3;
> Introductory Conversation, 4–9;
> Cato's Defence of Old Age, 10–85.

After § 9 Cato continues to express his views on old age without interruption to the end, and the dialogue thus becomes
really a monologue.

2. *Analysis.*

Preliminary . . . . 1·3.

Cicero, addressing Atticus, states his purpose in writing the
book and the effect of the work on himself (1, 2), the reasons

---

[1] See Introduction to the Laelius, pp. vi, vii.

for putting the sentiments on old age into the mouth of Cato, and the circumstances of the supposed conversation (3).

Scipio declares his admiration of Cato's vigorous and happy old age. Cato replies that the secret lies in following the guidance of Nature (4, 5). Laelius then asks Cato to point out the road to such an old age as his own (6). This the old man promises to do, but first remarks that the faults charged against old age are generally due to defects of character (7). Laelius suggests that prosperity makes Cato's declining years pleasant. Cato admits that there may be some truth in this, but maintains that right character alone can make old age tolerable (8, 9).

B. Refutation of charges made against old age . . . 15-85
Statement of the four charges commonly made against old age: it withdraws men from active life, it weakens the physical powers, it takes away capacity for enjoyment, and it involves the anticipation of death   15

  A. Refutation of the first charge, that old age withdraws from active life.
    (a). There are employments suited to old age which are as necessary to the well-being of society as those which require greater physical powers . . 15-20
    (b). The special objection that old men have weak memories is answered by showing that this is due either to an original defect or to insufficient exercise 21-22

M. TULLI CICERONIS

CATO MAIOR

DE SENECTUTE.

I.　　*O Tite, si quid ego adiuero curamve levasso*
　　　　quae nunc te coquit et versat in pectore fixa,
　　　　ecquid erit praemi?

Licet enim mihi versibus isdem affari te, Attice, quibus
affatur Flamininum

　　　　ille vir haud magna cum re, sed plenus fidei,

quamquam certo scio non, ut Flamininum,

　　　　sollicitari te, Tite, sic noctesque diesque,

novi enim moderationem animi tui et aequitatem, teque
non cognomen solum Athenis deportasse, sed humanitatem et prudentiam intellego. Et tamen te suspicor
isdem rebus quibus me ipsum interdum gravius com-
moveri, quarum consolatio et maior est et in aliud
tempus differenda. Nunc autem visum est mihi de
senectute aliquid ad te conscribere. Hoc enim onere, 2
quod mihi commune tecum est, aut iam urgentis aut
certe adventantis senectutis et te et me ipsum levari
volo: etsi te quidem id modice ac sapienter, sicut
omnia, et ferre et laturum esse certo scio. Sed mihi,
cum de senectute vellem aliquid scribere, tu occurrebas

dignus eo munere, quo uterque nostrum communiter
uteretur. Mihi quidem ita iucunda huius libri confectio
fuit, ut non modo omnis absterserit senectutis molestias,
sed effecerit mollem etiam et iucundam senectutem.
Numquam igitur laudari satis digne philosophia poterit,
cui qui pareat omne tempus aetatis sine molestia possit
3 degere. Sed de ceteris et diximus multa et saepe dicemus : hunc librum ad te de senectute misimus. Omnem
autem sermonem tribuimus non Tithono, ut Aristo Cius,
parum enim esset auctoritatis in fabula, sed M. Catoni
seni, quo maiorem auctoritatem haberet oratio : apud
quem Laelium et Scipionem facimus admirantis, quod
is tam facile senectutem ferat, eisque eum respondentem
qui si eruditius videbitur disputare quam consuevit ipse
in suis libris, attribuito litteris Graecis, quarum constat
eum perstudiosum fuisse in senectute. Sed quid opus
est plura? Iam enim ipsius Catonis sermo explicabit
nostram omnem de senectute sententiam.

4 II. Scipio. Saepe numero admirari soleo cum hoc
C. Laelio cum ceterarum rerum tuam excellentem, M.
Cato, perfectamque sapientiam, tum vel maxime quod
numquam tibi senectutem gravem esse senserim, quae
plerisque senibus sic odiosa est, ut onus se Aetna gravius
dicant sustinere.

Cato. Rem haud sane, Scipio et Laeli, difficilem
admirari videmini. Quibus enim nihil est in ipsis opis
ad bene beateque vivendum, eis omnis aetas gravis est :
qui autem omnia bona a se ipsi petunt, eis nihil potest
malum videri quod naturae necessitas afferat. Quo in
genere est in primis senectus, quam ut adipiscantur
omnes optant, eandem accusant adeptam : tanta est
stultitiae inconstantia atque perversitas. Obrepere

aiunt eam citius quam putassent. Primum quis coegit
eos falsum putare? Qui enim citius adulescentiae
senectus quam pueritiae adulescentia obrepit? Deinde
qui minus gravis esset eis senectus, si octingentesimum
annum agerent, quam si octogesimum? Praeterita
enim aetas quamvis longa, cum effluxisset, nulla consolatione permulcere posset stultam senectutem. Quocirca ς
si sapientiam meam admirari soletis, quae utinam digna
esset opinione vestra nostroque cognomine, in hoc
sumus sapientes, quod naturam optimam ducem tamquam deum sequimur eique paremus : a qua non veri
simile est, cum ceterae partes aetatis bene descriptae
sint, extremum actum tamquam ab inerti poeta esse
neglectum. Sed tamen necesse fuit esse aliquid extremum et, tamquam in arborum bacis terraeque fructibus,
maturitate tempestiva quasi vietum et caducum, quod
ferundum est molliter sapienti. Quid est enim aliud
Gigantum modo bellare cum dis nisi naturae repug-
nare ?

LAELIUS.   Atqui, Cato, gratissimum nobis, ut etiam 6
pro Scipione pollicear, feceris, si, quoniam speramus,
volumus quidem certe, senes fieri, multo ante a te
didicerimus quibus facillime rationibus ingravescentem
aetatem ferre possimus.

CATO.   Faciam vero, Laeli, praesertim si utrique vestrum, ut dicis, gratum futurum est.

LAELIUS.   Volumus sane, nisi molestum est, Cato,
tamquam longam aliquam viam confeceris, quam nobis
quoque ingrediundum sit, istuc, quo pervenisti, videre
quale sit.

III. CATO.   Faciam ut potero, Laeli. Saepe enim 7
interfui querellis aequalium meorum, pares autem vetere

proverbio cum paribus facillime congregantur, quae C.
Salinator, quae Sp. Albinus, homines consulares, nostri
fere aequales, deplorare solebant, tum quod voluptatibus carerent, sine quibus vitam nullam putarent, tum
quod spernerentur ab·eis, a quibus essent coli soliti;
qui mihi non id videbantur accusare, quod esset accusandum. Nam,si id culpa senectutis accideret, eadem
mihi usu venirent reliquisque omnibus maioribus natu,
quorum ego multorum cognovi senectutem sine querella,
qui se et libidinum vinculis laxatos esse non moleste
ferrent nec a suis despicerentur. Sed omnium istius
modi querellarum in moribus est culpa, non in aetate.
Moderati enim et nec difficiles nec inhumani senes
tolerabilem senectutem agunt, importunitas autem et
inhumanitas omni aetati molesta est.

8   LAELIUS. Est, ut dicis, Cato; sed fortasse dixerit
quispiam tibi propter opes et copias et dignitatem tuam
tolerabiliorem senectutem videri, id autem non posse
multis contingere.

CATO. Est istuc quidem, Laeli, aliquid, sed nequa-
quam in isto sunt omnia; ut Themistocles fertur Seriphio cuidam in iurgio respondisse, cum ille dixisset
non eum sua, sed patriae gloria splendorem assecutum:
'nec hercule', inquit, 'si ego Seriphius essem, nec tu,
si Atheniensis, clarus umquam fuisses'. Quod eodem
modo de senectute dici potest; nec enim in summa
inopia levis esse senectus potest, ne sapienti quidem,
9 nec insipienti etiam in summa copia non gravis. Aptis-
sima omnino sunt, Scipio et Laeli, arma senectutis artes
exercitationesque virtutum, quae in omni aetate cultae,
cum diu multumque vixeris, mirificos ecferunt fructus,
non solum quia numquam deserunt, ne extremo quidem

tempore aetatis, quamquam id quidem maximum est,
verum etiam quia conscientia bene actae vitae mul-
torumque bene factorum recordatio iucundissima est.

IV.   Ego Q. Maximum, eum qui Tarentum recepit, 10
senem adulescens ita dilexi, ut aequalem.   Erat enim
in illo viro comitate condita gravitas, nec senectus
mores mutaverat.   Quamquam eum colere coepi non
admodum grandem natu, sed tamen iam aetate provec-
tum.   Anno enim post consul primum fuerat quam
ego natus sum, cumque eo quartum consule adulescentulus miles ad Capuam profectus sum quintoque anno
post ad Tarentum.   Quaestor deinde quadriennio post
factus sum, quem magistratum gessi consulibus Tuditano et Cethego, cum quidem ille admodum senex
suasor legis Cinciae de donis et muneribus fuit.   Hic
et bella gerebat ut adulescens, cum plane grandis esset,
et Hannibalem iuveniliter exsultantem patientia sua
molliebat; de quo praeclare familiaris noster Ennius :

> *unus homo nobis cunctando restituit rem ;*
> *noenum rumores ponebat ante salutem ;*
> *ergo plusque magisque viri nunc gloria claret.*

Tarentum vero qua vigilantia, quo consilio recepit ! 11
Cum quidem me audiente Salinatori, qui amisso oppido
fugerat in arcem, glorianti atque ita dicenti, 'mea opera,
Q. Fabi, Tarentum recepisti', 'certe', inquit ridens,
'nam nisi tu amisisses, numquam recepissem'.   Nec
vero in armis praestantior quam in toga ; qui consul
iterum, Sp. Carvilio collega quiescente, C. Flaminio
tribuno plebis, quoad potuit, restitit agrum Picentem et
Gallicum viritim contra senatus auctoritatem dividenti ;

augurque cum esset, dicere ausus est optimis auspiciis
ea geri, quae pro rei publicae salute gererentur; quae
contra rem publicam ferrentur, contra auspicia ferri.
12 Multa in eo viro praeclara cognovi, sed nihil admirabilius quam quo modo ille mortem fili tulit, clari viri
et consularis. Est in manibus laudatio, quam cum
legimus, quem philosophum non contemnimus? Nec
vero ille in luce modo atque in oculis civium magnus,
sed intus domique praestantior. Qui sermo, quae praecepta! Quanta notitia antiquitatis, scientia iuris auguri!
Multae etiam, ut in homine Romano, litterae : omnia
memoria tenebat non domestica solum, sed etiam externa bella. Cuius sermone ita tum cupide fruebar,
quasi iam divinarem, id quod evenit, illo exstincto fore
unde discerem neminem.

13   V. Quorsus igitur haec tam multa de Maximo? Quia
profecto videtis nefas esse dictu miseram fuisse talem
senectutem. Nec tamen omnes possunt esse Scipiones
aut Maximi, ut urbium expugnationes, ut pedestris
navalisve pugnas, ut bella a se gesta, ut triumphos
recordentur. Est etiam quiete et pure atque eleganter
actae aetatis placida ac lenis senectus, qualem accepimus Platonis, qui uno et octogesimo anno scribens
est mortuus, qualem Isocrati, qui eum librum, qui Panathenaicus inscribitur, quarto nonagesimo anno scripsisse
dicit vixitque quinquennium postea; cuius magister
Leontinus Gorgias centum et septem complevit annos,
neque umquam in suo studio atque opere cessavit.
Qui, cum ex eo quaereretur cur tam diu vellet esse in
vita, 'nihil habeo,' inquit, 'quod accusem senectutem'.
14 Praeclarum responsum et docto homine dignum! Sua
enim vitia insipientes et suam culpam in senectutem

conferunt, quod non faciebat is, cuius modo mentionem
feci, Ennius:

> *sic ut fortis ecus, spatio qui saepe supremo*
> *vicit Olumpia, nunc senio confectus quiescit.*

Equi fortis et victoris senectuti comparat suam; quem
quidem probe meminisse potestis; anno enim undevi-
cesimo post eius mortem hi consules, T. Flamininus et
M'. Acilius, facti sunt; ille autem Caepione et Philippo
iterum consulibus mortuus est, cum ego quinque et sexa-
ginta annos natus legem Voconiam magna voce et bonis
lateribus suasissem. Annos septuaginta natus, tot enim
vixit Ennius, ita ferebat duo quae maxima putantur
onera, paupertatem et senectutem, ut eis paene delectari
videretur.

Etenim, cum complector animo, quattuor reperio 15
causas cur senectus misera videatur: unam, quod avocet
a rebus gerendis; alteram, quod corpus faciat infirmius;
tertiam, quod privet omnibus fere voluptatibus; quar-
tam, quod haud procul absit a morte. Earum, si placet, causarum quanta quamque sit iusta una quaeque
videamus.

VI. A rebus gerendis senectus abstrahit. Quibus?
An eis, quae iuventute geruntur et viribus? Nullaene
igitur res sunt seniles, quae vel infirmis corporibus
animo tamen administrentur? Nihil ergo agebat Q.
Maximus, nihil L. Paulus, pater tuus, socer optimi viri
fili mei? Ceteri senes, Fabricii Curii Coruncanii, cum
rem publicam consilio et auctoritate defendebant, nihil
agebant? Ad Appi Claudi senectutem accedebat etiam
ut caecus esset; tamen is, cum sententia senatus in- 16

clinaret ad pacem cum Pyrrho foedusque faciendum,
non dubitavit dicere illa, quae versibus persecutus est
Ennius :

> *quo vobis mentes, rectae quae stare solebant*
> *antehac, dementis sese flexere viai ?*

ceteraque gravissime, notum enim vobis carmen est, et
tamen ipsius Appi exstat oratio. Atque haec ille egit
septemdecim annis post alterum consulatum, cum inter
duos consulatus anni decem interfuissent censorque
ante superiorem consulatum fuisset, ex quo intellegitur
Pyrrhi bello grandem sane fuisse, et tamen sic a patribus
17 accepimus. Nihil igitur afferunt qui in re gerenda
versari senectutem negant, similesque sunt ut si qui
gubernatorem in navigando nihil agere dicant, cum alii
malos scandant, alii per foros cursent, alii sentinam
exhauriant, ille clavum tenens quietus sedeat in puppi,
non faciat ea, quae iuvenes. At vero multo maiora et
meliora facit. Non viribus aut velocitate aut celeritate
corporum res magnae geruntur, sed consilio auctoritate
sententia, quibus non modo non orbari, sed etiam augeri
18 senectus solet; nisi forte ego vobis, qui et miles et
tribunus et legatus et consul versatus sum in vario
genere bellorum, cessare nunc videor, cum bella non
gero. At senatui quae sint gerenda praescribo et quo
modo ; Carthagini male iam diu cogitanti bellum multo
ante denuntio, de qua vereri non ante desinam quam
19 illam exscisam esse cognovero. Quam palmam utinam
di immortales, Scipio, tibi reservent, ut avi relliquias
persequare, cuius a morte tertius hic et tricesimus annus
est, sed memoriam illius viri omnes excipient anni con-
sequentes. Anno ante me censorem mortuus est,

novem annis post meum consulatum, cum consul iterum
me consule creatus esset.   Num igitur, si ad centesi-
mum annum vixisset, senectutis eum suae paeniteret?
Nec enim excursione nec saltu, nec eminus hastis aut
comminus gladiis uteretur, sed consilio ratione sententia,
quae nisi essent in senibus, non summum consilium
maiores nostri appellassent senatum.   Apud Lacedae- 20
monios quidem ei, qui amplissimum magistratum gerunt,
ut sunt, sic etiam nominantur senes.   Quod si legere
aut audire voletis externa, maximas res publicas ab
adulescentibus labefactatas, a senibus sustentatas et
restitutas reperietis.

> *Cedo qui vestram rem publicam tantam amisistis tam cito?*

sic enim percontantur in Naevi poetae Ludo.   Respon-
dentur et alia et hoc in primis:

> *proveniebant oratores novi, stulti adulescentuli.*

Temeritas est videlicet florentis aetatis, prudentia senes-
centis.

VII.   At memoria minuitur.   Credo, nisi eam ex- 21
erceas, aut etiam si sis natura tardior.   Themistocles
omnium civium perceperat nomina; num igitur censetis
eum, cum aetate processisset, qui Aristides esset Lysimachum salutare solitum?   Equidem non modo eos novi
qui sunt, sed eorum patres etiam et avos, nec sepulcra
legens vereor, quod aiunt, ne memoriam perdam; his
enim ipsis legendis in memoriam redeo mortuorum.
Nec vero quemquam senem audivi oblitum, quo loco
thesaurum obruisset.   Omnia quae curant meminerunt,
vadimonia constituta, quis sibi, cui ipsi debeant.   Quid 22
iuris consulti, quid pontifices, quid augures, quid phi-

losophi senes? Quam multa meminerunt! Manent
ingenia senibus, modo permaneat studium et industria,
neque ea solum claris et honoratis viris, sed in vita
etiam privata et quieta. Sophocles ad summam senectutem tragoedias fecit; quod propter studium cum rem
neglegere familiarem videretur, a filiis in iudicium vo-
catus est, ut, quem ad modum nostro more male rem
gerentibus patribus bonis interdici solet, sic illum quasi
desipientem a re familiari removerent iudices. Tum
senex dicitur eam fabulam quam in manibus habebat et
proxime scripserat, Oedipum Coloneum, recitasse iudi-
cibus quaesisseque num illud carmen desipientis videre-
23 tur, quo recitato sententiis iudicum est liberatus. Num
igitur hunc, num Homerum Hesiodum Simoniden
Stesichorum, num quos ante dixi Isocraten Gorgian,
num philosophorum principes, Pythagoran Democritum,
num Platonem Xenocraten, num postea Zenonem
Cleanthen, aut eum, quem vos etiam vidistis Romae,
Diogenen Stoicum coegit in suis studiis obmutiscere
senectus? An in omnibus studiorum agitatio vitae
24 aequalis fuit? Age, ut ista divina studia omittamus,
possum nominare ex agro Sabino rusticos Romanos,
vicinos et familiaris meos, quibus absentibus numquam
fere ulla in agro maiora opera fiunt, non serendis, non
percipiendis, non condendis fructibus. Quamquam in
aliis minus hoc mirum est, nemo enim est tam senex
qui se annum non putet posse vivere; sed idem in eis
elaborant, quae sciunt nihil ad se omnino pertinere :

serit arbores, quae alteri saeclo prosint,

25 ut ait Statius noster in Synephebis. Nec vero dubitat
agricola, quamvis sit senex, quaerenti cui serat respon-

dere: 'dis immortalibus, qui me non accipere modo
haec a maioribus voluerunt, sed etiam posteris prodere'.
    VIII. Et melius Caecilius de sene alteri saeculo pro-
spiciente, quam illud idem :

> *edepol, senectus, si nil quicquam aliud viti*
> *adportes tecum, cum advenis, unum id sat est,*
> *quod diu vivendo multa quae non volt videt.*

Et multa fortasse quae volt, atque in ea, quae non volt,
saepe etiam adulescentia incurrit. Illud vero idem
Caecilius vitiosius :

> *tum equidem in senecta hoc deputo miserrimum,*
> *sentire ea aetate eumpse esse odiosum alteri.*

Iucundum potius quam odiosum ! Ut enim adulescenti- 26
bus bona indole praeditis sapientes senes delectantur,
leviorque fit senectus eorum qui a iuventute coluntur et
diliguntur, sic adulescentes senum praeceptis gaudent,
quibus ad virtutum studia ducuntur, nec minus intellego
me vobis quam mihi vos esse iucundos. Sed videtis, ut
senectus non modo languida atque iners non sit, verum
etiam sit operosa et semper agens aliquid et moliens,
tale scilicet, quale cuiusque studium in superiore vita
fuit.   Quid, qui etiam addiscunt aliquid, ut et Solonem
versibus gloriantem videmus, qui se cotidie aliquid
addiscentem dicit senem fieri, et ego feci, qui litteras
Graecas senex didici, quas quidem sic avide arripui
quasi diuturnam sitim explere cupiens, ut ea ipsa mihi
nota essent, quibus me nunc exemplis uti videtis. Quod
cum fecisse Socraten in fidibus audirem, vellem equidem etiam illud, discebant enim fidibus antiqui, sed in
litteris certe elaboravi.

27   IX. Nè nunc quidem viris desidero adulescentis, is
enim erat locus alter de vitiis senectutis, non plus quam
adulescens tauri aut elephanti desiderabam. Quod est,
eo decet uti et quidquid agas agere pro viribus. Quae
enim vox potest esse contemptior quam Milonis Croto-
niatae? Qui cum iam senex esset athletasque se exer-
centis in curriculo videret, aspexisse lacertos suos dicitur
illacrimansque dixisse, ' at hi quidem mortui iam sunt '.
Non vero tam isti, quam tu ipse, nugator, neque enim
ex te umquam es nobilitatus, sed ex lateribus et lacertis
tuis.   Nihil Sex. Aelius tale, nihil multis annis ante Ti.
Coruncanius, nihil modo P. Crassus, a quibus iura civibus praescribebantur, quorum usque ad extremum spiri-
28 tum est provecta prudentia. Orator metuo ne languescat
senectute : est enim munus eius non ingeni solum, sed
laterum etiam et virium. Omnino canorum illud in voce
splendescit etiam nescio quo pacto in senectute, quod
equidem adhuc non amisi, et videtis annos. Sed tamen
est decorus seni sermo quietus et remissus, facitque per-
saepe ipsa sibi audientiam diserti senis composita et
mitis oratio, quam si ipse exsequi nequeas, possis tamen
Scipioni praecipere et Laelio. Quid enim est iucundius
29 senectute stipata studiis iuventutis? An ne illas quidem
viris senectuti relinquimus, ut adulescentis doceat, insti-
tuat, ad omne offici munus instruat ? Quo quidem opere
quid potest esse praeclarius ? Mihi vero et Cn. et P.
Scipiones et avi tui duo L. Aemilius et P. Africanus
comitatu nobilium iuvenum fortunati videbantur, nec
ulli bonarum artium magistri non beati putandi, quamvis
consenuerint vires atque defecerint. Etsi ipsa ista de-
fectio virium adulescentiae vitiis efficitur saepius quam
senectute ; libidinosa enim et intemperans adulescentia

effetum corpus tradit senectuti. Cyrus quidem apud 30
Xenophontem eo sermone, quem moriens habuit, cum
admodum senex esset, negat se umquam sensisse senectutem suam imbecilliorem factam quam adulescentia
fuisset. Ego L. Metellum memini puer, qui, cum quadriennio post alterum consulatum pontifex maximus
factus esset, viginti et duos annos ei sacerdotio praefuit,
ita bonis esse viribus extremo tempore aetatis, ut adulescentiam non requireret. Nihil necesse est mihi de
me ipso dicere, quamquam est id quidem senile aeta-
tique nostrae conceditur. X. Videtisne, ut apud Home- 31
rum saepissime Nestor de virtutibus suis praedicet?
Tertiam enim aetatem hominum videbat, nec erat ei
verendum ne vera praedicans de se nimis videretur aut
insolens aut loquax. Etenim, ut ait Homerus, ex eius
lingua melle dulcior fluebat oratio; quam ad suavitatem
nullis egebat corporis viribus. Et tamen dux ille Grae-
ciae nusquam optat ut Aiacis similis habeat decem, sed
ut Nestoris, quod si sibi acciderit, non dubitat quin
brevi sit Troia peritura. Sed redeo ad me. Quartum 32
ago annum et octogesimum: vellem equidem idem posse
gloriari quod Cyrus, sed tamen hoc queo dicere, non
me quidem eis esse viribus, quibus aut miles bello
Punico aut quaestor eodem bello aut consul in Hispania
fuerim aut quadriennio post, cum tribunus militaris
depugnavi apud Thermopylas M'. Glabrione consule;
sed tamen, ut vos videtis, non plane me enervavit, non
afflixit senectus: non curia viris meas desiderat, non
rostra, non amici, non clientes, non hospites. Nec enim
umquam sum assensus veteri illi laudatoque proverbio,
quod monet mature fieri senem, si diu velis senex esse.
Ego vero me minus diu senem esse mallem quam esse

senem ante quam essem. Itaque nemo adhuc convenire
33 me voluit cui fuerim occupatus. At minus habeo virium
quam vestrum utervis. Ne vos quidem T. Ponti centurionis viris habetis : num idcirco est ille praestantior ?
Moderatio modo virium adsit et tantum quantum potest
quisque nitatur, ne ille non magno desiderio tenebitur
virium. Olympiae per stadium ingressus esse Milo
dicitur, cum umeris sustineret bovem : utrum igitur has
corporis an Pythagorae tibi malis viris ingeni dari ?
Denique isto bono utare, dum adsit, cum absit, ne
requiras : nisi forte adulescentes pueritiam, paulum
aetate progressi adulescentiam debent requirere. Cursus est certus aetatis et una via naturae eaque simplex,
suaque cuique parti aetatis tempestivitas est data, ut et
infirmitas puerorum et ferocitas iuvenum et gravitas
iam constantis aetatis et senectutis maturitas naturale
34 quiddam habet, quod suo tempore percipi debeat. Audire te arbitror, Scipio, hospes tuus avitus Masinissa
quae faciat hodie nonaginta natus annos : cum ingressus iter pedibus sit, in equum omnino non ascendere ;
cum autem equo, ex equo non descendere ; nullo imbri,
nullo frigore adduci ut capite operto sit ; summam
esse in eo corporis siccitatem, itaque omnia exsequi
regis officia et munera. Potest igitur exercitatio et
temperantia etiam in senectute conservare aliquid
pristini roboris.

XI. Ne sint in senectute vires : ne postulantur quidem vires a senectute. Ergo et legibus et institutis
vacat aetas nostra muneribus eis quae non possunt
sine viribus sustineri. Itaque non modo quod non
possumus, sed ne quantum possumus quidem cogimur.
35 At multi ita sunt imbecilli senes, ut nullum offici aut

omnino vitae munus exsequi possint. At id quidem
non proprium senectutis vitium est, sed commune valetudinis. Quam fuit imbecillus P. Africani filius, is qui
te adoptavit, quam tenui aut nulla potius valetudine!
Quod ni ita fuisset, alterum illud exstitisset lumen
civitatis; ad paternam enim magnitudinem animi doc-
trina uberior accesserat. Quid mirum igitur in senibus,
si infirmi sunt aliquando, cum id ne adulescentes quidem effugere possint? Resistendum, Laeli et Scipio,
senectuti est, eiusque vitia diligentia compensanda sunt,
pugnandum tamquam contra morbum sic contra senectutem, habenda ratio valetudinis, utendum exercitationi- 36
bus modicis, tantum cibi et potionis adhibendum, ut
reficiantur vires, non opprimantur. Nec vero corpori
solum subveniendum est, sed menti atque animo multo
magis. Nam haec quoque, nisi tamquam lumini oleum
instilles, exstinguuntur senectute. Et corpora quidem
exercitationum defetigatione ingravescunt, animi autem
exercitando levantur. Nam quos ait Caecilius 'comicos stultos senes,' hos significat credulos obliviosos dis-
solutos, quae vitia sunt non senectutis, sed inertis
ignavae somniculosae senectutis. Ut petulantia, ut
libido magis est adulescentium quam senum, nec tamen
omnium adulescentium, sed non proborum, sic ista
senilis stultitia, quae deliratio appellari solet, senum 37
levium est, non omnium. Quattuor robustos filios,
quinque filias, tantam domum, tantas clientelas Appius
regebat et caecus et senex; intentum enim animum
tamquam arcum habebat nec languescens succumbebat
senectuti. Tenebat non modo auctoritatem, sed etiam
imperium in suos: metuebant servi, verebantur liberi,
carum omnes habebant; vigebat in illo animus patrius

38 et disciplina. Ita enim senectus honesta est, si se ipsa
defendit, si ius suum retinet, si nemini emancipata est,
si usque ad ultimum spiritum dominatur in suos. Ut
enim adulescentem in quo est senile aliquid, sic senem
in quo est aliquid adulescentis probo, quod qui sequitur,
corpore senex esse poterit, animo numquam erit. Sep-
timus mihi liber Originum est in manibus; omnia
antiquitatis monumenta colligo; causarum illustrium,
quascunque defendi, nunc cum maxime conficio orationes; ius augurium pontificium civile tracto; multum
etiam Graecis litteris utor, Pythagoriorumque more,
exercendae memoriae gratia, quid quoque die dixerim
audierim egerim commemoro vesperi. Hae sunt exerci-
tationes ingeni, haec curricula mentis; in his desudans
atque elaborans corporis viris non magno opere desidero. Adsum amicis, venio in senatum frequens ultro-
que affero res multum et diu cogitatas easque tueor
animi, non corporis viribus. Quas si exsequi nequirem,
tamen me lectulus meus oblectaret ea ipsa cogitantem,
quae iam agere non possem; sed ut possim facit acta
vita. Semper enim in his studiis laboribusque viventi
non intellegitur quando obrepat senectus: ita sensim
sine sensu aetas senescit nec subito frangitur, sed
diuturnitate exstinguitur.

39   XII. Sequitur tertia vituperatio senectutis, quod
eam carere dicunt voluptatibus. O praeclarum munus
aetatis, si quidem id aufert a nobis, quod est in adulescentia vitiosissimum! Accipite enim, optimi adulescentes, veterem orationem Archytae Tarentini, magni
in primis et praeclari viri, quae mihi tradita est cum
essem adulescens Tarenti cum Q. Maximo. Nullam
capitaliorem pestem quam voluptatem corporis homini-

bus dicebat a natura datam, cuius voluptatis avidae
libidines temere et ecfrenate ad potiendum incitarentur.
Hinc patriae proditiones, hinc rerum publicarum ever- 40
siones, hinc cum hostibus clandestina colloquia nasci;
nullum denique scelus, nullum malum facinus esse, ad
quod suscipiendum non libido voluptatis impelleret;
stupra vero et adulteria et omne tale flagitium nullis excitari aliis illecebris nisi voluptatis; cumque homini sive
natura sive quis deus nihil mente praestabilius dedisset,
huic divino muneri ac dono nihil tam esse inimicum quam
voluptatem. Nec enim libidine dominante temperan- 41
tiae locum esse, neque omnino in voluptatis regno
virtutem posse consistere. Quod quo magis intellegi
posset, fingere animo iubebat tanta incitatum aliquem
voluptate corporis, quanta percipi posset maxima:
nemini censebat fore dubium quin tam diu, dum ita
gauderet, nihil agitare mente, nihil ratione, nihil cogitatione consequi posset. Quocirca nihil esse tam de-
testabile tamque pestiferum quam voluptatem, si quidem
ea, cum maior esset atque longior, omne animi lumen
exstingueret. Haec cum C. Pontio Samnite, patre eius,
a quo Caudino proelio Sp. Postumius T. Veturius consules superati sunt, locutum Archytam Nearchus Taren-
tinus hospes noster, qui in amicitia populi Romani
permanserat, se a maioribus natu accepisse dicebat,
cum quidem ei sermoni interfuisset Plato Atheniensis,
quem Tarentum venisse L. Camillo Ap. Claudio consulibus reperio. Quorsus hoc? Ut intellegeretis, si 42
voluptatem aspernari ratione et sapientia non posse-
mus, magnam esse habendam senectuti gratiam, quae
efficeret ut id non liberet quod non oporteret. Impedit
enim consilium voluptas, rationi inimica est, mentis ut

ita dicam praestringit oculos, nec habet ullum cum
virtute commercium.   Invitus feci ut fortissimi viri T.
Flaminini fratrem L. Flamininum e senatu eicerem septem annis post quam consul fuisset, sed notandam
putavi libidinem.   Ille enim cum esset consul in Gallia
exoratus in convivio a scorto est ut securi feriret
aliquem eorum qui in vinculis essent, damnati rei
capitalis.   Hic Tito fratre suo censore, qui proximus
ante me fuerat, elapsus est, mihi vero et Flacco neutiquam probari potuit tam flagitiosa et tam perdita libido,
quae cum probro privato coniungeret imperi dedecus.

43   XIII.   Saepe audivi e maioribus natu, qui se porro
pueros a senibus audisse dicebant, mirari solitum C.
Fabricium quod, cum apud regem Pyrrhum legatus
esset, audisset a Thessalo Cinea esse quendam Athenis
qui se sapientem profiteretur, eumque dicere omnia
quae faceremus ad voluptatem esse referenda.   Quod
ex eo audientis M'. Curium et Ti. Coruncanium optare
solitos ut id Samnitibus ipsique Pyrrho persuaderetur,
quo facilius vinci possent cum se voluptatibus dedissent.
Vixerat M'. Curius cum P. Decio, qui quinquennio ante
eum consulem se pro re publica quarto consulatu
devoverat : norat eundem Fabricius, norat Coruncanius, qui cum ex sua vita tum ex eius quem dico
Deci facto iudicabant esse profecto aliquid natura pulchrum atque praeclarum, quod sua sponte expeteretur
quodque spreta et contempta voluptate optimus quisque
44 sequeretur.   Quorsum igitur tam multa de voluptate ?
Quia non modo vituperatio nulla, sed etiam summa
laus senectutis est, quod ea voluptates nullas magno
opere desiderat.   Caret epulis exstructisque mensis et
frequentibus poculis.   Caret ergo etiam vinulentia et

cruditate et insomniis. Sed si aliquid dandum est
voluptati, quoniam eius blanditiis non facile obsistimus,
divine enim Plato escam malorum appellat voluptatem
quod ea videlicet homines capiantur ut pisces, quamquam immoderatis epulis caret senectus, modicis tamen
conviviis delectari potest. C. Duellium M. F., qui
Poenos classe primus devicerat, redeuntem a cena
senem saepe videbam puer ; delectabatur cereo funali
et tibicine, quae sibi nullo exemplo privatus sumpserat:
tantum licentiae dabat gloria. Sed quid ego alios ? 45
Ad me ipsum iam revertar. Primum habui semper
sodalis — sodalitates autem me quaestore constitutae
sunt sacris Idaeis Magnae Matris acceptis — epulabar
igitur cum sodalibus, omnino modice, sed erat quidam
fervor aetatis, qua progrediente omnia fiunt in dies
mitiora. Neque enim ipsorum conviviorum delectationem voluptatibus corporis magis quam coetu amicorum
et sermonibus metiebar ; bene enim maiores accubitionem epularem amicorum, quia vitae coniunctionem
haberet, convivium nominaverunt, melius quam Graeci,
qui hoc idem tum compotationem, tum concenationem
vocant, ut, quod in eo genere minimum est, id maxime
probare videantur.

XIV. Ego vero propter sermonis delectationem tem- 46
pestivis quoque conviviis delector, nec cum aequalibus
solum, qui pauci admodum restant, sed cum vestra
etiam aetate atque vobiscum, habeoque senectuti magnam gratiam, quae mihi sermonis aviditatem auxit,
potionis et cibi sustulit. Quod si quem etiam ista delectant, ne omnino bellum indixisse videar voluptati,
cuius est fortasse quidam naturalis modus, non intellego
ne in istis quidem ipsis voluptatibus carere sensu senec-

tutem. Me vero et magisteria delectant a maioribus
instituta et is sermo, qui more maiorum a summo adhi-
betur in poculo, et pocula, sicut in Symposio Xenophontis est, minuta atque rorantia, et refrigeratio aestate
et vicissim aut sol aut ignis hibernus. Quae quidem
etiam in Sabinis persequi soleo conviviumque vicinorum
cotidie compleo, quod ad multam noctem quam maxime
possumus vario sermone producimus. At non est
47 voluptatum tanta quasi titillatio in senibus. Credo,
sed ne desideratio quidem ; nihil autem est molestum
quod non desideres. Bene Sophocles, cum ex eo quidam iam affecto aetate quaereret, utereturne rebus
veneriis, 'di meliora !' inquit ; 'ego vero istinc sicut a
domino agresti ac furioso profugi.' Cupidis enim rerum
talium odiosum fortasse et molestum est carere, satiatis
vero et expletis iucundius est carere quam frui ; quamquam non caret is, qui non desiderat ; ergo hoc non
48 desiderare dico esse iucundius. Quod si istis ipsis
voluptatibus bona aetas fruitur libentius, primum par-
vulis fruitur rebus, ut diximus, deinde eis, quibus senectus, etiam si non abunde potitur, non omnino caret. Ut
Turpione Ambivio magis delectatur qui in prima cavea
spectat, delectatur tamen etiam qui in ultima, sic adulescentia voluptates propter intuens magis fortasse
laetatur, sed delectatur etiam senectus, procul eas
49 spectans, tantum quantum sat est. At illa quanti sunt,
animum tamquam emeritis stipendiis libidinis ambitionis,
contentionum inimicitiarum, cupiditatum omnium secum
esse secumque, ut dicitur, vivere ! Si vero habet aliquod tamquam pabulum studi atque doctrinae, nihil est
otiosa senectute iucundius. Videbamus in studio di-
metiendi paene caeli atque terrae Gallum familiarem

patris tui, Scipio. Quotiens illum lux noctu aliquid
describere ingressum, quotiens nox oppressit cum mane
coepisset! Quam delectabat eum defectiones solis et
lunae multo ante nobis praedicere! Quid in levioribus 50
studiis, sed tamen acutis? Quam gaudebat Bello suo
Punico Naevius, quam Truculento Plautus, quam Pseudolo! Vidi etiam senem Livium, qui, cum sex annis
ante quam ego natus sum fabulam docuisset Centone
Tuditanoque consulibus, usque ad adulescentiam meam
processit aetate. Quid de P. Licini Crassi et pontifici
et civilis iuris studio loquar aut de huius P. Scipionis,
qui his paucis diebus pontifex maximus factus est?
Atque eos omnis, quos commemoravi, his studiis flagrantis senes vidimus. M. vero Cethegum, quem recte
suadae medullam dixit Ennius, quanto studio exerceri
in dicendo videbamus etiam senem! Quae sunt igitur
epularum aut ludorum aut scortorum voluptates cum
his voluptatibus comparandae? Atque haec quidem
studia doctrinae, quae quidem prudentibus et bene
institutis pariter cum aetate crescunt, ut honestum illud
Solonis sit, quod ait versiculo quodam, ut ante dixi,
senescere se multa in dies addiscentem, qua voluptate
animi nulla certe potest esse maior.

XV. Venio nunc ad voluptates agricolarum, quibus 51
ego incredibiliter delector, quae nec ulla impediuntur
senectute et mihi ad sapientis vitam proxime videntur
accedere. Habent enim rationem cum terra, quae
numquam recusat imperium nec umquam sine usura
reddit quod accepit, sed alias minore, plerumque maiore
cum faenore; quamquam me quidem non fructus modo,
sed etiam ipsius terrae vis ac natura delectat. Quae
cum gremio mollito ac subacto sparsum semen excepit,

primum id occaecatum cohibet, ex quo occatio quae
hoc efficit nominata est; deinde tepefactum vapore et
compressu suo diffundit et elicit herbescentem ex eo
viriditatem, quae nixa fibris stirpium sensim adolescit
culmoque erecta geniculato vaginis iam quasi pubescens
includitur; e quibus cum emersit, fundit frugem spici
ordine structam et contra avium minorum morsus muni-
52 tur vallo aristarum.   Quid ego vitium ortus satus incrementa commemorem?   Satiari delectatione non
possum, ut meae senectutis requietem oblectamentum-
que noscatis.   Omitto enim vim ipsam omnium quae
generantur e terra, quae ex fici tantulo grano aut ex
acini vinaceo aut ex ceterarum frugum aut stirpium
minutissimis seminibus tantos truncos ramosque procreet; malleoli plantae sarmenta viviradices propagines
nonne efficiunt ut quemvis cum admiratione delectent?
Vitis quidem quae natura caduca est et, nisi fulta est,
fertur ad terram, eadem, ut se erigat, claviculis suis
quasi manibus quidquid est nacta complectitur, quam
serpentem multiplici lapsu et erratico, ferro amputans
coercet ars agricolarum, ne silvescat sarmentis et in
53 omnis partis nimia fundatur.   Itaque ineunte vere in
eis quae relicta sunt exsistit tamquam ad articulos
sarmentorum ea quae gemma dicitur, a qua oriens uva
se ostendit, quae et suco terrae et calore solis augescens
primo est peracerba gustatu, dein maturata dulcescit
vestitaque pampinis nec modico tepore caret et nimios
solis defendit ardores: qua quid potest esse cum fructu
laetius, tum aspectu pulchrius?   Cuius quidem non
utilitas me solum, ut ante dixi, sed etiam cultura et
natura ipsa delectat: adminiculorum ordines, capitum
iugatio, religatio et propagatio vitium, sarmentorum ea,

quam dixi, aliorum amputatio, aliorum immissio. Quid
ego irrigationes, quid fossiones agri repastinationesque
proferam, quibus fit multo terra fecundior? Quid de 54
utilitate loquar stercorandi? Dixi in eo libro, quem de
rebus rusticis scripsi. De qua doctus Hesiodus ne
verbum quidem fecit, cum de cultura agri scriberet.
At Homerus, qui multis, ut mihi videtur, ante saeculis
fuit, Laerten lenientem desiderium, quod capiebat e
filio, colentem agrum et eum stercorantem facit. Nec
vero segetibus solum et pratis et vineis et arbustis res
rusticae laetae sunt, sed hortis etiam et pomariis, tum
pecudum pastu, apium examinibus, florum omnium
varietate. Nec consitiones modo delectant, sed etiam
insitiones, quibus nihil invenit agri cultura sollertius.

XVI. Possum persequi permulta oblectamenta rerum 55
rusticarum, sed ea ipsa quae dixi sentio fuisse longiora.
Ignoscetis autem, nam et studio rerum rusticarum
provectus sum, et senectus est natura loquacior, ne ab
omnibus eam vitiis videar vindicare. Ergo in hac vita
M'. Curius, cum de Samnitibus, de Sabinis, de Pyrrho
triumphavisset, consumpsit extremum tempus aetatis ;
cuius quidem ego villam contemplans, abest enim non
longe a me, admirari satis non possum vel hominis ipsius
continentiam vel temporum disciplinam. Curio ad 56
focum sedenti magnum auri pondus Samnites cum
attulissent, repudiati sunt ; non enim aurum habere
praeclarum sibi videri dixit, sed eis qui haberent aurum
imperare. Poteratne tantus animus efficere non iucundam senectutem? Sed venio ad agricolas, ne a me
ipso recedam. In agris erant tum senatores, id est
senes, si quidem aranti L. Quinctio Cincinnato nuntia-
tum est eum dictatorem esse factum, cuius dictatoris

iussu magister equitum C. Servilius Ahala Sp. Maelium
regnum appetentem occupatum interemit. A villa in
senatum arcessebatur et Curius et ceteri senes, ex quo
qui eos arcessebant viatores nominati sunt. Num
igitur horum senectus miserabilis fuit, qui se agri cultione oblectabant? Mea quidem sententia haud scio
an nulla beatior possit esse, neque solum officio, quod
hominum generi universo cultura agrorum est salutaris,
sed et delectatione quam dixi, et saturitate copiaque
rerum omnium, quae ad victum hominum, ad cultum
etiam deorum pertinent, ut, quoniam haec quidam
desiderant, in gratiam iam cum voluptate redeamus.
Semper enim boni assiduique domini referta cella vi-
naria, olearia, etiam penaria est, villaque tota locuples
est, abundat porco haedo agno gallina, lacte caseo
melle. Iam hortum ipsi agricolae succidiam alteram
appellant. Conditiora facit haec supervacaneis etiam
57 operis aucupium atque venatio. Quid de pratorum
viriditate aut arborum ordinibus aut vinearum oliveto-
rumve specie plura dicam? Brevi praecidam. Agro
bene culto nihil potest esse nec usu uberius nec specie
ornatius, ad quem fruendum non modo non retardat,
verum etiam invitat atque allectat senectus. Ubi enim
potest illa aetas aut calescere vel apricatione melius
vel igni, aut vicissim umbris aquisve refrigerari salu-
58 brius? Sibi habeant igitur arma, sibi equos, sibi hastas,
sibi clavam et pilam, sibi venationes atque cursus;
nobis senibus ex lusionibus multis talos relinquant et
tesseras; id ipsum ut lubebit, quoniam sine eis beata
esse senectus potest.

59   XVII. Multas ad res perutiles Xenophontis libri
sunt, quos legite quaeso studiose, ut facitis. Quam

copiose ab eo agri cultura laudatur in eo libro, qui est
de tuenda re familiari, qui Oeconomicus inscribitur!
Atque ut intellegatis nihil ei tam regale videri quam
studium agri colendi, Socrates in eo libro loquitur cum
Critobulo Cyrum minorem Persarum regem, praestan-
tem ingenio atque imperi gloria, cum Lysander Lace-
daemonius, vir summae virtutis, venisset ad eum Sardis
eique dona a sociis attulisset, et ceteris in rebus com-
munem erga Lysandrum atque humanum fuisse et ei
quendam consaeptum agrum diligenter consitum osten-
disse. Cum autem admiraretur Lysander et proceritates
arborum et directos in quincuncem ordines et humum
subactam atque puram et suavitatem odorum qui affla-
rentur ex floribus, tum eum dixisse mirari se non modo
diligentiam sed etiam sollertiam eius a quo essent illa
dimensa atque discripta; et Cyrum respondisse 'atqui
ego ista sum omnia dimensus, mei sunt ordines, mea
discriptio; multae etiam istarum arborum mea manu
sunt satae.' Tum Lysandrum, intuentem purpuram eius
et nitorem corporis ornatumque Persicum multo auro
multisque gemmis, dixisse 'recte vero te, Cyre, beatum
ferunt, quoniam virtuti tuae fortuna coniuncta est!'
Hac igitur fortuna frui licet senibus, nec aetas impedit 60
quo minus et ceterarum rerum et in primis agri colendi
studia teneamus usque ad ultimum tempus senectutis.
M. quidem Valerium Corvinum accepimus ad centesi-
mum annum perduxisse, cum esset acta iam aetate in
agris eosque coleret, cuius inter primum et sextum consulatum sex et quadraginta anni interfuerunt. Ita quantum spatium aetatis maiores ad senectutis initium esse
voluerunt, tantus illi cursus honorum fuit; atque huius
extrema aetas hoc beatior quam media, quod auctori-

tatis habebat plus, laboris minus; apex est autem senec-
61 tutis auctoritas.   Quanta fuit in L. Caecilio Metello,
quanta in A. Atilio Calatino !   In quem illud elogium :

> *hunc unum plurimae consentiunt gentes*
> *populi primarium fuisse virum.*

Notum est totum carmen incisum in sepulcro.   Iure
igitur gravis, cuius de laudibus omnium esset fama consentiens.   Quem virum nuper P. Crassum, pontificem
maximum, quem postea M. Lepidum eodem sacerdotio
praeditum vidimus !   Quid de Paulo aut Africano loquar,
aut, ut iam ante, de Maximo ?   Quorum non in sententia solum, sed etiam in nutu residebat auctoritas.   Habet senectus, honorata praesertim, tantam auctoritatem,
ut ea pluris sit quam omnes adulescentiae voluptates.

62   XVIII.   Sed in omni oratione mementote eam me
senectutem laudare, quae fundamentis adulescentiae
constituta sit.   Ex quo efficitur id, quod ego magno
quondam cum assensu omnium dixi, miseram esse senectutem quae se oratione defenderet.   Non cani nec
rugae repente auctoritatem arripere possunt, sed honeste
acta superior aetas fructus capit auctoritatis extremos.
63 Haec enim ipsa sunt honorabilia, quae videntur levia
atque communia, salutari appeti decedi assurgi deduci
reduci consuli, quae et apud nos et in aliis civitatibus,
ut quaeque optime morata est, ita diligentissime obser-
vantur.   Lysandrum Lacedaemonium, cuius modo feci
mentionem, dicere aiunt solitum Lacedaemonem esse
honestissimum domicilium senectutis ; nusquam enim
tantum tribuitur aetati, nusquam est senectus honora-
tior.   Quin etiam memoriae proditum est, cum Athenis
ludis quidam in theatrum grandis natu venisset, magno

consessu locum nusquam ei datum a suis civibus, cum
autem ad Lacedaemonios accessisset, qui, legati cum
essent, certo in loco considerant, consurrexisse omnes
illi dicuntur et senem sessum recepisse; quibus cum 64
a cuncto consessu plausus esset multiplex datus, dixisse
ex eis quendam Atheniensis scire quae recta essent, sed
facere nolle.   Multa in nostro collegio praeclara, sed
hoc, de quo agimus, in primis, quod, ut quisque aetate
antecedit, ita sententiae principatum tenet, neque solum
honore antecedentibus, sed eis etiam, qui cum imperio
sunt, maiores natu augures anteponuntur.   Quae sunt
igitur voluptates corporis cum auctoritatis praemiis comparandae?   Quibus qui splendide usi sunt, ei mihi
videntur fabulam aetatis peregisse nec tamquam inexer-
citati histriones in extremo actu corruisse.

   At sunt morosi et anxii et iracundi et difficiles senes. 65
Si quaerimus, etiam avari; sed haec morum vitia sunt,
non senectutis.   Ac morositas tamen et ea vitia, quae
dixi, habent aliquid excusationis, non illius quidem
iustae, sed quae probari posse videatur: contemni se
putant, despici, illudi; praeterea in fragili corpore odiosa
omnis offensio est; quae tamen omnia dulciora fiunt et
moribus bonis et artibus, idque cum in vita tum in
scaena intellegi potest ex eis fratribus qui in Adelphis
sunt.   Quanta in altero diritas, in altero comitas! Sic
se res habet: ut enim non omne vinum, sic non omnis
natura vetustate coacescit.   Severitatem in senectute
probo, sed eam, sicut alia, modicam; acerbitatem nullo
modo; avaritia vero senilis quid sibi velit, non intellego.
Potest enim quicquam esse absurdius quam, quo viae 66
minus restet, eo plus viatici quaerere?

   XIX.   Quarta restat causa, quae maxime angere at-

que sollicitam habere nostram aetatem videtur, appro-
pinquatio mortis, quae certe a senectute non potest esse
longe. O miserum senem, qui mortem contemnendam
esse in tam longa aetate non viderit ! Quae aut plane
neglegenda est, si omnino exstinguit animum, aut etiam
optanda, si aliquo eum deducit ubi sit futurus aeternus.
67 Atqui tertium certe nihil inveniri potest. Quid igitur
timeam, si aut non miser post mortem, aut beatus etiam
futurus sum ? Quamquam quis est tam stultus, quamvis
sit adulescens, cui sit exploratum se ad vesperum esse
victurum ? Quin etiam aetas illa multo pluris quam
nostra casus mortis habet : facilius in morbos incidunt
adulescentes, gravius aegrotant, tristius curantur. Itaque
pauci veniunt ad senectutem ; quod ni ita accideret,
melius et prudentius viveretur. Mens enim et ratio et
consilium in senibus est, qui si nulli fuissent, nullae
omnino civitates fuissent. Sed redeo ad mortem impendentem. Quod est istud crimen senectutis, cum id ei
68 videatis cum adulescentia esse commune ? Sensi ego
in optimo filio, tu in exspectatis ad amplissimam dignitatem fratribus, Scipio, mortem omni aetati esse com-
munem. At sperat adulescens diu se victurum, quod
sperare idem senex non potest. Insipienter sperat ;
quid enim stultius quam incerta pro certis habere, falsa
pro veris ? At senex ne quod speret quidem habet.
At est eo meliore condicione quam adulescens, quoniam
id quod ille sperat hic consecutus est : ille volt diu
69 vivere, hic diu vixit. Quamquam, o di boni, quid est in
hominis natura diu ? Da enim supremum tempus, ex-
spectemus Tartessiorum regis aetatem : fuit enim, ut
scriptum video, Arganthonius quidam Gadibus, qui
octoginta regnaverat annos, centum viginti vixerat.

Sed mihi ne diuturnum quidem quicquam videtur, in
quo est aliquid extremum ; cum enim id advenit, tum
illud, quod praeteriit, effluxit ; tantum remanet, quod
virtute et recte factis consecutus sis. Horae quidem
cedunt et dies et menses et anni, nec praeteritum tempus umquam revertitur nec quid sequatur sciri potest.
Quod cuique temporis ad vivendum datur, eo debet esse
contentus. Neque enim histrioni, ut placeat, peragenda 70
fabula est, modo in quocunque fuerit actu probetur ;
neque sapientibus usque ad 'plaudite' veniendum est,
breve enim tempus aetatis satis longum est ad bene
honesteque vivendum ; sin processerit longius, non
magis dolendum est, quam agricolae dolent praeterita
verni temporis suavitate aestatem autumnumque venisse.
Ver enim tamquam adulescentia significat ostenditque
fructus futuros ; reliqua autem tempora demetendis
fructibus et percipiendis accommodata sunt. Fructus 71
autem senectutis est, ut saepe dixi, ante partorum bonorum memoria et copia. Omnia autem, quae secundum
naturam fiunt, sunt habenda in bonis ; quid est autem
tam secundum naturam quam senibus emori? Quod
idem contingit adulescentibus adversante et repugnante
natura. Itaque adulescentes mihi mori sic videntur, ut
cum aquae multitudine flammae vis opprimitur, senes
autem sic, ut cum sua sponte, nulla adhibita vi, con-
sumptus ignis exstinguitur, et quasi poma ex arboribus,
cruda si sunt, vix evelluntur, si matura et cocta, de-
cidunt, sic vitam adulescentibus vis aufert, senibus
maturitas ; quae quidem mihi tam iucunda est, ut, quo
propius ad mortem accedam, quasi terram videre videar
aliquandoque in portum ex longa navigatione esse ven-
turus. XX. Senectutis autem nullus est certus termi- 72

nus, recteque in ea vivitur, quoad munus offici exsequi
et tueri possit mortemque contemnere, ex quo fit ut
animosior etiam senectus sit quam adulescentia et
fortior.   Hoc illud est, quod Pisistrato tyranno a So-
lone responsum est, cum illi quaerenti qua tandem re
fretus sibi tam audaciter obsisteret respondisse dicitur
'senectute.'   Sed vivendi est finis optimus, cum integra
mente certisque sensibus opus ipsa suum eadem quae
coagmentavit natura dissolvit.   Ut navem, ut aedificium
idem destruit facillime qui construxit, sic hominem
eadem optime quae conglutinavit natura dissolvit.   Iam
omnis conglutinatio recens aegre, inveterata facile divel-
litur.   Ita fit ut illud breve vitae reliquum nec avide
appetendum senibus nec sine causa deserendum sit ;
73 vetatque Pythagoras iniussu imperatoris, id est dei, de
praesidio et statione vitae decedere. Solonis quidem
sapientis est elogium, quo se negat velle suam mortem
dolore amicorum et lamentis vacare.   Volt, credo, se
esse carum suis.   Sed haud scio an melius Ennius :

> *nemo me lacrumis decoret, neque funera fletu*
> *faxit.*

Non censet lugendam esse mortem, quam immortalitas
74 consequatur.   Iam sensus moriendi aliquis esse potest,
isque ad exiguum tempus, praesertim seni : post mortem
quidem sensus aut optandus aut nullus est.   Sed hoc
meditatum ab adulescentia debet esse, mortem ut negle-
gamus ; sine qua meditatione tranquillo animo esse
nemo potest.   Moriendum enim certe est, et incertum
an hoc ipso die.   Mortem igitur omnibus horis impen-
75 dentem timens qui poterit animo consistere ?   De qua
non ita longa disputatione opus esse videtur, cum re-

corder non L. Brutum, qui in liberanda patria est inter-
fectus, non duos Decios, qui ad voluntariam mortem
cursum equorum incitaverunt, non M. Atilium, qui ad
supplicium est profectus ut fidem hosti datam conser-
varet, non duos Scipiones, qui iter Poenis vel corporibus
suis obstruere voluerunt, non avum tuum L. Paulum,
qui morte luit collegae in Cannensi ignominia temerita-
tem, non M. Marcellum, cuius interitum ne crudelissimus quidem hostis honore sepulturae carere passus est,
sed legiones nostras, quod scripsi in Originibus, in eum
locum saepe profectas alacri animo et erecto, unde se
redituras numquam arbitrarentur. Quod igitur adulescentes, et ei quidem non solum indocti sed etiam rustici
contemnunt, id docti senes extimescent? Omnino, ut 76
mihi quidem videtur, rerum omnium satietas vitae facit
satietatem. Sunt pueritiae studia certa : num igitur ea
desiderant adulescentes? Sunt ineuntis adulescentiae :
num ea constans iam requirit aetas, quae media dicitur?
Sunt etiam eius aetatis : ne ea quidem quaeruntur in
senectute. Sunt extrema quaedam studia senectutis :
ergo, ut superiorum aetatum studia occidunt, sic occidunt
etiam senectutis ; quod cum evenit, satietas vitae tempus
maturum mortis affert.

XXI. Non enim video, cur, quid ipse sentiam de 77
morte, non audeam vobis dicere, quod eo cernere mihi
melius videor, quo ab ea propius absum. Ego vestros
patres, P. Scipio tuque, C. Laeli, viros clarissimos mihi-
que amicissimos, vivere arbitror et eam quidem vitam,
quae est sola vita nominanda. Nam dum sumus inclusi
in his compagibus corporis, munere quodam necessitatis et gravi opere perfungimur ; est enim animus cae-
lestis ex altissimo domicilio depressus et quasi demersus

in terram, locum divinae naturae aeternitatique contra-
rium.   Sed credo deos immortalis sparsisse animos in
corpora humana, ut essent qui terras tuerentur quique
caelestium ordinem contemplantes imitarentur eum vitae
modo atque constantia.   Nec me solum ratio ac dispu-
tatio impulit ut ita crederem, sed nobilitas etiam sum-
morum philosophorum et auctoritas.

78   Audiebam Pythagoran Pythagoriosque, incolas paene
nostros, qui essent Italici philosophi quondam nominati,
numquam dubitasse quin ex universa mente divina deli-
batos animos haberemus.   Demonstrabantur mihi praeterea quae Socrates supremo vitae die de immortalitate
animorum disseruisset, is qui esset omnium sapientissi-
mus oraculo Apollinis iudicatus.   Quid multa?   Sic
mihi persuasi, sic sentio, cum tanta celeritas animorum
sit, tanta memoria praeteritorum futurorumque prudentia, tot artes tantae scientiae, tot inventa, non posse eam
naturam, quae res eas contineat, esse mortalem; cumque
semper agitetur animus nec principium motus habeat,
quia se ipse moveat, ne finem quidem habiturum esse
motus, quia numquam se ipse sit relicturus; et cum
simplex animi natura esset neque haberet in se quicquam
admixtum dispar sui atque dissimile, non posse eum
dividi, quod si non posset, non posse interire; magno-
que esse argumento homines scire pleraque ante quam
nati sint, quod iam pueri, cum artis difficilis discant, ita
celeriter res innumerabilis arripiant, ut eas non tum
primum accipere videantur, sed reminisci et recordari.

79 Haec Platonis fere. XXII. Apud Xenophontem autem
moriens Cyrus maior haec dicit: ' nolite arbitrari, o mihi
carissimi filii, me, cum a vobis discessero, nusquam aut
nullum fore.   Nec enim, dum eram vobiscum, animum

meum videbatis, sed eum esse in hoc corpore ex eis
rebus quas gerebam intellegebatis.   Eundem igitur esse
creditote, etiam si nullum videbitis.   Nec vero clarorum 80
virorum post mortem honores permanerent, si nihil
eorum ipsorum animi efficerent, quo diutius memoriam
sui teneremus.   Mihi quidem numquam persuaderi potuit animos dum in corporibus essent mortalibus vivere,
cum excessissent ex eis emori ; nec vero tum animum
esse insipientem cum ex insipienti corpore evasisset, sed
cum omni admixtione corporis liberatus purus et integer
esse coepisset, tum esse sapientem.   Atque etiam, cum
hominis natura morte dissolvitur, ceterarum rerum per-
spicuum est quo quaeque discedat, abeunt enim illuc
omnia, unde orta sunt ; animus autem solus nec cum
adest nec cum discessit apparet.   Iam vero videtis nihil
esse morti tam simile quam somnum.   Atqui dormien- 81
tium animi maxime declarant divinitatem suam ; multa
enim, cum remissi et liberi sunt, futura prospiciunt ; ex
quo intellegitur quales futuri sint, cum se plane corporis
vinculis relaxaverint.   Qua re, si haec ita sunt, sic me
colitote,' inquit, 'ut deum, sin una est interiturus animus
cum corpore, vos tamen, deos verentes, qui hanc omnem
pulchritudinem tuentur et regunt, memoriam nostri pie
inviolateque servabitis.'

XXIII.   Cyrus quidem haec moriens ; nos, si placet, 82
nostra videamus.   Nemo umquam mihi, Scipio, persua-
debit aut patrem tuum Paulum, aut duos avos Paulum
et Africanum, aut Africani patrem aut patruum, aut multos praestantis viros, quos enumerare non est necesse,
tanta esse conatos quae ad posteritatis memoriam per-
tinerent, nisi animo cernerent posteritatem ad ipsos
pertinere.   Anne censes, ut de me ipse aliquid more

3

senum glorier, me tantos labores diurnos nocturnosque
domi militiaeque suscepturum fuisse, si isdem finibus
gloriam meam quibus vitam essem terminaturus? Nonne
melius multo fuisset otiosam et quietam aetatem sine
ullo labore et contentione traducere? Sed nescio quo
modo animus erigens se posteritatem ita semper prospi-
ciebat, quasi, cum excessisset e vita, tum denique victu-
rus esset. Quod quidem ni ita se haberet ut animi
immortales essent, haud optimi cuiusque animus maxime
83 ad immortalitatis gloriam niteretur. Quid quod sapien-
tissimus quisque aequissimo animo moritur, stultissimus
iniquissimo, nonne vobis videtur is animus, qui plus
cernat et longius, videre se ad meliora proficisci, ille
autem, cuius obtusior sit acies, non videre? Equidem
efferor studio patres vestros quos colui et dilexi videndi,
neque vero eos solum convenire aveo, quos ipse cognovi,
sed illos etiam, de quibus audivi et legi et ipse conscripsi; quo quidem me proficiscentem haud sane quid
facile retraxerit, nec tamquam Pelian recoxerit. Et si
quis deus mihi largiatur ut ex hac aetate repuerascam
et in cunis vagiam, valde recusem, nec vero velim quasi
84 decurso spatio ad carceres a calce revocari. Quid habet
enim vita commodi? Quid non potius laboris? Sed
habeat sane; habet certe tamen aut satietatem aut modum. Non libet enim mihi deplorare vitam, quod multi
et ei docti saepe fecerunt, neque me vixisse paenitet,
quoniam ita vixi, ut non frustra me natum existimem, et
ex vita ita discedo tamquam ex hospitio, non tamquam
e domo; commorandi enim natura divorsorium nobis,
non habitandi dedit. O praeclarum diem cum in illud
divinum animorum concilium coetumque proficiscar
cumque ex hac turba et colluvione discedam! Proficis-

car enim non ad eos solum viros, de quibus ante dixi,
verum etiam ad Catonem meum, quo nemo vir melior
natus est, nemo pietate praestantior, cuius a me corpus
est crematum, quod contra decuit ab illo meum, animus
vero non me deserens sed respectans, in ea profecto loca
discessit quo mihi ipsi cernebat esse veniendum.   Quem
ego meum casum fortiter ferre visus sum, non quo aequo
animo ferrem, sed me ipse consolabar existimans non
longinquum inter nos digressum et discessum fore.

His mihi rebus, Scipio, id enim te cum Laelio admi- 85
rari solere dixisti, levis est senectus, nec solum non
molesta, sed etiam iucunda.   Quod si in hoc erro, qui
animos hominum immortalis esse credam, libenter erro
nec mihi hunc errorem, quo delector, dum vivo, extorqueri volo ; sin mortuus, ut quidam minuti philosophi
censent, nihil sentiam, non vereor ne hunc errorem
meum philosophi mortui irrideant.   Quod si non sumus
immortales futuri, tamen exstingui homini suo tempore
optabile est.   Nam habet natura, ut aliarum omnium
rerum, sic vivendi modum.   Senectus autem aetatis est
peractio tamquam fabulae, cuius defetigationem fugere
debemus, praesertim adiuncta satietate.

Haec habui de senectute quae dicerem, ad quam utinam veniatis, ut ea, quae ex me audistis, re experti probare possitis!

NOTES TO CATO MAIOR.

—◆◇◆—

CATO MAIOR DE SENECTUTE (CATO THE ELDER
ON OLD AGE). CATO MAIOR was probably intended by
Cicero as the principal title. He twice gives the work this
name, in Laelius 4 and Att. 14, 21, 1. In the former passage
he adds the descriptive words, addressed to Atticus, *qui est
scriptus ad te de senectute*. In a third notice, De Div. 2, 3, he
gives the description without the title, *liber is quem ad nostrum Atticum de senectute misimus*. It is likely that Cicero
intended the essay to be known as the CATO MAIOR DE SE-
NECTUTE, the full title corresponding with LAELIUS DE AMI-
CITIA. The word *maior* was necessary to distinguish the book
from Cicero's eulogy of the younger Cato (Uticensis), which
seems to have gone by the name of CATO simply.

P. 1.—**1.** **O Tite** etc.: the lines are a quotation from the *Annales*
of Q. Ennius (born at Rudiae in Calabria 239 B. C., died 169), an epic
poem in hexameter verse, the first great Latin poem in that metre,
celebrating the achievements of the Roman nation from the time of
Aeneas to the poet's own days. The incident alluded to in Ennius'
verses is evidently the same as that narrated by Livy 32, cc. 9, 10.
Titus Quinctius Flamininus, who commanded in 198 B. C. the Roman
army opposed to Philip of Macedon, found the king strongly posted
on the mountains between Epirus and Thessaly. For forty days Flamininus lingered, hoping to find some path which would give him ac-
cess to the enemy's quarters. A shepherd who knew every nook of
the mountains came before the general, and promised to lead the Roman soldiers to the ground above Philip's camp. This was done, and

Flamininus drove the Macedonians into Thessaly. It is the shepherd who in the first line addresses Flamininus by his first name Titus. Cicero here cleverly applies the lines to his life-long friend T i t u s Pomponius Atticus. He several times takes the two words '*O Tite*' to designate the whole treatise; cf. Att. 16, 11, 3 '*O Tite*' *tibi prodesse laetor.* —— **quid**: accusative of respect or extent; so *nihil* in 30, *aliquid* in 82. A.* 240, *a*; G. 331, 3; H. 378, 2. —— **adiŭero**: for *adiŭvero*, the long vowel having become short after the falling out of the *v* between the two vowels. Catullus 66, 18 has *iŭerint* at the end of a pentameter verse, and the same scanning is found in Plautus and Terence. A. 128, *a*; G. 151, 1; H. 235. —— **levasso**: a form of *levavero*, which was originally *levaveso*. For the formation of this class of future-perfects see Peile, *Introduction to Greek and Latin Etymology*, p. 295, ed. 3; also Roby, *Gram.* 1, p. 199, who has a list of examples; he supports a different view from that given above; cf. A. 128, *e*, 3; G. 191, 5; H. 240, 4. —— **coquit**: 'vexes.' This metaphorical use of *coquere* occurs in poetry and late prose; cf. Plaut. Trin. 225 *egomet me coquo et macero et defetigo;* Verg. Aen. 7, 345 *quam . . . femineae ardentem curaeque iraeque coquebant;* Quint. 12, 10, 77 *sollicitudo oratorem macerat et coquit.* —— **versāt**: we have here the original quantity of the vowel preserved, as in *ponebāt* below, 10; the *a* in *versat* was originally as long as the *a* in *versās*. Plautus has some parallels to this scanning (see Corssen, Aussprache 11², 488), but it is rarely imitated by poets of the best period. Horace, however, has *arāt*, Odes 3, 16, 26. A. 375, *g*, 5; H. 580, III. n. 2. —— **praemi**: the genitive in *ī-ī* from nouns in *ium* only began to come into use at the end of the Republic. A. 40, *b*; G. 29, Rem. 1; H. 51, 5. —— **isdem**: Cicero may have written *isdem* or *eisdem* (two syllables), but he probably did not write the form most commonly found in our texts, *iisdem*. H. p. 74, foot-note 2. —— **Flamininum**: T. Quinctius Flaminīnus first served against Hannibal during the Second Punic War. He was present at the capture of Tarentum in 209 B. C., and in 208 was military tribune under Marcellus. After being employed on minor business of state, he became quaestor in 199, and, immediately after his year of office, consul, passing over the aedileship and praetorship, and attaining the consulship at the extraordinarily early age of 30. In 197 he won the

---

* A. = Allen and Greenough's Grammar, Revised Ed.; G. = Gildersleeve's Grammar; H. = Harkness's Grammar, Rev. Ed. of 1881. In quoting from the works of Cicero reference is made to sections, not to chapters.

great **victory** of Cynoscephalae over the Macedonians, which ended
the **war**. At the Isthmian games in the spring of 196 Flamininus made
his famous proclamation of freedom to all the Greeks. He returned
to Rome in 194 to enjoy a splendid triumph. For the rest of his life
he was employed chiefly on diplomatic business concerning Greece
and the East. One of his embassies was to Prusias, king of Bithynia,
to call on him to surrender Hannibal, who was living at his court in
advanced old age; this led to Hannibal's suicide. Flamininus was
censor in 189 (see below, 42), and lived on till some time after 167, in
which year he became augur; but the date of his death is unknown.
He was a man of brilliant ability both as general and as diplomat, and
also possessed much culture and was a great admirer of Greek literature. —— **ille vir** etc.: *i. e.* the shepherd mentioned in n. on line 1.
Livy 32, 11, 4 says that Flamininus sent to the master of the shepherd,
Charopus, an Epirote prince, to ask how far he might be trusted.
Charopus replied that Flamininus might trust him, but had better keep
a close watch on the operations himself. —— **haud magna cum re :**
'of no great property'; *re = re familiari,* as is often the case elsewhere
in both verse and prose. Cf. pro Caelio 78 *hominem sine re. Cum*
is literally 'attended by'; it is almost superfluous here, since *vir haud
magna re* would have had just the same meaning. Madvig, Gram.
§ 258 has similar examples. —— **plenus :** final *s* was so lightly pronounced that the older poets felt justified in neglecting it in their
scanning. It was probably scarcely pronounced at all by the less
educated Romans, since it is often wholly omitted in inscriptions, and
has been lost in modern Italian. Cicero, Orator 161, says that the
neglect to pronounce final *s* is 'somewhat boorish' (*subrusticum*),
though formerly thought 'very refined' (*politius*). Even Lucretius
sometimes disregards it in his scanning. In the ordinary literary
Latin a large number of words has lost an original *s; e. g.* all the
nouns of the *-a* declension. A. 375, *a*; G. 722; H. 608, 1, n. 3. ——
fidēi : this form of the genitive of *fides* is found also in Plautus, Aulu-
laria 575, and Lucretius 5, 102. *Fidĕi* as genitive seems only to occur
in late poets, but as dative it is found in a fragment of Ennius. *Fidē*
as genitive occurs in Horace and Ovid. H. 585, III. 1; Roby, 357, (*c*).
—— **quamquam :** see n. on 2 *etsi.* —— **sollicitari** etc.: Cicero probably has not quoted the line as Ennius wrote it. The word *sic,* at least,
is evidently inserted on purpose to correspond with *ut* before *Flamininum.* —— **noctesque diesque :** the use of *que . . . que* for *et . . . et* is

almost entirely poetical, Sallust being the only prose writer of the best period in whose works the usage is beyond doubt. *Noctes* is put before *dies* here, as in *noctes diesque* (Verr. 5, 112), *noctes et dies* (Brut. 308 *etc.*), *noctes ac dies* (Arch. 29); cf. also Verg. Aen. 6, 127; and νύκτας τε καὶ ἦμαρ in Iliad 5, 490; but the collocations *dies noctesque, dies et noctes* are far commoner in Cicero. Madvig (Emend. Liv. p. 487 n., ed. 2) says that in writers of Livy's time and earlier, when an action is mentioned which continues throughout a number of days and nights, either *dies et noctes* and the like phrases are used, or *die et nocte* and the like; but not *diem noctemque* or *diem et noctem*, which expression, he says, would imply that the action continued only throughout *one* day and *one* night. But Madvig has overlooked De Or. 2, 162 *eandem incudem diem noctemque tundentibus;* also three passages of Caesar: viz. Bell. Gall. 7, 42, 6 and 7, 77, 11; Bell. Civ. 1, 62, 1; to which add a passage in the Bell. Hisp. 38. Though *diem noctemque* does often mean 'throughout *one* day and *one* night' (as *e. g.* in Nep. Them. 8, 7), yet it would seem that the other sense cannot be excluded. —— **moderationem...aequitatem:** 'the self-control and even balance of your mind'. *Moderatio* is in Cic. a common translation of σωφροσύνη. *Aequitas* is not used here in its commonest sense of 'reasonableness' or 'equity', but as the noun corresponding to *aequus* in the ordinary phrase *aequus animus* (Horace, '*aequam memento rebus in arduis servare mentem*'); cf. Tusc. 1, 97 *hanc maximi animi aequitatem in ipsa morte,* said of Socrates' undisturbed composure just before his execution. —— **animi tui:** for the position of these words between *moderationem* and *aequitatem,* to both of which nouns they refer (a form of speech called by the Latin grammarians *coniunctio*), see note on Laelius 8 *cum summi viri tum amicissimi.* —— **cognomen:** *i. e.* the name *Atticus,* which Cicero's friend did not inherit, but adopted. For the word *cognomen* cf. n. on 5. —— **deportasse:** it should be noted that the verb *deportare* is nearly always in the best writers used of bringing things from the provinces to Italy or Rome, and not *vice versa,* the Romans using 'down' (*de*) of motion towards the capital. *Italia deportare* occurs in Tacitus and late writers, but only in the sense of banishing a person (cf. Ann. 14, 45). So *decedere de provincia* is common, but not *Roma decedere.* As to the form *deportasse,* it may be remarked that Cic. in the vast majority of instances uses the contracted and not the full forms of the infinitives corresponding to perfects in *-avi.* So *putassent* in 4. An extensive collection of examples

of this and similar contractions may be found in Frohwein, Die Per-
fectbildungen auf -vi bei Cicero; Gera, 1874. —— **humanitatem:**
'culture'; *i. e.* learning resulting in gentleness and refinement of
character. —— **prudentiam:** φρόνησιν or practical wisdom. Corn.
Nepos (or his imitator) in his life of Atticus 17, 3 says of him *prin-
cipum philosophorum ita percepta habuit praecepta ut his ad vitam agen-
dam non ad ostentationem uteretur.* —— **isdem rebus:** *i. e.* the state
of public affairs at the time; see Introd. —— **quibus me ipsum:**
strictly speaking the construction is inaccurate, since *suspicor com-
moveri* must be supplied, and Cicero does not really mean to say that
he merely *conjectures* himself to be seriously affected by the state of
public affairs; *ego ipse commoveor* would have accurately expressed
his meaning. The accusative is due to the attraction of *te* above.
—— **maior** = *difficilior* as often; *e. g.* Lael. 29 *quod maius est.* ——
visum est mihi conscribere: = *placuit mihi*, 'I have determined
to write'. The best writers rarely use the impersonal *videtur etc.*
followed by an infinitive. When the usage occurs *videtur mihi etc.*
generally have the meaning (as here) of δοκεῖ μοι κ. τ. λ. = 'I have
made up my mind'. Cf. Tusc. 5, 12 *Non mihi videtur ad beate
vivendum satis posse virtutem*; ib. 5, 22 (a curious passage) *mihi
enim non videbatur quisquam esse beatus posse cum esset in malis; in
malis autem sapientem esse posse;* Off. 3, 71 *malitia quae volt
illa quidem videri se esse prudentiam* ('craft which desires that people
should believe it to be wisdom'); Liv. 1, 10, 7 *dis visum nec irritam
conditoris templi vocem esse*... ('the gods decided that the word of the
founder of the shrine should not remain of no effect'). It would be
difficult, if not impossible, to find a passage in a writer before silver
Latin times where the best texts still exhibit anything like *videtur eum
facere* for *is videtur facere.* H. 534, 1, n. 1; Roby, 1353. —— **aliquid
ad te:** 'some work dedicated to you'; so below, 3; cf. also Lael. 4
ut de amicitia scriberem aliquid; ib. *Catone maiore qui est scriptus ad te
de senectute;* Div. 2, 3 *liber is quem ad nostrum Atticum de senectute
misimus.*

2. aut ... aut certe: so often in Cic.; *certe*, 'at any rate'. ——
senectutis: at the time the words were written Cic. was 62 years old,
Atticus three years older. For the meaning of *senectus* see n. on 4.
—— **levari volo:** the best Latin writers frequently use the passive
infinitive after verbs expressing desire, where moderns would incline
to the active; here Cic. instead of saying 'I wish to relieve yourself

and me of the burden' says 'I wish yourself and me to be relieved'.
—— etsi: = καίτοι 'and yet'. This use of *etsi* to introduce a clause
correcting the preceding clause, though not uncommon (*e. g.* below
29; Tusc. 1, 99; 3, 17; 4, 63; 5, 55), is far less common than that of
quamquam, which we have in 1, 9, 10, 24, 47, 67, 69. —— te quidem:
'you at all events', 'you for one'. —— modice ac sapienter: *modice*
recalls *moderationem* above (*modice* and *moderate* are used with exactly
the same sense by Cic.), while *sapienter* recalls *aequitatem*, since *sapientia* produces stability and an even balance of the mind. In De Or.
1, 132 we have *modice et scienter*. —— sicut omnia: cf. Fin. 1, 7 *fa-
cete is quidem sicut alia ;* also below, 65 *sicut alia.* —— et ferre et
laturum esse: Tischer rightly remarks that when a verb is repeated
thus with a variation of tense Cic. very nearly always uses *et ... et*, and
not a single *et* merely. The contrast between the two tenses is thus
made more pointed. Cf. 3 *et diximus et dicemus.* —— certo scio:
one of the best MSS., followed by some editors, has here *certe scio*.
The latter phrase would mean 'I am sure that I know' (a sense which
seems out of place here); the former 'I have certain or sure knowledge'. Observe that *certe* may be used with all verbs, while *certo* is
only used with *scire*. A. 151, *c.* —— sed: the idea implied is, 'but
though I well know you do not need such consolation, I have yet
resolved to address my book to you'. —— occurrebas dignus: a condensed construction for *occurrebat te dignum esse.*

P. 2. — munere ... uteretur: 'a gift such as we both might make
use of in company'. —— mihi quidem: this forms a correction
upon *uterque nostrum* above: 'whatever you may think of the work,
I at least have found the writing of it pleasant'. —— confectio:
'composition'; 'completion'; a word scarcely found in the classical Latin except in Cicero's writings. Cf. De Or. 2, 52 *anna-
lium confectio;* pro. Font. 3 *confectio tabularum* ('account-books').
—— fuit ut absterserit: the sequence of tenses *fuit ut abstergeret*
would have been equally admissible, but the meaning would have been
slightly different. With the perfect the sense is 'was so pleasant that
it *has* wiped away'; with the imperfect 'was so pleasant that it *did*
(while I was writing) wipe away'. The metaphor in *absterserit* is common: *e. g.* Tusc. 3, 43 *luctum omnem absterseris*. With this statement
of Cicero's concerning the effect the work had on himself contrast Att.
14, 21, 3 *legendus mihi saepius est Cato maior ad te missus. A m a r i o-
r e m enim me s e n e c t u s f a c i t. Stomachor omnia.* —— omnis: acc.

pl. A. 55, *c*; **G.** 60, 1 ; **H.** 67. —— **effecerit mollem** : so 56 *poteratne tantus animus efficere non iucundam senectutem;* but 56 *conditiora f a c i t haec aucupium. Efficio* gives more emphatically than *facio* the idea of the completion of the action. Cf. Lael. 73 *efficere aliquem consulem*, ' to carry through a man's election as consul ' ; *facere aliquem consulem* being merely ' to vote for a man's election to the consulship '. —— **satis digne** : ' as she deserves ', lit. ' in a sufficiently worthy manner '. Some editors have thought *digne* superfluous and wished to cast it out, but we have *satis digne* elsewhere, as in Verr. Act. II. 1, 82 ; cf. also Sex. Rosc. 33 *pro dignitate laudare satis commode.* —— **qui pareat...degere** : a conditional sentence of irregular form (*qui = siquis ; cui*, simply connective, = *et ei*). Cf. Div. 1, 127 *qui enim teneat causas rerum futurarum, idem necesse est omnia teneat quae futura sint ;* also the examples in Roby's Grammar, 1558. A. 310, *a*, 307, *b*; G. 594, 1, 598; H. 507, II. and III. 2. Some, however, make *possit* a subjunctive of characteristic or of cause with *cui*, and *pareat* a subjunctive by attraction. —— **omne tempus aetatis** : ' every season of life '; so in 55 *extremum tempus aetatis;* 70 *breve tempus aetatis.* The opposite phrase *aetas temporis* is very rare ; it occurs in Propertius 1, 4, 7.

3. ceteris : neuter adjective used as a noun, equivalent to *ceteris rebus* ' the other matters ' ; *i. e.* the political troubles hinted at above. The best writers do not often use the neuter adjective as noun in the *oblique* cases unless there is something in the context to show the gender clearly, as in 24 *aliis...eis quae;* we have, however, below in 8, *isto = ista re ;* 72, *reliquum ;* 77, *caelestium = rerum caelestium ;* and in 78, *praeteritorum futurorumque ;* see other instances in n. on Lael. 50 *similium.* The proleptic or anticipatory use of *ceteris* should also be noticed ; its sense is not fully seen till we come to *hunc librum ;* the same use occurs below in 4, 5, 59, 60 ; so *aliis* in 24; cf. also n. on Lael. 7 *reliqua.* —— **diximus ... dicemus** : when a clause or phrase consists of four parts, which go in pairs (as here *diximus, dicemus* on one side, and *multa, saepe* on the other), the Latins frequently arrange the words so as to put one pair between the two members of the other pair, as here. This usage is called by grammarians *chiasmus.* Thus if we denote the four parts by *AA', BB', chiasmus* requires the order *ABB'A'* or *BAA'B'.* See examples in 8, 20, 22, 38, 44, 71. For the more complicated forms of chiasmus consult Nägelsbach, Stil. §§ 167, 169. A. 344, *f*; G. 684; H. 562. —— **librum ... misimus** : observe the omission of a particle at the beginning of the clause; the contrast between *ceteris* and *hunc librum* is made stronger by the omission. For this *asyndeton adversativum* see n. on Lael. 5 *Laelium...putes.* For tense of *misimus*, 'I send', see A. 282; G. 244; H. 472, 1. —— **omnem:** see n. on 62. —— **tribuimus:** perfect tense like *misimus.* —— **Tithono...Aristo:** see Introd. —— **Cius:** Greek Κεῖος (a native of Ceos), not to be confused with Χῖος (a native of Chios), or Κῶος (a native of Cos). Cicero generally denotes the Greek diphthong ει by *ī* not *ē*. This Aristo was a Peripatetic. —— **parum...auctoritatis:** observe how often Cicero takes trouble to separate words which are, grammatically, closely connected. So above, *omnis...molestias; 7 multorum...senectutem; 9 mirificos ...fructus; 21 civium...nomina; 33 minus...virium; 53 multo... fecundior;* etc. etc. See also n. on 15 *quam sit iusta.* A. 344, *c, d, e*; H. 561, III. —— **esset:** condition omitted. A. 311; G. 602; H. 510. —— **maiorem auctoritatem:** cf. Lael. 4. —— **apud quem:** 'at whose house'; so 55 *a me,* 'from my house'. A. 153; G. 417; H. 446, n. 4. —— **Laelium...Scipionem:** see Introd. —— **facimus admirantis:** 'we represent as expressing astonishment'. For *facere*, in this sense, Cic. more often uses *inducere* 'to bring on the stage', as in Lael. 4 *Catonem induxi senem disputantem.* Cf. however 54 *Homerus Laerten colentem agrum facit;* also Brut. 218; Orat. 85. Instead of *facimus* we might have expected either *fecimus* to correspond with *misimus* and *tribuimus* above, or *faciemus* to correspond with *videbitur* below. On the use of the participle see A. 292, *e*; G. 536; H. 535, I. 4. —— **eruditius disputare:** Cic. not infrequently in his dialogues makes people talk with more learning than they really possessed. He several times confesses this as regards Lucullus and Catulus in the Academica, and as regards Antonius in the De Oratore. —— **ferat:** subjunctive because embodying the sentiment of Laelius and Scipio. Roby, 1744; Madvig, 357; H. 516, II. —— **suis libris** etc.: for the allusions here to Cato's life, works, and opinions see Introd. —— **quid opus est plura?** *sc. dicere;* cf. the elliptic phrases *quid multa? sc. dicam* in 78; also below, 10 *praeclare.* A. 206, *c*; H. 368, 3, n. 2.

4. saepe numero soleo: 'it is my frequent custom'. *Numero* is literally 'by the count or reckoning', and in *saepe numero* had originally the same force as in *quadraginta numero* and the like; but the phrase came to be used merely as a slight strengthening of *saepe.* —— **cum hoc...cum ceterarum:** the use of *cum* in different senses in the same clause, which seems awkward, is not uncommon; cf. below, 67

The spelling *quum* was certainly not used by Cicero, and probably by no other Latin writer of the best period. H. 311, foot-note 4. It is worth remarking that *cum* the conjunction and *cum* the preposition, though spelt alike, are by origin quite distinct. The former is derived from the pronominal stem *ka* or *kva*, and is cognate with *qui ;* the latter comes from the root *sak* 'to follow', and is cognate with Gk. σύν, Lat. *sequor*, etc. See Vaniček, Etymologisches Wörterbuch, pp. 96, 984. —— **rerum . . . sapientiam:** 'wisdom *in* affairs'; the objective genitive. —— **excellentem:** in sense much stronger than our 'excellent'; *excellentem perfectamque* 'pre-eminent and indeed faultless'. —— **quod . . . senserim:** this clause takes the place of an object to *admirari*. The subjunctive is used because the speaker reports his own reason for the wonder, formerly felt, as if according to the views of another person, and without affirming his holding the same view at the time of speaking. Madvig, 357, *a*, Obs. 1. A. 341, *d*, Rem. —— **odiosa:** this word is not so strong as our 'hateful', but rather means 'wearisome', 'annoying'. In Plautus the frequent expression *odiosus es* means, in colloquial English, 'you bore me'. Cf. 47 *odiosum et molestum ;* 65 *odiosa offensio*. —— **onus Aetna gravius:** a proverbial expression with an allusion to Enceladus, who, after the defeat of the Giants by Juppiter, was said to have been imprisoned under Mt. Aetna. Cf. Eurip. Hercules Furens, 637 ; also Longfellow's poem, Enceladus. —— **haud sane difficilem:** 'surely far from difficult'; cf. 83 *haud sane facile*. —— **quibus:** a *dativus commodi*, 'those for whom there is no aid in themselves'. Cf. Lael. 79 *quibus in ipsis*. —— **bene beateque vivendum:** 'a virtuous and happy life'; 'virtue and happiness'; so *bene honesteque* below, 70. —— **qui . . . petunt:** these are the αὐτάρκεις, men sufficient for themselves, '*in se toti teretes atque rotundi*'. We have here a reminiscence of the Stoic doctrine about the wise man, whose happiness is quite independent of everything outside himself, and is caused solely by his own virtue. Cicero represents the same Stoic theory in Lael. 7. Cf. Juv. Sat. 10, 357–362; also Seneca, De Cons. Sap. VIII., De Prov. I. 5. —— **a se ipsi:** 'themselves from themselves,' so in 78 *se ipse moveat . . . se ipse relicturus sit ;* 84 *me ipse consolabar*. Expressions like *a se ipsis* are quite uncommon in Cicero. Cf. n. on Lael. 5 *te ipse cognosces ;* also see below, 38 *se ipsa ;* 78 *se ipse*. —— **naturae necessitas:** 'the inevitable conditions of nature'. Cf. 71 *quid est tam secundum naturam quam senibus emori ?* —— **afferat:** subjunctive because *nihil quod = nihil tale ut*. A. 320, *a*; G. 633, 634; H. 503, I. —— **quo in genere:** *sc. rerum;* with this phrase the defining genitive is commonly omitted by Cicero. So below, 45 *in eo genere.* —— **ut ... adeptam:** notice the chiasmus. —— **eandem:** *idem* is used in the same way, to mark an emphatic contrast, in 24, 52, 68, 71. —— **adeptam:** this is probably the only example in Cicero of the passive use of *adeptus,* which occurs in Sallust, Ovid, Tacitus, etc.; and in this passage the use cannot be looked on as certain, since one of the very best and several of the inferior MSS. read *adepti.* Cicero, however, uses a good many deponent participles in a passive sense (cf. below, 59 *dimensa;* 74 *meditatum;* see also a list, Roby, 734), and some of them occur very rarely. Thus *periclitatus, arbitratus, depastus* as passives are found each in only one passage. —— **inconstantia:** 'instability', 'inconsistency'. *Constantia,* unwavering firmness and consistency, is the characteristic of the wise man; cf. Acad. 2, 23 *sapientia...quae ex sese habeat constantiam;* also Lael. 8 and 64.

P. 3. — **aiunt:** *sc. stulti.* —— **putassent:** the subjunctive is due to the indirect discourse. Where we say 'I should not have thought,' the Latins say, in direct narration, '*non putaram,*' *i. e.* 'I never had thought' (so Off. 1, 81 and often in Cicero's letters). Translate, 'more quickly than they had ever expected'. Cf. Att. 6, 1, 6 *accipiam equidem dolorem mihi illum irasci sed multo maiorem non esse eum talem qualem putassem.* See Zumpt, Gram., 518. —— **falsum putare:** 'to form a mistaken judgment'. For *falsum* as noun equivalent to ψεῦδος, cf. 6 *gratissimum;* also n. on 3 *ceteris.* —— **qui citius ·** lit. 'in what way quicker'; cf. Tusc. 5, 89 *qui melius.* H. 188, II. 2. —— **adulescentia ... senectus ... pueritia:** boyhood was generally at Rome supposed to last till the 17th year (the time for assuming the *toga virilis* and for beginning military service). *Iuventus* is usually the age from 17 to 45, during which men were liable to be called on for active service. Ordinarily, in colloquial language, *adulescentia* is the earlier portion of *iuventus,* say the years from 17 to 30 (cf. 33), but Cicero seems here to make *adulescentia* co-extensive with *iuventus.* From 45 to 60 is the *aetas seniorum,* the period during which citizens in early Rome might be called out for the defence of the city, but not for active service. *Senectus* was commonly reckoned as beginning at 60; but in § 60 Cicero includes in *senectus* the *aetas seniorum,* and probably intended to include it here. In Tusc. 1, 34 Cic. reckons three ages *pueritia adulescentia senectus* as here; below in 74, four periods, or five.

—— quamvis : = *quantumvis*. —— effluxisset : subjunctive because of the mood of *posset*, to which it stands in subordinate relation. *Cum* here is purely temporal. See Roby, 1778 ; A. 342 ; G. 666 ; H. 529, II. —— posset : see n. on *esset* above, 3.

5. si...soletis...sumus : the apodosis and protasis do not strictly correspond ; the sense really required is 'if that wisdom for which you admire me does exist, it lies in this ', etc. —— utinam... esset : *esset* here gives a greater appearance of modesty than would have been expressed by *sit :* ' would it were, as it certainly is not '. A. 267 ; G. 253 ; H. 483, 2. —— cognomine : Cato bore the title *sapiens* even in his lifetime ; see Introd. *Cognomen* is used in good Latin to denote both the family name and the acquired by-name ; in late Latin this latter is denoted by *agnomen*. —— in hoc sapientes : but above, 4 *rerum sapientiam*, not *in rebus*. The genitive construction is not found with *sapiens* used as noun or adjective till late Latin times. —— naturam ducem etc. : Cato's claim to the title of *sapiens* does not rest on any deep knowledge of philosophy, but on practical wisdom or common sense and experience in affairs. Cf. Lael. 6 and 19. In this passage Cicero has put into Cato's mouth phrases borrowed from the Stoic philosophy, which declared the life of virtue to be life in accordance with nature (*naturae convenienter vivere* or ὁμολογουμένως τῇ φύσει ζῆν). Cf. 71, n. on *secundum naturam*. —— tamquam deum : observe *deum* not *deam*, because nature is compared with, and not identified with, a divine being. Cf. Fin. 5, 43 *eam (rationem) quasi deum ducem subsequens*. —— aetatis : here = *vitae*, life as a whole. Cf. 2 *omne tempus aetatis* and n. ; also 13 *aetatis...senectus ;* 33, 64, 82. —— descriptae : ' composed '; literally ' written out '. The reading *discriptae*, which many editions give, does not so well suit the passage. *Discribere* is to map out, plan, arrange, put in order (see 59 *discripta* and *discriptio*) ; the point here lies, however, not in the due arrangement of the different scenes of a play, but in the careful working out of each scene. *Ab ea* must be supplied after *descriptae* from *a qua* above. —— actum : the common comparison of life with a drama is also found in 64, 70, 85. —— inerti : the sense of ' ignorant ', ' inartistic ' (*in, ars*), has been given to this by some editors (cf. Hor. Ep. 2, 2, 126 *praetulerim scriptor delirus inersque videri*, and Cic. Fin. 2, 115 *artes, quibus qui carebant, inertes a maioribus nominabantur*), but the meaning ' inactive ', ' lazy ', ' slovenly ' seems to suit *neglectum* better. —— poeta : nature is here the dramatist, the drama is life, the

actors are human beings. —— **sed tamen** etc. : 'but for all that it
was inevitable that there should be something with the nature of an
end.' So 69 *in quo est aliquid extremum* ; 43 *aliquid pulchrum*. ——
arborum bacis : the word *baca* (the spelling *bacca* has little or no
authority) is applied to all fruits growing on bushes or trees ; cf. Tusc.
1, 31 *arbores seret diligens agricola, quarum aspiciet bacam ipse numquam.* —— **terraeque fructibus :** here = cereals, roots, vegetables,
and small fruits.   No sharp distinction can be drawn between *fruges*
and *fructus* (*e. g.* in Div. 1, 116 we have *fruges terrae bacasve arborum*),
though *fructus* as commonly used is the more general word of the two.
—— **maturitate . . . caducum :** 'a time of senility, so to speak, and
readiness to drop, that comes of a seasonable ripeness'.   *Vietus* is
literally 'twisted' or 'bent', being originally the passive participle of
viere.   The comparison of old age with the ripeness of fruit recurs in
71.   Cf. Plin. Ep. 5, 14, 5 *non tam aetatis maturitate quam vitae.* ——
ferundum : the form in *-undus* is archaic, and generally used by Cic.
in quoting or imitating passages of laws, sacred formulae, and the like.
H. 239. —— **molliter :** here 'gently', 'with resignation' ; though *molliter ferre* often has another meaning, viz. to bear pain or trouble in
an *unmanly* fashion.   Cf. *facillime ferre* below. —— **quid est aliud**
etc. : The words perhaps imply the rationalistic explanation of myths
which the Greeks had begun to teach to the Romans during Cato's
lifetime.   Trans. 'what else but resistance to nature is equivalent to
warring against the gods', and *not* 'what else does warring with the
gods mean but to resist nature'.   In comparisons of this sort the
Latins generally put the things compared in a different order from
that required by English idiom.   Thus in Div. 2, 78 *quid est aliud
nolle moneri a Iove nisi efficere ut aut ne fieri possit auspicium aut, si
fiat, videri ;* S. Rosc. 54 *quid est aliud iudicio ac legibus ac maiestate
vestra abuti ad quaestum ac libidinem, nisi hoc modo accusare ;* Phil. 1,
22 ; 2, 7 ; 5, 5 ; 10, 5. —— **Gigantum modo :** see n. on 4 *Aetna gravius.* —— **dis :** for the form *dis* see n. on 25.

   6. atqui : in the best Latin *atqui* does not introduce a statement
contradicting the preceding statement, but one that *supplements* it.
Here it may be translated 'True, but'.   Cf. 66, 81. —— **gratissimum :** equivalent to *rem gratissimam*.   With the thought cf. Rep. 1,
34 *gratum feceris si explicaris ;* Lael. 16 *pergratum feceris si dispu-
taris.* —— **ut . . . pollicear :** so Acad. 1, 33 *nos vero volumus, ut pro
Attico respondeam ;* Brut. 122 *nobis vero placet, ut pro Bruto etiam re*

spondeam ; Lael. 32 *tu vero perge ; pro hoc enim respondeo.* A. 317, *c* ; H. 499, 2, n. —— **senes fieri :** if the infinitive had depended on *speramus* alone and *volumus* had not intervened, Cicero would probably have written *nos futuros esse senes.* —— **multo ante :** *sc. quam id factum erit :* so Balb. 41 *re denique multo ante* (*sc. quam factum est*) *audita,* and very often in Cicero. —— **didicerimus :** as this corresponds with *feceris,* it would have been formally correct to write here *nos docueris.* —— **quibus...possimus :** 'what considerations will enable us most easily to support the growing burden of age'. —— **futurum est =** μέλλει εἶναι : this form of the future is used in preference to the simple *erit* because it is desired to represent the event as *on the very point of fulfilment,* and therefore sure of fulfilment. *Erit* would have implied much less certainty. Trans. 'I will do so, if my action *is going to give* you pleasure'. Cf. 67 *beatus futurus sum ;* also 81, 85. See Roby, 1494. —— **nisi molestum est :** a common expression of courtesy, like 15 *nisi alienum putas, si placet ;* cf. Hor. Sat. 2, 8, 4 *si grave non est.* —— **tamquam longam viam :** Cicero here puts into Laelius' mouth almost the very words addressed by Socrates to the aged Cephalus in the introduction to Plato's Republic, 328 E. Observe the succession of similar sounds in t*amquam,* aliqu*am,* long*am,* vi*am.* —— **viam conficeris :** so pro Quint. 79 *conficere* DCC *milia passuum ; conficere iter* is a common phrase. For mood see A. 312; G. 604; H. 513, II. —— **quam...ingrediundum sit :** this construction, the neuter of the gerundive with *est* followed by an accusative case, is exceedingly rare excepting in two writers, Lucretius and Varro. See the full list of examples given by Roby, Gram., Pref. to vol. 2, p. LXXII. A. 294, *c* ; H. 371, I. 2, 2), n. The best texts of Cicero now give only one example of a construction at all resembling this, viz. pro Scauro 13 *obliviscendum vobis putatis matrum in liberos, virorum in uxores scelera ?* The supposition of some scholars, that in this passage Cic. used the construction in imitation of the archaic style of Cato, is not likely to be true, seeing that in Cato's extant works the construction does not once occur. For the form *-undum* see n. on 5 *ferundum.* —— **istuc :** not adverb, but neuter pronoun, as in 8. The kind of construction, *istuc videre quale sit* for *videre quale istuc sit,* is especially common in Cicero.

7. faciam ut potero : 'I will do it as well as I can'. Observe the future *potero* where English idiom would require a present. So Rep. 1, 38 *hic Scipio, faciam quod voltis, ut potero.* —— **saepe enim :**

enim introduces a reason, not for the words *ut potero*, but for *faciam* : — 'I will grant your request because I have often heard complaints about old age and therefore have thought of the matter'. —— **pares autem** etc.: parenthetical. —— **vetere proverbio**: the saying is as old as Homer, Od. 17, 218 ὡς αἰεὶ τὸν ὅμοιον ἄγει θεὸς ὡς τὸν ὅμοιον; cf. also Plat., Rep. 329 A, Symp. 195 B, Phaedr. 240 C.

P. 4. — **facillime**: 'most cheerfully', 'most eagerly'; a common meaning of the word in Cic., *e. g.* Fam. 2, 16, 2 *in maritimis facillime sum*, *i. e.* 'I find most pleasure in staying by the sea'. —— **quae**: a kind of explanation of *querellis*: — 'lamentations, viz. such utterances as' etc.; see n. on Lael. 14 *quae*; cf. Fam. 2, 8, 2 *sermonibus de re publica....quae nec possunt scribi nec scribenda sunt.* A. 199, *b*; G. 616, 3, I.; H. 445, 5. —— **C. Salinator**: probably C. Livius Salinator, praetor in 191 B. C. (Livy 35, 24), who was entrusted with the equipment of the Roman fleets during the war against Antiochus. He was born about 230, and was therefore a little younger than Cato; cf. *fere aequales* below. Salinator was consul in 188, and died in 170. For the name Salinator cf. n. on 11. —— **Sp. Albinus**: Sp. Postumius Albinus was consul in 186, and was with his colleague appointed to investigate the great Bacchanalian conspiracy of that year (Livy 39, cc. 1 seq.). Albinus died in 180. He was probably a little younger than Salinator. He can scarcely have been fifty years of age at his death. —— **tum ... tum**: 'now ... again'; so in 45. —— **carerent**: see n. on 3 *ferat.* —— **vitam nullam putarent**: 'they considered life to be not life at all'. For *vitam nullam* cf. Lael. 86 *sine amicitia vitam esse nullam* ; also the Greek phrase βίος ἀβίωτος ; and below, 77 *vitam quae est sola vita nominanda* ; also 82. A. 239; H. 373, 1, n. 2. *Putarent* = 'thought, as they said'. —— **id quod esset accusandum**: the subjunctive *esset* is used because a *class* of things is referred to, 'nothing of a nature to deserve complaint'; *id quod erat*, etc. would have meant merely 'that one thing which was matter for complaint'. A. 320; G. 634, Rem. 1; H. 503, I. —— **usu venirent**: the phrase *usu venire* differs very little in meaning from *accidere*. *Usu* is commonly explained as an ablative ('in practice', 'in experience'), but is quite as likely to be a dative of the sort generally called predicative ('to come as matter of experience'); cf. Verg. Aen. 1, 22 *venire excidio* ; Plin. N. H. 28, 106 *odio* ; Caes. B. G. 5, 27 *subsidio.* —— **quorum ... multorum** : the first genitive is dependent on the second, so that *quorum = e quibus.* Notice the separation of *quorum* from *multorum*, and of *multorum* from *senectutem*. —— sine querella : attribute of *senectutem*. A. 217, Rem.; H. 359, n. 1, 4), and ·n. 3. This form of attributive phrase, consisting of a preposition with a noun, is common; cf. 24 *ex agro Sabino rusticos Romanos ; 40 cum hostibus clandestina colloquia. Querella* is better spelling than *querela.* See Roby, 177, 2. —— qui : 'men of such nature as to...' —— et...nec : Roby, 2241. The reason for the departure from the ordinary sequence of particles lies in the words *non moleste. Nec...et* is common; see 51, 53. —— libidinum vinculis etc. : Cic. is here thinking of the conversation between Socrates and Cephalus in Plato, Rep. 329 D, for which see Introd. —— moderati : 'self-controlled '; cf. n. on 1 *moderationem ; difficiles,* 'peevish'; *inhumani,* 'unkindly'; *importunitas,* 'perversity'. *Importunitas* seems to be used as the substantive corresponding in sense with the adjective *difficilis. Difficultas,* in the sense of 'peevishness', probably occurs only in Mur. 19.

8. dixerit quispiam : 'some one will say presently'; a gentle way of introducing one's own objection. The mood of *dixerit* is probably indicative, not subjunctive ; see the thorough discussion in Roby, Gram , Vol. 2, Pref., p. CIV. *et seq.* —— opes et copias : 'resources and means '. *Opes* has a wider meaning than *copias* (mere material wealth) and includes all sources of power, influence, and authority as well as wealth. Thus in Lael. 22 the end of *divitiae* is said to be enjoyment ; of *opes,* worship (*opes ut colare*). *Dignitas* is social position. —— id : remark the singular pronoun, which indicates that the preceding clause is now taken as conveying one idea. Trans. 'such fortune '. —— contingere : 'to fall to one's lot ' is the phrase in English which most closely represents *contingere.* This verb is not, as is often assumed, used merely of *good* fortune ; it implies in itself nothing concerning the *character* of events, whether they be good or bad, but simply that the events take place *naturally* and were to be expected. See n. on Lael. 8, where the word is distinctly used in connection with *bad* fortune, as it is, strikingly, in 71 below. —— est...omnia : 'your statement indeed amounts to something, but it by no means comprises every consideration '. The phrase *esse aliquid,* 'to be of some importance ', is often used by Cic. both of things and of persons ; cf. Tusc. 5, 104 *eos aliquid esse,* also n. on 17 *nihil afferunt.* So *esse aliquis* of persons, as in the well-known passage of Iuvenal, 1, 72 *aude aliquid brevibus Gyaris et carcere dignum si vis esse aliquis.* For the general sense cf. Tusc. 3, 52 *est id quidem magnum, sed non sunt in hoc omnia ;*

so De Or. 2, 215; ib. 3, 221; Leg. 2, 24 *in quo sunt omnia*. —— **isto**:
the use of the neuter pronoun in the oblique case as substantive is
noticeable. —— **Themistocles** etc.: Cicero borrows the story from
Plato (Rep. 329 E *et seq.*), but it was first told by Herodotus, 8, 125
who gave a somewhat different version. Themistocles had received
great honors at Sparta when Athenian ambassador there; an envious
man declaring that the honors were paid really to Athens and not to
Themistocles, the statesman answered οὔτ' ἂν ἐγώ, ἐὼν Βελβινίτης (*i. e.*
an inhabitant of the small island of Belbina lying to the S. of Cape
Sunium) ἐτιμήθην οὕτω πρὸς Σπαρτιητέων, οὔτ' ἂν σύ, ἄνθρωπε, ἐὼν
'Αθηναῖος. —— **Seriphio**: Seriphus is a small island belonging to the
Cyclad group and lying almost due N. of Melos, and due E. of the
Scyllaean promontory. Seriphus is often taken by ancient writers as
a specimen of an insignificant community (*e. g.* Aristoph. Acharn. 542;
Cic. N. D. 1, 88), but it had the honor of being one of the three island
states which refused to give earth and water to the Persian envoys,
the other two being the adjacent islands of Melos and Siphnus (Herodotus, 8, 46). —— **iurgio**: *iurgium* is a quarrel which does not go
beyond words; *rixa* a quarrel where the disputants come to blows.
—— **si ego**: but further on, *tu si*. The contrast would certainly be
more perfect if *ego si* were read, as has been proposed, in place of *si
ego*. —— **quod eodem modo...dici**: Cic. commonly says *quod ita
dicendum* and the like; see n. on 35 *quod ni ita fuisset*. Cato means
that just as Themistocles' success was due to two things, his own
character and his good fortune, so two things are necessary to make
old age endurable, viz. moderate fortune and wisdom. He then in 9
insists that of these two conditions wisdom is far the more important.
—— **nec...levis...nec...non gravis**: notice the chiasmus.

9. omnino: here = παντάπασι 'undoubtedly', in a strongly affirma
tive sense, as in 76; but in 28 (where see n.) it is concessive. ——
cum diu multumque vixeris: literally 'when you have lived long
and much', *i. e.* when you have not only had a long life but have done
a great deal in the course of it. The phrases *diu multumque, multum
et diu* are common in Cic., as below, 38; Acad. 1, 4; Div. 2, 1; Off.
1, 118; Leg. Agr. 2, 88; De Or. 1, 152. For mood see A. 309, *a*; H.
518, 2. —— **ecferunt**: *ecferunt* for *efferunt* (*ec = ex = ecs*; so ἐκ = ἐξ
= ἐκς) was old-fashioned in Cicero's time, but forms of the sort, as
below, 39 *ecfrenate*, according to the evidence of the best MSS., occur
in a good many passages. See Neue, Formenlehre, Vol. 2, pp. 766

seq., ed. 2. —— **numquam deserunt**: the omission of the object after *deserunt* is not common. With the general sense of this passage cf. Arch. 16 *litterarum studia adulescentiam alunt, s e n e c t u t e m o b l e c t a n t, secundas res ornant, adversis perfugium ac solacium praebent, delectant domi, non impediunt foris, pernoctant nobiscum, peregrinantur, rusticantur.*

P. 5. — 10. Q. Maximum: the famous Q. Fabius Maximus Verrucosus Ovicula Cunctator, hero of the Second Punic War. —— **eum ... recepit**: this clause has often been suspected to be an insertion of the writers of MSS. But (1) the capture of Tarentum in 209 B.C. was Fabius' crowning achievement, and 'captor of Tarentum' was often added to his name as a title of honor; see *e. g.* De Or. 2, 273; and (2) there were several other persons of distinction bearing the name Q. Maximus about the same time, so that some special mark was wanted for the sake of clearness. Notice *recepit* 'recovered', Tarentum having been lost by the Romans to Hannibal in 212 B.C. —— **senem adulescens**: observe the emphasis given by placing close together the two words of opposite meaning. —— **erat ... gravitas**: 'that hero possessed dignity tempered by courtesy'. Expressions like *erat in illo gravitas* are common in Cicero; *e. g.* Mur. 58 *erat in Cotta summa eloquentia.* The metaphor in *condīta,* 'seasoned', is also common; cf. Lael. 66 *condimentum amicitiae.* —— **quamquam**: 'though indeed', introducing a necessary correction of the last words *nec senectus mores mutaverat.* For this corrective *quamquam* cf. n. on 2. —— **consul primum**: B. C. 233. —— **grandem natu**: although the phrases *maior, maximus, parvus, minor, minimus natu* are of frequent occurrence, yet *magnus natu* is not Latin, *grandis natu* being always used instead. The historians sometimes use *magno natu esse* or *in magno natu esse.* —— **anno post**: the word *unus* is not usually attached to *annus* except where there is a strong contrast between one and a larger number of years. *Anno post* must not be translated 'during the year after'; but either 'a year after', *anno* being regarded as the ablative of measure or excess, literally 'later by a year', or 'at the end of a year', the ablative being one of limitation, and *fuerat* being equivalent to *factus erat* 'had been elected'. So *quinto anno* below, 'at the end of the fifth year', *i. e.* 'five years after'. —— **adulescentulus miles**: See n. on 21 *quemquam senem.* Translate 'when quite a youth I marched with him to Capua as a private soldier'. G. 324; H. 363, 3, 2). *Miles* here = *gregarius miles.* ——

quem magistratum : *sc. quaesturam,* to be understood from *quaestor.*
Cf. Mur. 18 *quaesturam una petiit et sum ego factus* (*sc. quaestor*) *prior.*

—— **Tuditano et Cethego :** when the *praenomina* of the consuls are
given the names generally stand side by side without *et ;* when they
are omitted *et* is generally inserted. Cf. n. on 50 *Centone Tuditanoque,* etc. —— **cum quidem :** the *quidem* simply adds a slight emphasis to *cum ;* 'at the very time when', ἐπειδή γε. —— **suasor :** *suasor
legis* was any person who publicly (*i. e.* before the senate or people in
contio assembled) spoke in favor of a measure, *dissuasor* any one who
spoke against it. Cf. 14 *suasissem.* —— **legis Cinciae :** a law passed
in 204 B. C. by M. Cincius Alimentus, a plebeian tribune, whereby advo-
cates were forbidden to take fees from their clients, and certain limi-
tations were placed on gifts of property by private persons. —— **cum
... esset :** '*though* he was'; so below 11, 30, etc. —— **grandis :** =
grandis natu. —— **iuveniliter :** Hannibal was 29 years of age when
he entered Italy in 218. —— **exsultantem :** 'wildly roaming'. The
word in its literal sense is used of a horse galloping at its own will
over a plain. The metaphorical use is common in Cicero; cf. Acad.
2, 112 *cum sit c a m p u s in quo e x s u l t a r e possit oratio, cur eam
tantas in angustias compellimus ?* —— **patientia :** 'endurance', 'persist-
ence'; it is not equivalent to our 'patience'. —— **praeclare :** *sc. dicit ;*
cf. n. on 3. —— **familiaris :** see Introd. —— **unus homo** etc. : these
lines were famous, and were not only often quoted with the name of
Ennius attached (as in Off. 1, 84; Livy 30, 26), but also imitated or
adapted without mention of his name, as being too familiar to need
it; cf. Att. 2, 19, 2; Ovid, Fast. 2, 241; Verg. Aen. 6, 846; Suet. Tib.
21. —— **cunctando :** Cf. Polybius 3, 105, 8. On Fabius' military
policy consult Mommsen, Hist. of Rome, Bk. III. ch. 5. —— **rem :**
here = *rem publicam.* —— **noenum :** the older form from which *non*
is an abbreviation; = *ne-oinom, n-oinom,* literally 'not one thing'; cf.
nihil = *ne-hilum* 'not a whit', also the rare word *ningulus* = *ne oin-
culus,* 'not even a little one'. —— **rumores :** 'fame', 'public opinion'.
—— **ponebāt :** for the long vowel cf. n. on 1, l. 2 *versat.* —— **plusque :**
MSS. *postque ; plusque* is the emendation of Bernays. *Plusque magisque* is a variation upon the ordinary phrases *plus plusque, magis
magisque.*

11. Salinatori : there can be no doubt that Cicero is guilty of a
blunder here, and in De Or. 2, 273 where the story also occurs. Livy
(27, 34, 7) gives M. Livius Macatus as the name of the Roman com-

mander who held the citadel of Tarentum while Hannibal was in possession of the town. Cicero probably found the commander described by the annalists merely as M. Livius (so in Livy 24, 20, 13; 26, 39, 1), and then jumped to the conclusion that he was the famous M. Livius Salinator. This man, the father of the Salinator mentioned in 7, was consul in 219 and subdued the Illyrians, but was condemned for misappropriation of public moneys and went into exile. In 210 he was induced to return by the desire of the senate. In 207 he became consul with C. Claudius Nero, and defeated Hasdrubal in the great battle of the Metaurus. In 204 Livius was censor with Nero as his colleague, and won his name *Salinator* by imposing a tax on salt. The title was bestowed in ridicule, but clung to the family. Salinator was a relative of M. Livius Macatus. See Liv. 27, 34, 7. —— **ita dicenti** etc.: the anecdote is told by Livy, 27, 25, 5 and Plutarch, Fab. 23. Both, however, refer the story not to the time at which Tarentum was taken, but to the year after, when altercations about it took place in the senate. —— **toga**: here put for ' civil life', the *toga* being replaced in time of war by the *sagum.* Cf. in Pisonem 73 *pacis est insigne et oti toga, contra autem arma tumultus atque belli;* De Or. 3, 167 '*togam*', *pro* '*pace*', '*arma*', *ac* '*tela*', *pro* '*bello*'. We have the same contrast between *arma* and *toga* in Cicero's own much-derided verse, *cedant arma togae, concedat laurea laudi,* which is defended by him, in Pis. 73 and Off. 1, 77. —— **consul iterum** etc.: as the second consulship of Fabius was in 228 B. C., while the law of Flaminius was passed in 232 (according to Polybius), it is very difficult to understand the statement here made. It is possible that Flaminius was one of the commissioners for executing his own law, and that its execution lasted over the time of Fabius' second consulship. The Flaminius here mentioned is the same who fell as consul in 217 at the battle of lake Trasimenus. He held large and statesman-like views on the policy of securing Italy by planting Romans and Latins in the territory then recently taken from the Gauls, in the neighborhood of Ariminum. This particular measure was carried against the will of the senate, and was the first law passed, since the *lex Hortensia* of 287, in defiance of its wishes. It was also the first agrarian law since the Licinio-Sextian law of 367. Polybius dates the decline of the Roman constitution from the passing of the *lex Flaminia.* Cf. ' Rheinisches Museum ', 1843, p. 573. ——
Sp. Carvilio quiescente: this Sp. Carvilius was consul in 234 when

he conquered the Corsicans and Sardinians. In 228 he was again consul, and died as augur in 212. He is said, but erroneously, to have been the first Roman who divorced his wife. In 216, just after the battle of Cannae, he made a most remarkable proposal, to fill up the gaps which that battle had made in the numbers of the senate by selecting two members from each of the Latin communities. It was almost the only occasion in the course of Roman history when anything like modern representative government was advocated. Carvilius was not sprung from one of the noble families, who for the most part monopolized the higher offices of state; it is therefore not surprising that he should have sympathized with Flaminius. —— **contra senatus auctoritatem**: 'against the expressed wish of the senate'. *Senatus auctoritas* is, strictly speaking, an opinion of the senate not formally embodied in a decree, *senatus consultum*. Cicero, in Invent. 2, 52 says Flaminius carried his law *contra v o l u n t a t e m omnium optimatium*. —— **dividenti**: 'when he tried to divide'. The participle is here equivalent to *cum* with the imperfect indicative (*dividebat*). So in 54 *lenientem*. A. 290, *a*; G. 668; H. 549, 1.

P. 6. — **cum esset**: '*though* he was'. What Fabius declared was really that the *auspicia* were a political instrument in the hands of the aristocrats, rather than a part of religion. Fabius, according to Liv. 30, 26, 7, was augur for 62 years before his death, and had no doubt had a large experience in the manipulation of the *auspicia* for political purposes. Compare Homer, Iliad, 12, 243; also Cic. Phil. 11, 28 *Iuppiter ipse sanxit ut omnia quae rei publicae salutaria essent legitima et iusta haberentur* Consult Mommsen, Hist. of Rome, Bk. IV. Ch. 12.

12. **admirabilius**: 'more amazing'. The Latin word has a much stronger meaning than the English word derived from it. —— **quo modo tulit**: = *eum modum quo tulit*, so that the clause is not really dependent on *cognovi*, nor *tulit* irregularly put for *tulerit*. In Lael. 9 Laelius exclaims, of Cato himself, *quo modo, ut alia omittam, mortem fili tulit*. And no doubt Cic. meant here to make Cato allude to *his* loss, described in 84. —— **fili**: see n. on 1 *praemi*. —— **consularis**: the son of Fabius was consul in 213 with Ti. Sempronius Gracchus. —— **est in manibus**: 'is in every one's hands', 'is commonly read'. The expression is common enough in this sense; *e. g.* Lael. 96 *in manibus est oratio*. —— **laudatio**: *sc. funebris*, the funeral speech. This composition was read in Cicero's time (see Tusc. 3, 70; Fam. 4,

6, 1) and existed in the time of Plutarch. See Plutarch's life of Fab.
24. —— **quem philosophum**: many of the ancient philosophers
wrote popular treatises in which the principles of philosophy were
applied to the alleviation of sorrow. The most famous of these in
Cicero's time was Crantor's περὶ πένθους, which Cicero used largely in
writing his *Tusculan Disputations*, and also in his *De Consolatione* on
the death of his daughter. —— **in luce ... civium**: 'in public and
under the gaze of his fellow-countrymen'. Do not translate *in oculis*
by the English phrase 'in the eyes of', which has another sense. The
metaphor in *lux* is often used by Cicero, as Qu. Fr. 1, 1, 7 *in luce
Asiae, in oculis provinciae*. —— **notitia**: *notitia* is general knowledge,
often merely the result of superficial observation; *scientia* is thorough
knowledge, the result of elaboration and generalization. —— **multae
litterae**: 'great literary attainments'. In this sense *magnae* could
not be used to represent 'great'. Note the ellipsis of *erant*. —— **ut
in homine Romano**: 'considering that he was a Roman', or 'for a
Roman'. On the backwardness of the Romans in literary pursuits
see Teuffel, Hist. of Rom. Lit., § 2; cf. also Ritter, Hist. of Ancient
Philosophy, Vol. IV. pp. 1-13, Eng. ed. In parenthetic clauses like
this, the introductory *ut* may convey two very different meanings
according to the context. Thus in Acad. 2, 98 *homo acutus, ut Poenus*
is 'a keen-witted man, *as might be expected of* a Carthaginian' (cf.
Colum. 1, 3, 8 *acutissimam gentem Poenos*) while Nepos, Epam. 5, 2
exercitatum in dicendo ut Thebanum implies that oratory was *not* to be
expected of a Theban. —— **domestica ... externa bella**: here the
domestica bella are those wars which belong to the history of Rome;
the *externa bella* those wars which belong to the history of other states;
but usually *domestica bella* are civil wars, *externa* foreign wars in which
Rome is engaged; *e. g.* Leg. agr. 2, 90 *omnibus domesticis externisque
bellis;* in Catil. 2, 11 *omnia sunt externa unius virtute pacata: domesticum bellum manet, intus insidiae sunt.* The practice of reading military history was common among Roman commanders; see for instance
Acad. 2, 3 of Lucullus; the practice is ridiculed by Marius in Sall.
Iug. 85. —— **ita**: *ita* does not qualify *cupide*, and has not the sense of
tam; it means rather 'in this state', 'under these conditions'; the
words from *quasi* to the end of the sentence really form an explanation of *ita*. This mode of expression is often found; *ita* and *sic* frequently look on to clauses introduced by *quasi, si, ut, cum* etc. Cf.
below 26 *sic ... quasi ... cupiens* (where see n.); Sall. Iug. 85, 19

ita aetatem agunt quasi vestros honores contemnunt, ita hos petunt quasi honeste vixerint. —— **divinarem**: see references on 6 *confeceris.* —— **illo exstincto**: Fabius died in 203 B. C. —— **fore unde discerem neminem**: cf. Acad. 1, 8 *quae nemo adhuc docuerat nec erat unde studiosi scire possent. Unde* of persons (here = *a quo*) is common in both verse and prose (so ὅθεν and ὅθενπερ, vid. Liddell and Scott in vv.); cf. Horace 1, 12, 17 *unde nil maius generatur ipso;* 1, 28, 28; Cic. de Or. 1, 67 *ille ipse unde cognorit;* ib. 2, 285. So *ubi* = *apud quem* in Verr. 4, 29; *quo* = *ad quos* below, 83, and in Verr. 4, 38; cf. also n. on *istinc* in 47. For mood of *discerem* see A. 320; G. 634; H. 503, I.

13. quorsus igitur haec: *sc. dixi.* —— **tam multa**: this takes the place of *tot*, which, like *quot*, cannot be used as a substantive. —— **Scipiones**: 'men like Scipio', *i. e.* the elder Africanus; so 15 *Fabricii Curii Coruncanii.* Cicero has here put his own opinion of Scipio into the mouth of Cato, who, during a large part of his life, was a staunch and even bitter opponent of Scipio, and therefore not likely to couple him with Fabius. Cf. Introd. —— **ut ... recordentur**: the repetition of *ut* with each clause for the sake of effect may be compared with the repetition of *nihil* in 15, 27, 41; of *non* in 32; of *hinc* in 40; of *sibi* in 58. —— **pedestris**: for *terrestris;* the usage is very common; so in Greek πεζομαχία and ναυμαχία, πεζομαχεῖν and ναυμαχεῖν are often contrasted (see Liddell and Scott). It is not recorded by historians that either Scipio or Fabius took part personally in naval warfare. —— **recordentur**: this verb implies the habitual dwelling of the memory upon the past. —— **quiete et pure atque eleganter**: the enumeration consists of two branches connected by *et*, the second branch being subdivided into two members connected by *atque.* Had each of the adverbs been intended to stand on exactly the same footing Cic. would have written *et* instead of *atque*, or else would have omitted the copula altogether; see n. on 53 *capitum iugatio.* In enumerations of the form $A + (B_1 + B_2)$, the + outside the bracket is expressed by *et*, the + inside the bracket generally being expressed by *ac*, for which *atque* is substituted when the following word (*i. e.* B_2) begins with a vowel, a guttural (*c, q, g*) or *h*, before which sounds *ac* was not written. —— **pure atque eleganter**: 'sinlessly and gently'. *Pure* implies moral stainlessness, *eleganter*, literally 'in choice fashion', implies daintiness combined with simplicity in regard to the external conditions of life. The same ideas are put

together in Sull. 79 *cum summa elegantia atque integritate vixistis.* ——
aetatis: see n. on 5. —— **placida ac lenis**: 'quiet and mild'; *placida* refers to the external surroundings, *lenis* to the temper and character. ——**accepimus**: *sc. fuisse ;* for the ellipsis of the infinitive cf.
n. on 22 *videretur.* —— **uno et octogesimo**: but below *quarto*
(not *quattuor*) *nonagesimo.* In the compound *ordinal* numbers corresponding to those *cardinal* numbers which are made up of one and a
multiple of ten, the Latins use *unus* oftener than *primus*, which would
be strictly correct; so in English 'one and eightieth' for 'eighty-first'.
The ordinary Grammar rule (Roby, Vol. 1, p. 443 'the *ordinal* not the
cardinal is used in giving the date') requires slight correction. For
the position of the words see G. 94, 3; H. 174, foot-note 3. —— **scribens est mortuus**: 'died while still engaged upon his works'; cf. 23
num Platonem ... coegit in suis studiis obmutiscere senectus ? Diog.
Laert. 3, 2 quoting Hermippus (a Greek writer on biography who
lived about the time of the Second Punic war), says that Plato died in
the middle of a marriage-feast at which he was a guest. Val. Max. 8,
7, 3 gives a slightly different account. —— **Isocrati**: this form of the
genitive of Greek proper names in *-es* was probably used by Cicero
rather than the form in *-is ;* see Madvig on Fin. 1, 14; Neue, Formenlehre, 1² 332. Isocrates, the greatest teacher of rhetoric of his time,
lived from 436 to 338, when he died by voluntary starvation owing to
his grief at the loss of Greek freedom through the battle of Chaeronea.
Milton, Sonnet x. 'That dishonest victory At Chaeronea, fatal to liberty, Kill'd with report that old man eloquent'. —— **eum ... inscribitur**: the periphrasis is common, and the verb *inscribere* is nearly
always in the present tense (in later prose as well as in Cicero) as in
59. This is sometimes the case even where the neighboring verbs
are in past tenses, as in Acad. 1, 12 *nec se tenuit quin contra suum
doctorem librum etiam ederet qui Sosus inscribitur*. The present
seems to mean that the name mentioned is continually given to each
copy of the book as produced; where the continuing multiplication of
copies is not looked to, we have the perfect, as Att. 8, 5, 2 *tu fascicu-
lum* (bundle of letters) *qui est inscriptus 'des M'. Curio', velim cures ad
eum perferendum.* Cf. also De Or. 2, 61 *deceptus indicibus librorum
qui sunt fere inscripti* ('to which the authors — once for all — have
given the titles') *de virtute, de iustitia*, etc.; so Div. 2, 1 *eo libro qui
est inscriptus Hortensius.* —— **dicit**: the 'Panathenaicus', an enco-
mium of Athens written for recitation at the great festival of the

Panathenaea, is among the works of Isocrates which we still possess. In c. 1 Isocrates says τοῖς ἔτεσι ἐνενήκοντα καὶ τετταρσίν, ὧν ἐγὼ τυγχάνω γεγονώς. —— vixitque: 'and yet he lived'. The *que* here has a slight adversative force, as is often the case with *et*. Cf. n. on 28, 43, 73 —— Gorgias: the greatest of the sophists, born at Leontini in Sicily about 485 B. C.; his death took place, according to the varying accounts, in 380, 378, or 377. In his old age he lived in Thessaly, where Isocrates studied with him; see Or. 176; Fin. 2, 1. For the adjective *Leontinus* placed before the name rather than after cf. 43 *Thessalo Cinea*. —— centum et septem annos: Kennedy, Gram., § 34, vii, *c*, says, 'in compound numbers above 100 the larger number, with or without *et*, generally precedes the smaller'; cf. Roby, Vol. 1, p. 443. —— cesso: does not correspond in meaning with our 'cease', *i. e.* 'to come to a standstill'; *cesso* is 'I am in a state of rest', 'I am idle'. —— quaereretur: the past tense, though the principal verb, *inquit*, is in the present, because the present is the *historical* present and so equivalent to a past tense. Cf. Roby, 1511–1514; Kennedy, 229, 2. A. 287, *e*; G. 511, Rem. 1; H. 495, II. The idiom by which the imperfect stands where we should expect a tense of completed action, should be noticed; cf. Tusc. 2, 60 *quem cum rogaret, respondit.* The explanation of the imperfect in such cases is that it marks out, more clearly than the pluperfect would, the fact that the action of the principal verb and the action of the dependent verb are practically contemporaneous. In our passage if *quaesitum esset* had been written it would have indicated merely that at some quite indefinite time after the question was put the answer was given. Cf. N. D. 1, 60 *auctore ...obscurior.* —— cur ... vita: a hint at suicide, which the ancients thought a justifiable mode of escape from troubles, particularly those of ill health or old age. See n. on 73 *vetat Pythagoras. Esse in vita* is stronger than *vivere;* cf. Qu. Fr. 1, 3, 5. —— nihil habeo quod accusem: 'I have no reason to reproach'. Cf. the common phrase *quid est quod...? Quod*, adverbial acc. A. 240, *a*; G. 331, R. 3; H. 378, 2. For mood of *accusem* see H. 503, I. n. 2, and references on 12 *discerem.* —— praeclarum responsum: *est* is not required, because *responsum* is in apposition to the last part of the preceding sentence. Similar appositions occur in Laelius, 67, 71, 79. —— docto: applied especially to philosophers, but also to poets. The word implies *cultivation* as well as mere *knowledge;* 'a learned man', merely as such, is '*homo litteratus*'; cf. n. on 54.

P. 7.—14. cuius ... feci: 'the aforesaid' is in good Latin always expressed by a parenthesis like this and not by a participle in agreement with the noun. The phrases '*ante dictus*', '*supra dictus*', belong to silver Latin, where they are common. Cf. 23 *quos ante dixi.* —— **sic ut** etc.: the lines are from the Annals of Ennius, for which see n. on 1. —— **ecus:** Ennius did not write *uu*, nor most likely did Cicero; the former may have written either *ecus, equos,* or *equs.* The last form Vahlen prints in his edition of Ennius. —— **spatio supremo:** 'at the end of the race-course', 'at the goal', or it may be 'at the last turn round the course', the race requiring the course to be run round several times; cf. Homer's πύματον δρόμον in Iliad 23, 768. So 83 *decurso spatio;* Verg. Aen. 5, 327 *iamque fere spatio extremo fessique sub ipsam finem adventabant.* —— **vicit Olympia:** a direct imitation of the Greek phrase νικᾶν 'Ολύμπια, to win a victory at an Olympic contest. So Horace Ep. 1, 1, 50 has *coronari Olympia* = στεφανοῦσθαι 'Ολύμπια. The editors print *Olympia,* but the use of *y* to represent Greek *v* did not come in till long after the time of Ennius. —— **senio:** differs from *senectute* in implying not merely old age, but the weakness which usually accompanies it. —— **confectus:** for the disregard of the final *s* in scanning cf. n. on 1, l. 6. —— **equi victoris:** for the almost adjectival use of the substantive *victor,* cf. Verg. Aen. 7, 656 *victores equos;* ib. 12, 751 *venator canis;* ib. 10, 891; 11, 89, and Georg. 2, 145 *bellator equus,* in Theocritus 15, 51 πολεμισταὶ ἵπποι. The feminine nouns in *-trix* are freely used as adjectives both in verse and in prose. A. 88, *c*; H. 441, 3. —— **quem quidem:** the same form of transition is used in 26, 29, 46, 53. The whole of this passage to *suasissem* is an exhibition of antiquarian learning quite unnatural and inappropriate in a dialogue. —— **probe meminisse potestis:** cf. De Or. 3, 194 *quem tu probe meministi;* Fin. 2, 63 *L. Thorius quem meminisse tu non potes. Memini* can take a *personal* accusative only when the person who remembers was a contemporary of the person remembered; otherwise the gen. follows. Cf. Roby, 1333; A. 219, Rem.; H. 407, n. 1. —— **hi consules:** 'the present consuls'. —— **T. Flamininus:** commonly said to be the son of the great Flamininus (1, l. 1). He was altogether undistinguished, as also were the Acilius and the Caepio here mentioned. This passage gives the imagined date of the dialogue as 150 B.C. —— **Philippo:** this was Q. Marcius Philippus, who was consul in 186 and took part in the suppression of the great Bacchanalian conspiracy of that year. For the next 17 years he was a leading senator and much engaged in diplomacy in the East. In 169 he was again consul and commanded against Perseus in the early part of the war. —— **cum ... legem Voconiam ... suasissem:** 'after I had spoken publicly in favor of the law of Voconius'. For *suasissem* cf. 10 *suasor* with n. The *Lex Voconia de mulierum hereditatibus* aimed at securing the continuance of property in families. By its provisions no man who possessed property valued in the censors' lists at 100,000 sesterces or more, could appoint a woman or women as his *heres* or *heredes ;* further, no person or persons, male or female, could receive under the will legacies amounting in all to a larger sum than that received by the principal heir or heirs. Every Roman will named a *heres* or *heredes*, on whom devolved all the privileges and duties of the deceased, with such duties as were enjoined by the will; particularly the duty of paying the legacies left to those who were not *heredes.* See Maine, Ancient Law, Ch. 6; also Hunter, Introd. to Roman Law, Ch. 5. —— **magna:** in Latin the word *magnus* is the only equivalent of our 'loud'. —— **lateribus:** 'lungs'. Cic. and the best writers rarely use *pulmones* for 'lungs'; the few passages in which it occurs either refer to victims sacrificed at the altar, or are medical or physiological descriptions. 'Good lungs' is always *'bona latera'* never *pulmones.* —— **duo ... senectutem:** Ennius is said to have kept a school in his later days, and to have lived in a cottage with one servant only.

15. etenim: this word generally introduces either an explanation or a proof of a preceding statement. Here the words are elliptic, and the real connection with what precedes can only be made clear by a paraphrase. 'Ennius seemed to delight in old age. And no wonder, since there are four causes which make men think old age wretched, and no one of these will bear examination'. *Etenim* may generally be translated 'indeed', or 'in fact'. —— **cum complector animo:** 'when I grasp them in my thoughts'. The object of *complector* is to be supplied from *causas.* —— **avocet:** *sc. senes.* The subjunctives denote that these are the thoughts not of the speaker, but of the persons who do think old age a wretched thing. See n. on 3 *ferat ;* but cf. Kennedy, Grammar, pref., p. 30. —— **alteram ... tertiam:** in enumerations of more than two things *unus* and *alter* generally take the place of *primus* and *secundus ;* in Cic. these latter rarely occur under such circumstances. Cf. Att. 3, 15, 1 ; Fin. 5, 9; Off. 1, 152; Cluent. 178. —— **infirmius:** *sc. quam antea erat.* —— **quam sit iusta:**

Cicero generally separates from the words they qualify *quam, tam, ita,
tantus, quantus*, often, as here, by one small word. Cf. below, 35
quam fuit imbecillus ; 40 *tam esse inimicum*. —— **quibus:** the preposition *a* is often omitted; cf. in Pis. 91 *Arsinoen ... Naupactum fateris
ab hostibus esse captas. Quibus hostibus? Nempe eis*, etc.; Tusc. 3,
37 *sed traducis cogitationes meas ad voluptates. Quas?* Even when
relative and antecedent are in the same sentence the preposition is
not often repeated; *e. g.* Fin. 5, 68 *eodem in genere quo illa*. —— **an
eis :** *an* always introduces a question which is not independent, but
follows upon a previous question either expressed or implied. Here
quibus implies *omnibusne*. Cf. div. in Caec. 52 *quid enim dices ? An
id quod dictitas ...* where *quid* implies *nihilne ;* also below, 23, 29 *anne.*
A. 211, *b* ; G. 459; H. 353, 2, n. 4. —— **iuventute et viribus:**
commonly explained as a hendiadys, *i. e.* as put for *iuventutis viribus ;*
but Cic. no more meant this than we mean 'the strength of youth'
when we speak of 'youth and strength'. Real instances of hendiadys
are much rarer than is generally supposed. —— **quae:** = *tales ut.* ——
L. Paulus: this is L. Aemilius Paulus Macedonicus, consul in 182
B. C., and again in 168 when he finished the third Macedonian war by
utterly defeating Perseus at Pydna. For his connection with Scipio
and Cato see Introd. —— **pater tuus:** *i. e. Scipio ;* so in 29 *avi tui,*
and in 75 *avum tuum*, without mention of young Scipio's name, but
in 49 *patris tui, Scipio ;* so 77. —— **Fabricii** etc.: for the plurals see
n. on 13. C. Fabricius Luscinus, consul in 282, 278, and 273 B. C.,
censor in 275, held the command against Pyrrhus. The Roman writers, Cicero especially, are never tired of eulogizing him as a pattern
of old-fashioned Roman virtue. Manius Curius Dentatus, consul in
290, 275, and 274 practically, if not formally, ended the third Samnite
war, and also commanded against Pyrrhus; see 55. He was famed
for his sturdy Roman simplicity and frugality. Tiberius Coruncanius
as consul in 280 crushed an Etruscan insurrection. In 252 he became
the first plebeian pontifex maximus. These three men are very frequently mentioned together by Cicero; cf. below, 43, Lael. 18. ——
nihil agebant: observe that *nihil agebat* is put at the beginning of the
first sentence, *nihil agebant* at the end of the second ; chiasmus.

16. A. Claudi: Appius Claudius, the head of the most strongly
aristocratic family in Rome, was censor in 311 B. C., when he con-
structed the *via Appia*, and consul in 307 and 296. He had to be
carried into the senate-house in order to oppose the peace with Pyr-

rhus. —— **accedebat ut**: *accedit* is far oftener followed by a clause with *quod* and indicative than by a clause with *ut* and subjunctive. When the *quod*-clause follows, it contains a fact looked at merely as a fact and nothing more; but the *ut*-clause views the fact as consequent upon, or dependent on some other fact. Here the blindness is regarded as being the consequence of old age; though Livy 9, 29, 11 and other authors attribute it to the anger of the gods, because as censor Appius had taken the administration of the worship of Hercules away from the ancient family of the Potitii, and had placed it in the hands of public slaves. The mental vigor of Appius in his old age is mentioned by Cic. in Tusc. 5, 112.

P. 8. — **cum Pyrrho**: note the position of the words between *pacem* and *foedus*, with both of which they go. This usage is called by the grammarians *coniunctio;* cf. n. on Lael. 8 *cum summi viri tum amicissimi;* also above, *quae iuventute geruntur et viribus;* below, 18 *quae sint gerenda praescribo et quo modo.* —— **foedus**: this seems opposed to *pacem* as a formal engagement is to a mere abstention from hostilities. —— **non dubitavit dicere**: when *dubitare* means 'to hesitate' (about a course of action), and the sentence is *negative*, or an interrogative sentence assuming a negative answer, the infinitive construction generally follows, as here; but the infinitive is rare in a *positive* sentence. When *dubitare* means to 'be in doubt' (as to whether certain statements are true or not), the regular construction is either *quin* with subj. or some form of indirect interrogative clause. Cf. below, 25. —— **quo vobis**: from the *Annales.* In *mentes dementis* we have *oxymoron* (an intentional contradiction in terms) as in 38 *sensim sine sensu;* 39 *munus...aufert.* On the case of *vobis,* see Roby, 1154; A. 235, *a;* H. 384, 4, n. 2. —— **antehac**: always a dissyllable in verse, and probably so pronounced in prose. —— **viai**: the old genitive. A. 36, *a;* G. 27, Rem. 1; H. 49, 2. The reading is not quite certain; if *viai* be read it is not altogether certain whether it depends on *quo* or on *sese flexere.* In the former construction we have a partitive gen. with an adv.; A. 216, *a,* 4; G. 371, Rem. 4; H. 397, 4; in the latter, a distinct Graecism like *desine querellarum* (Hor. Od. 2, 9, 17) and the like; A. 243, Rem.; G. 373, Rem. 6; H. 410, V. 4.

—— **et tamen**: the sense is incompletely expressed; in full it is 'and yet there is no need for me to refer to Appius' speech as given by Ennius, since the speech itself is in existence'. Exactly similar ellipses are found with *et tamen* in Fin. 1, 11 and 15; 2, §§ 15, 21, 64 and

85; Att. 7, 3, 10; Lucretius 5, 1177. In Munro's note on the last passage a collection of examples will be found. —— **Appi...oratio**: the speech was known to Cicero, and was one of the oldest monuments of prose composition in Latin extant in his time; see Brut. 61. Plutarch, Pyrrhus 19, gives an account of Appius' speech, which may be founded on the original; he mentions it also in his tract commonly called '*an seni sit gerenda res publica*', c. 21. Ihne (History of Rome, Vol. I. p. 521, Eng. ed.) doubts whether the speech, as Cic. knew it, was committed to writing by Appius himself. —— **haec ille egit**: 'he made this speech'. —— **septemdecim annis**: as the second (*alterum*) consulship was in 296, and the speech in 280, both these years are included in the reckoning by a usage very common in Latin. For the ablative cf. 19. —— **censor...ante consulatum**: this was unusual, and therefore to Claudius' honor. —— **grandem sane**: 'undoubtedly old'. —— **et tamen sic**: *i. e. eum tum grandem fuisse*. Lahmeyer wrongly says that *sic* points to the words *atque haec ille egit*. It may be noted that *sic* takes the place of an object after *accepimus*; cf. 77 *ita crederem*; 78 *sic mihi persuasi*; also 18 *male cogitanti*.

17. nihil afferunt: 'they bring forward nothing', *i. e.* what they bring forward is worthless; so in Greek οὐδὲν λέγειν, the opposite of which is λέγειν τι. Cf. 8 *est istuc aliquid*. —— **similes ut si**: a very rare construction. Equally unusual is *similes tamquam si* in Div. 2, 131. In Tusc. 4, 41 and Off. 1, 87 we find *similiter ut si*, in Fin. 2, 21 and 4, 31 *similiter* or *similis et si*, in N. D. 3, 8 *similiter ac si*; also in Liv. 5, 5, 12 *dissimilia ac si*, in 35, 42, 10 *idem ac si*. As regards the *ut* after *similes*, we may compare a few passages in which *simul ut* appears for *simul ac*; see Reid's n. on Academ. 2, 51. In the English Bible there are expressions like *similes sunt ut si qui dicant*, 'they are like as if some men should say'. —— **scandant**: '*cum* is used with the subjunctive when it expresses a kind of comparison, and especially a contrast, between the contents of a leading proposition and a subordinate ("whereas", etc.)'. Madvig, 358, Obs. 3. The underlying idea in this use is generally cause, sometimes concession. —— **per foros**: 'over the deck'. —— **ille**: for the omission of *sed* or *autem* (*asyndeton adversativum*) see n. on 3 *librum*, etc. —— **clavum**: 'tiller'. With this passage Lahmeyer well compares what Cicero says of himself in Fam. 9, 15, 3 *sedebamus in puppi et clavum tenebamus; nunc autem vix est in sentina locus*. —— **velocitate**: *velocitas* and *celeritas* differ very slightly; the former means rather speed of movement in one line, the latter rather power of rapid motion with frequent change of direction. The emphatic word in this clause is *corporum*. Cf. Off. 1, 79 *honestum ... animi efficitur non corporis viribus*. —— consilio ... sententia: *consilio*, advice; *auctoritate*, weight of influence; *sententia*, an opinion or vote formally given. —— quibus: in twofold relation; with *orbari*, abl. of separation, with *augeri*, of specification.

18. nisi forte: ironical, used to introduce a possible, but absurd objection to something which has gone before. The verb that follows is always in the indicative. —— miles etc.: 'as common soldier'; see n. on 10. —— in vario genere: we use the plural, 'in different kinds'. Cf. Acad. 2, 3 *in omni genere belli;* Deiot. 12 *in omni genere bellorum*. —— cessare: cf. n. on 13. —— at senatui etc.: exactly the same ideas are expressed, with the same mention of Cato's activity, in Off. 1, 79. —— male cogitanti: 'which has now for a long time been plotting mischief'; A. 290, *a*; G. 671, 221; H. 549, 4; 467, III. 2. Cf. pro Sulla 70 *nefarie cogitare;* for the use of the adverb see n. on 16 *sic*. On Cato's attitude toward Carthage see Introd. —— vereri: the construction is unusual. *Vereor* regularly takes after it an accusative, or else a clause with *ne* or *ut*. A passage much resembling this is Rab. Post. 10 *omnes qui aliquid de se verebantur;* cf. also Att. 10, 4, 6 *de vita sua metuere;* Verg. Aen. 9, 207 *de te nil tale verebar;* in all these examples the ablative with *de* denotes the quarter threatened, not, as here, the quarter from which the threat comes. —— exscisam: from *exscindo;* most edd. *excisam*, but to raze a city is *urbem exscindere* not *excidere; e. g.* Rep. 6, 11 *Numantiam exscindes*.

19. quam palmam etc.: a prophecy after the event, like that in Rep. 6, 11 *avi relliquias*, the finishing up of the Punic wars. For the use of *relliquias* cf. Verg. Aen. 1, 30 *Troas relliquias Danaum atque immitis Achilli;* ib. 598; ib. 3, 87. —— tertius: so all our MSS. This places the elder Scipio's death in 183, which agrees with Livy's account in 39, 50, 10. But the year before Cato's censorship was 185 not 183, hence some edd. read *quintus* and some *sextus* in place of *tertius*.

P. 9. — novem annis: as Cato's consulship was in 195 these words also apparently disagree with *tertius* above. *Novem annis post* means nine *full* years after, *i. e*, 185 not 186; cf. 42 *septem annis post*. —— enim: implies that the answer 'no' has been given to the question, and proceeds to account for that answer. —— **excursione :** a military term = 'skirmishing'; Cf. Div. 2, 26 *prima orationis e x c u r s i o.* —— **hastis :** loosely used for *pilis*. The long old Roman *hasta*, whence the name *hastati*, had long before Cato's time been discarded for the *pilum* or short javelin, which was thrown at the enemy from a distance, before the troops closed and used the sword. —— **consilium :** the repetition of *consilium* in a different sense from that which it had in the sentence before seems to us awkward; but many such repetitions are found in Cicero. *Consilium* corresponds to both 'counsel' and 'council'; the senate was originally *regium consilium*, the king's body of advisers. Here translate *summum consilium* 'the supreme deliberative body'. —— **senatum :** 'assembly of elders'. Cf. 56 *senatores, id est senes*. *Senatus* implies a lost verb *senā-re*, to be or grow old, from the stem of which both *senā-tus* and *senā-tor* are derived. This stem again implies a lost noun or adjective *senus*, old. The word *senatus* was collective, like *comitatus*, a body of companions, *exercitus*, a trained band etc.

20. amplissimum : 'most honorable'. —— **ut sunt...senes :** the Spartan γερουσία, as it is commonly called, consisted of 28 members, all over 60 years of age. Herodotus uses the term γέροντες (*senes*) for this assembly; Xenophon γεροντία. In the Laconian dialect γερωΐα was its name; we also find γεροντεύειν 'to be a senator'. For *ut ... sic* cf. Academ. 2, 14, *similiter vos cum perturbare, ut illi rem publicam, sic vos philosophiam velitis;* also Lael. 19. —— **audire :** like ἀκούω, used especially of historical matters, since instruction in them was almost entirely oral. Cf. ἀνήκοος = 'ignorant of history': —— **voletis :** see note on 7 *faciam ut potero ;* cf. Roby, 1464, *a* ; Madvig, 339, Obs. 1 ; A. 278, *b* ; G. 234, Rem. 1 ; H. 470, 2. —— **adulescentibus :** Cic., when he wrote this, was possibly thinking of Athens and Alcibiades. —— **labefactatas :** the verb *labefacio* is foreign to good prose, in which *labefacto* is used. —— **sustentatas :** Cic. does not use *sustentus*. In Mur. 3 *sustinenda* is followed by *sustentata* in the same sentence. —— **cedo ... cito :** the line is of the kind called tetrameter iambic acatalectic (or octonarius), and is scanned thus :—

$$\cup\cup\acute{=}\mid\overline{--}\mid\overline{-\acute{=}}\mid\cup\overline{-}\parallel\overline{-\acute{=}}\mid\overline{--}\mid\overline{-\acute{=}}\mid\cup\overline{-}.$$

In all kinds of iambic verse the old Romans freely introduced spondees where the Greeks used iambi; so in hexameters spondees for dactyls. Cf. Hor. Ep. ad. Pis. 254 *et seq.* —— **cědo :** = *dic ;* from *ce,*

the enclitic particle involved in *hic* = (*hi-ce*) etc. and *da*, the root of *do*.
So *cette* = *ce-dăte* = *cedte*, then *cette* by assimilation of *d* to *t*. The
original meaning would thus be 'give here', and in this sense the word
is often used. See Lex. *Dare* is commonly put for *dicere*, as *accipere*
is for *audire*. —— qui : 'how'. —— tantam : = τοσαύτην οὖσαν. ——
Naevi: Naevius lived about 264–194 B. C. His great work was a
history of the First Punic War written in Saturnian verse, the rude
indigenous metre of early Roman poetry. He wrote also plays, —
tragedies and comedies, both *palliatae* and *praetextae*. For an account
of him see Cruttwell, History of Roman Literature; also, Sellar, Roman Poets of the Republic, Ch. 3. If *Ludo* be read, it may be either
from the Latin *ludus* (Naevius entitled a comedy *Ludius*) or from
Λυδός, Lydian. —— poetae : Naevius seems to have been in the habit
of adding *poeta* to his name. It appears in the well-known epitaph
said to have been written by himself, also in the lines written against
him by the family poet of the Metelli : '*malum dabunt Metelli Naevio
poetae*'. The name *poeta* was new in Naevius' time and was just dis-
placing the old Latin name *vates ;* see Munro on Lucr. 1, 102. ——
proveniebant etc.: the same metre as above, divided thus by Lahmeyer : —

provéni | ebant | orát | ores ‖ noví | stulti adu ‖ lescén | tuli.

The whole line has the look of being translated from the Greek :
προὔβαινον (εἰς τὸ βῆμα) ῥήτορες καινοί τινες, μειράκια γελοῖα.   Lr. takes
provenire in the sense of 'to grow up', comparing Plin. Ep. I, 13, 1
magnum proventum ('crop') *poetarum annus hic attulit ;* Sall. Cat. 8,
3 *provenere ibi scriptorum magna ingenia*. —— videlicet : 'you see'.
   21. at : = ἀλλὰ γάρ; used, as in 32, 35, 47, 65, and 68, to introduce
the supposed objection of an opponent. —— credo : 'of course'. Cf.
47 where *credo* follows *at* as here. —— exerceas : the subject is the
indefinite 'you' equivalent to 'one', τὶς : 'unless one were to practise
it'. So 28 *nequeas ;* 33 *requiras*. Cf. also Plin. Ep. 8, 14, 3 *difficile
est tenere quae acceperis, nisi exerceas*. For the mood see A. 309, *a*; G.
598, 597, Rem. 3; H. 508, 5, 2). —— tardior : 'unusually dull'; cf.
Academ. 2, 97 *Epicurus quem isti tardum putant*. —— Themistocles :
famed for his memory. —— civium : 'fellow-countrymen'; *perceperat*:
'had grasped' or 'mastered'. —— qui...solitum : 'that he often
addressed as Lysimachus some one who for all that was Aristides'.
The direct object of *salutare* is omitted. For *qui* = *tametsi is* cf. Att.

1, 13, 3 *nosmet ipsi, qui Lycurgei f u i s s e m u s, cotidie demitigamur;*
also De Or. 1, 82. —— **esset:** A. 342; G. 631; H. 529, II. and n. 1, 1).
—— **Lysimachum:** for *ut L.* or *pro Lysimacho.* So Arch. 19 *Ho-*
merum Chii suum vindicant (= *ut suum* or *pro suo*). Lysimachus was
the father of Aristides. —— **sunt:** = *vivunt,* as often; so in 32 *esse*
= *vivere;* 54 *fuit* = *vixit;* 56, 60, 69. —— **sepulcra legens:** Cato
was a great antiquarian; cf. 38 *Originum.* —— **in memoriam redeo**
mortuorum: the genitive as with *memini, recordari* etc.   For the
phrase cf. Verr. 1, 120 *redite in memoriam, iudices, quae libido istius*
fuerit; also below, 59 *in gratiam redire cum voluptate.* Here translate 'I refresh my memory of the dead'. —— **quemquam senem:**
the best writers do not use *quisquam* as an adjective, but there is no
need to alter *senem* into *senum* as some editors do, since *senem* is a
substitute for a clause *cum senex esset;* 'I never heard that anybody
because he was an old man...'. *Senes* must be so taken in 22, since
pontifices etc. cannot stand as adjectives. Cf. n. on 10 *adulescentulus*
miles. —— **vadimonia:** 'their appointments to appear in court, the
debts due to them and the debts they owe'. When the hearing of a
suit had to be adjourned, the defendant was bound over either on his
own recognizance merely (*pure*) or along with sureties (*vades*) to appear in court on the day appointed for the next hearing, a sum or sums
of money being forfeited in case of his non-appearance. The engagement to appear was technically called *vadimonium;* when the defendant entered into the engagement he was said *vadimonium promittere;*
if he kept the engagement, *v. obire* or *sistere;* if he failed in it, *v. dese-*
rere. The plural *vadimonia* is here used because a number of suits
is meant; the word *constituta* is chosen as a more general term than
promissa, and as referring to the circumstances of both plaintiff and
defendant. Strictly speaking, it is the presiding judge who *vadimonia*
constituit. On this account *vadimonia constituta* should be translated
as above 'appointments', and not '*bonds*' or '*engagements*' to appear
in court.

P. 10. — **22.** quid ... senes: *sc. tibi videntur;* 'what do you
think of old men as lawyers, etc.?' So without ellipsis, Fam. 9, 21, 1
quid tibi ego in epistulis videor? —— ingenia: = *suum cuique ingenium;*
'old men retain their wits'. —— **permaneat:** A. 266, *d*; G. 575; H.
513, I. —— **studium et industria:** 'earnestness and activity'; not a
case of hendiadys, as some editors make it. Cf. n. on 15 *iuventute et*
viribus. —— **neque ea solum:** = οὐδὲ ταῦτα μόνον, 'and that not

only '. —— **honoratis**: this does not correspond to our 'honored', but implies that the persons have held high offices (*honores*); cf. 61 *senectus honorata præsertim*. Here translate 'statesmen'. —— **in vita ...quieta**: 'in an unofficial and retired life'. There is chiasmus here, since *privata* is contrasted with *honoratis* and *quieta* with *claris*. —— **summam senectutem**: Sophocles died at the age of 90 in 405 B. C. —— **quod propter studium**: 'from his devotion to this occupation'. —— **filiis**: except Plutarch, who probably follows Cicero's words, all the authorities tell the story of the poet's eldest son Iophon only. The tale is full of improbabilities. —— **rem**: = *rem familiarem* as in 1. —— **patribus bonis interdici solet**: 'fathers are often prevented from managing their property'. For the construction cf. the expression *interdicere alicui aqua et igni*: *interdici* is here used impersonally with *patribus* in the dat.; A. 230; H. 384, 5; *bonis* is abl. of separation (deprivation). The fragment of the XII tables here referred to is thus given in Dirksen's edition: *sei fouriosos aut prodicos* (*prodigus*) *escit* (*erit*) *adcnatorum centiliomque* (*gentiliumque*) *eius potestas estod, i. e.* the agnates (male relatives whose kinship with the *furiosus* is derived through males) and members of his *gens* are to administer his property. We have preserved the form in which the judgment was made by the *praetor urbanus* (Paulus, Sent. 3, 4a, 7): '*quando tibi tua bona paterna avitaque n e q u i t i a tua disperdis liberosque tuos ad egestatem perducis, ob eam rem tibi ea re commercioque interdico*'. —— **quasi desipientem**: '*ὡς παραφρονοῦντα*' says the author of the anonymous life of Sophocles. Cf. Xenophon, Mem. 1, 2, 49. —— **in manibus habebat**: 'had on hand' *i. e.* in preparation. *Est in manibus* in 12 has a different meaning. —— **scripserat**: he had written it but not finally corrected it. —— **recitasse**: the common version of the story states that not the whole play was read but only the fine chorus beginning *εὐίππου, ξένε, τᾶσδε χώρας*. —— **videretur**: *sc. esse;* the infinitive is often omitted thus after verbs of desiring, thinking etc., also verbs of speaking and hearing; cf. Lael. 18 *eam sapientiam interpretantur;* ib. 29 *quam natam volunt;* ib. 64 *homines ex maxime raro genere iudicare;* Acad. 2, 12 *viderenturne ea Philonis.*

23. Hesiodum: see n. on 54. —— **Simoniden**: Simonides of Ceos (not S. of Amorgos), one of the greatest Greek lyric poets, lived from 556 to about 469 B. C. —— **Stesichorum**: of Himera in Sicily, also a lyric poet; lived from about 630 to about 556 B. C. —— **Isocraten Gorgian**: nn. on 13. —— **philosophorum principes**: 'in the first rank of philosophers'. —— **Pythagoran**: neither the date of his birth nor that of his death can be determined; he 'flourished' about 530. He lived mostly in the Greek settlements of lower Italy, where his school existed for some centuries after his death. —— **Democritum**: of Abdera, one of the originators of the theory of atoms; said to have lived from 460 to 361 or 357 B.C. —— **Xenocraten**: after Plato, Speusippus was the first head of the Academic School; Xenocrates succeeded him. He lived from 397 to 315 or 313. —— **Zenonem**: of Citium in Cyprus, founder of Stoicism, born about 357, is said to have lived to the age of 98. —— **Cleanthen**: he followed Zeno in the presidency of the Stoic school. His age at death is variously given as 99 and as 80 years. —— **quem vidistis**: see Introd. It is rather curious that Cic. should make Cato speak with admiration of Diogenes, to whom he had shown great hostility. —— **Diogenen**: Cic. probably wrote in -*an*, -*en*, not in -*am*, -*em* the accusatives of Greek proper names in -*as*, -*es*. —— **Stoicum**: to distinguish him from Diogenes the Cynic. —— **agitatio**: Cic. uses *agitatio* and *actio* almost interchangeably; cf. *agitatio rerum* in De Or. 3, 88 with *actio rerum* in Acad. 2, 62 and elsewhere. *Actus* in this sense occurs only in silver Latin.

24. age: a common form of transition to a new subject; brief for 'hoc age', 'do this', *i. e.* 'attend to this that I am going to say'. The common use of ἄγε in Greek is exactly similar. —— **ut … omittamus**: Cf. n. on 52 *ut*. —— **possum nominare**: 'I am able to name'; in colloquial English 'I *might* name'. The Latins occasionally use also a hypothetical form, where *possim* or *possem* stands in the apodosis of a conditional sentence, the protasis of which is not expressed; but the missing protasis is generally easily supplied and was distinctly present to the writer's mind. *E. g.* in Tusc. 1, 88 we have *dici hoc in te non potest; posset in Tarquinio; at in mortuo ne intellegi quidem* (*potest*), where the reason for the change from *potest* to *posset* is quite evident. In translating from English into Latin it is far safer to use the indicative. Cf. 55 *possum persequi.* A. 311, *c*; G. 599, Rem. 3; H. 511, 1, n. 3, 476, 4. —— **ex agro … Romanos**: 'country-bred Romans (*i. e.* Roman citizens) belonging to the Sabine district'. The words *ex agro Sabino* form an attributive phrase qualifying *Romanos* just as *rusticos* does. —— **numquam fere**: 'scarcely ever'. —— **maiora opera**: 'farm work of any importance'. This use of *opera* is common in Vergil's Georgics. —— **non**: the repetition of the negative after *numquam* is common in Latin; in English *never* . . . *not* is found in dialects only. Cf. Lael. 48 *non tantum* . . . *non plus quam.* —— **serendis**: ablative of respect; 'as regards sowing'. See Roby, 1210; Kennedy, 149. —— **percipiendis**: so 70; cf. N. D. 2, 156 *neque enim serendi neque colendi, nec tempestive demetendi percipiendi-que fructus, neque condendi nec reponendi ulla pecudum scientia est.* —— **in aliis**: see n. on 3 *ceteris.* Notice the proleptic use. —— **idem**: a better form of the plural than *iidem*, commonly found in our texts. For the use here cf. n. on 4 *eandem.* —— **pertinere**: present for future. —— **serit . . . prosint**: the line is given as Ribbeck prints it. He scans it as a '*bacchius*', consisting of four feet, with the meas-urement ◡ – –, the last syllable of *saeclo* seeming to be shortened. Cicero quotes the same line in Tusc. 1, 31 adding *ut ait (Statius) in Synephebis, quid spectans nisi etiam postera saecla a d s e p e r t i n e r e? Saeclo* = 'generation'. For mood of *prosint* see A. 317; G. 632; H. 497, I. —— **Statius noster**: 'our fellow-countryman Statius'. So Arch. 22 *Ennius noster.* Caecilius Statius, born among the Insubres, wrote Latin comedies which were largely borrowed from the Greek of Menander. The original of the *Synephebi* was Menander's Συνέ-φηβοι 'young comrades'. See Sellar, Rom. Poets of the Rep., Ch. 7.

P. 11. — 25. dis: the spellings *diis, dii* which many recent editors still keep, are probably incorrect; at all events it is certain that the nominative and ablative plural of *deus* formed *monosyllables*, except occasionally in poetry, where *dei, deis* were used. Even these *dissyl-labic* forms scarcely occur before Ovid. —— **et**: emphatic at the be-ginning of a sentence: 'aye, and'. —— **melius**: *sc. dixit.* —— **illud**: 'the following'. A. 102, *b*; G. 292, 4; H. 450, 3. —— **idem**: *īdem*, not *ĭdem.* —— **edepol**: literally, 'ah, god Pollux', *e* being an interjec-tion, *de* a shortened form of the vocative of *deus, pol* abbreviated from *Pollux.* The asseveration is mostly confined to comedy. The lines come from a play by Statius called *Plocium* (πλοκίον 'necklace'), copied from one by Menander with the same title; see Ribbeck's 'Fragmenta.' The verses are iambic trimeters. A. 365; G. 754; H. 622. —— **nil quicquam**: see n. on 21 *quemquam senem*; cf. the com-mon expression *nemo homo ;* 84 *nemo vir* etc., where two substantival words are placed side by side. —— **viti**: see n. on 1, l. 3 *praemi. Viti* here = *mali ;* cf. Ter. Andr. 73 *ei vereor ne quid Andria adportet mali.* —— **sat est**: *sat* for *satis* in Cicero's time was old-fashioned

and poetical. —— **quod diu**: these words must be scanned as a spon-
dee. The *i* in *diu* here probably had the sound of our *y*. A. 347, *c*;
G. 717; H. 608, III. n. 2. Allen well compares a line of Publilius
Syrus *heu quam multa paenitenda incurrunt vivendo diu.* —— **volt**:
indefinite subject. —— **videt**: Tischer quotes Herod. I, 32 (speech of
Solon to Croesus) ἐν γὰρ τῷ μακρῷ χρόνῳ πολλὰ μὲν ἔστιν ἰδέειν, τὰ
μή τις ἐθέλει, πολλὰ δὲ καὶ παθέειν. —— **tum equidem** etc.:
these lines, as well as those above, occurred in a play of Statius called
Ephesio: see Ribbeck's 'Fragmenta'. —— **senecta**: not used by
prose writers before the time of silver Latin. —— **deputo**: this compound is used by the dramatists and then does not occur again till
late Latin times. —— **eumpse**: like *ipse* and *reapse* (for which see n.
on Lael. 47) this word contains the enclitic particle *pe* (probably another form of *que*), found in *nem-pe, quis-p-iam* etc., along with *se,*
which belongs to an old demonstrative pronoun once declined *sos, sa,
sum,* the masc. and fem. of which are seen in *ὁ, ἡ.* The form was no
doubt originally *eumpsum,* like *ipsom* (*ipsum*), but has passed into its
present form just as *ipsos* (nom.) became *ipso,* then *ipse.* The only
difference in sense between *eumpse* and the simple *eum* is that the
former is more emphatic. The pronoun *eumpse* is the subject of the
infinitive *sentire,* but the substantive, *senex,* to which the pronoun
refers, is not expressed. —— **odiosum**: cf. n. on 4.

26. iucundum … odiosum: elliptic, = '*iucundum' potius quam
'odiosum' senem esse dicendum est.* —— **ut … delectantur**: cf. Lael.
101; also below, 29. —— **sapientes senes**: neither of these words
is used as an adjective here; the whole expression = *sapientes, cum
facti sunt senes.* —— **levior**: cf. the fragm. of Callimachus: γηράσκει
δ' ὁ γέρων κεῖνος ἐλαφρότερον, τὸν κοῦροι φιλέουσι. —— **coluntur
et diliguntur**: *colere* rather implies the external marks of respect
(cf. *coli* in 7), *diligere* the inner feeling of affection. —— **praeceptis**
etc.: cf. Off. I, 122 *ineuntis enim aetatis inscitia senum constituenda et
regenda prudentia est.* —— **me … iucundos**: put for *me iucundum
esse quam vos mihi estis iucundi.* The attraction of a finite verb into
the infinitive after *quam* is not uncommon; cf. n. on I *quibus me
ipsum.* Roby, 1784, *b*; A. 336, *b*, Rem; H. 524, I, 2). *Minus,* be it
observed, does not qualify *intellego,* but *iucundos.* —— **sed**: here *ana-
leptic,* i. e. it introduces a return to the subject proper after a digres-
sion; so in 31. —— **videtis, ut … sit**: here *ut* = *quo modo;* 'how'.
senectus … cuiusque: the abstract *senectus* is put for *senes* as in 34;

hence *cuiusque, sc. senis*. So above *adulescentia = adulescentes*. ——
agens aliquid: this phrase differs from *agat* in that while the subjunctive would express the *fact* of action, the participial phrase expresses rather the constant *tendency* to act. *Agens aliquid* forms a
sort of attribute to *senectus*, parallel with *operosa*. *Moliri* differs from
agere in that it implies the bringing into existence of some object.
Cf. Off. 3, 102 *agere aliquid et moliri volunt;* Acad. 2, 22 *ut
moliatur aliquid et faciat;* N. D. 1, 2 *utrum di nihil agant, nihil
moliantur;* Mur. 82 *et agant et moliantur*. —— **quid ... aliquid**: for
the ellipsis in *quid qui* cf. n. on 22 *quid ... Addiscunt = προμανθάνουσι*
= learn on and on, go on learning. —— **ut ... videmus**: put, as
Allen observes, for *ut Solon fecit, quem videmus*. —— **Solonem**: see
also 50. The line (*versibus* here is an exaggeration; in 50 it is *versi-
culus*) is preserved by Plato in his Timaeus and by Plutarch, Sol. 31
γηράσκω δ᾽ ἀεὶ πολλὰ διδασκόμενος. The age of Solon at his death is
variously given as 80 or 100 years. —— **videmus**: the Latins frequently use 'we see' for 'we read'. See n. on Lael. 39, also below,
69 *ut scriptum video*. —— **gloriantem**: A. 292, *e*; G. 536, 527, Rem. 1;
H. 535, I. 4. Notice the change to the infinitive in *uti* below. ——
senex: *i. e. cum senex essem ;* so 27 *adulescens desiderabam ;* 30 *memini puer*. Plutarch (Cato 2) gives an account of Cato's study of
Greek in his old age. —— **sic**: this word does not qualify *avide*, but
refers on to *quasi*, so that *sic ... quasi cupiens =* 'thus, *viz.* like one
desiring'. Cf. n. on 12 *ita cupide fruebar quasi ;* also 35 *tamquam ...
sic*. *Quasi* serves to soften the metaphor in *sitim ;* cf. n. on Lael. 3.
—— **cupiens**: after *quasi* a finite verb (*cuperem*) would have been
more usual, as in 12 *ita ... quasi divinarem*. Cf. however 22 *quasi
desipientem.* —— **ea ipsa mihi**: for the juxtaposition of pronouns,
which is rather sought after in Latin, cf. 72 *ipsa suum eadem quae.*
—— **exemplis** : = *pro exemplis*, or *exemplorum loco* (cf. n. on 21 *Lysimachum*), so that those editors are wrong who say that we have here
an example of the antecedent thrust into the relative clause, as though
ea ipsa quibus exemplis were put for *ea ipsa exempla quibus*. —— **quod**:
= *ut cum iam senex esset disceret*. —— **Socraten**: Cic. probably learned
this fact from Plato's Menexenus 235 E and Euthydemus 272 C where
Connus is named as the teacher of Socrates in music. In the Euthydemus Socrates says that the boys attending Connus' lessons laughed
at him and called Connus γεροντοδιδάσκαλον. Cf. also Fam. 9, 22, 3
Socraten fidibus docuit nobilissimus fidicen ; is Connus vocitatus est ; Val.

Max. 8, 7, 8. —— in fidibus : 'in the case of the lyre'. Tücking
quotes Quintilian 9, 2, 5 *quod in fidibus fieri videmus* The Greek
word *cithara* is not used by Cicero and does not become common in
Latin prose till long after Cicero's time, though he several times uses
the words *citharoedus, citharista*, when referring to Greek professional
players. The word *lyra* too is rare in early prose ; it occurs in Tusc.
1, 4 in connection with a Greek, where in the same sentence *fides* is
used as an equivalent. —— audirem : for *audire = legendo cognoscere*
see n. on 20. —— vellem : *sc. si possem.* —— discebant ... antiqui :
doubts have been felt as to the genuineness of the clause. In Tusc.
4, 3 a passage of Cato is quoted which refers to the use of the *tibia*
among the ancient Romans ; immediately afterwards the antiquity of
practice on the *fides* at Rome is mentioned, though not expressly on
Cato's authority. The words cannot be said to be unsuited either to
the person or to the occasion. —— discebant ... fidibus : the verb
canere, which means 'to play' as well as 'to sing', must be supplied ;
fidibus is then an ablative of the means or instrument. There is the
same ellipsis of *canere* in the phrases *docere fidibus* (Fam. 9, 22, 3) and
scire fidibus (Terence, Eunuchus 133). Cf. Roby, 1217.

P. 12. — 27. ne ... quidem : these two words together correspond
to the Greek οὐδέ (οὐ = *ne*, δέ = *quidem*), and are best translated here
by 'nor' rather than by 'not even'. The rendering 'not even', though
required by some passages, will often misrepresent the Latin. ——
locus : *locus* (like τόπος in Greek) is a rhetorical term with a technical
meaning. The pleader is to anticipate the arguments he may find it
necessary to use in different cases, and is to arrange them under certain heads ; each head is called a τόπος or *locus*, meaning literally the
place where a pleader is to look for an argument when wanted. Hence
locus came to mean 'a cut-and-dried argument' or, as here, a 'com-
monplace'. It is often found in Cicero's rhetorical writings. ——
non plus quam : 'any more than'. After the negative *ne* above it is
impossible to translate *non* by a negative in English, though the repetition of the negative is common enough in Latin, as in some English
dialects. Cf. n. on 24. *Plus* here = *magis.* —— quod est : *sc. tibi*,
'what you have', so Paradoxa 18 and 52 *satis esse, quod est.* —— agas :
quisquis is generally accompanied by the indicative, as in Verg. Aen. 2,
49 *quidquid id est* etc. ; see Roby, 1697 ; A. 309, *c* ; G. 246, 4 ; H. 476,
3. The subjunctive is here used, with the imaginary second person,
to render prominent the hypothetical and indefinite character of the

verb statement. Roby, 1544-1546; Madvig, 370, 494, Obs. 5, (6). ——
vox: 'utterance'; the word is used only of speeches in some way
specially remarkable. —— **contemptior**: 'more despicable'. The
passive participe of *contemno* has the sense of an adjective in *-bilis*,
like *invictus* and many others. —— **Milonis**: the most famous of the
Greek athletes. He lived at the end of the sixth century B. C., and
the praises of his victories were sung by Simonides. It was under
his leadership that his native city Croton, in Magna Graecia, attacked
and destroyed Sybaris. Many stories are told by the ancients about
his feats of strength (see 33), and about his power of consuming food.
He is said to have been a prominent disciple of Pythagoras. —— **illa-
crimans**: beware of spelling *lacrima* with either *ch* for *c* or *y* for *i ;*
these spellings are without justification. The *y* rests on the absurd
assumption that the Latins borrowed their word *lacrima* straight from
the Greek δάκρυ. —— **dixisse**: combinations like *dicitur dixisse* are
exceedingly rare in good Latin. Cicero nearly always uses two different verbs; *i. e.* he says *aiunt dicere* and the like. —— **at**: there is an
ellipsis here such as 'those young men's muscles are powerful but...'.
This elliptic use of *at* is common in sudden exclamations of grief,
annoyance, surprise etc. —— **vero**: this is common in emphatic replies, whether the reply convey assent, or, as here, a retort. The
usage is well illustrated in Nägelsbach's Stilistik, § 197, 2. —— **tam**:
sc. mortui sunt. —— **nugator**: *nugari* = ληρεῖν, 'to trifle'. —— **ex te**:
Cato here identifies a man's person with his soul and intellect, the
body being regarded as a mere dress; cf. Rep. 6, 26 *mens cuiusque is
est quisque. Ex te*, literally, 'out of yourself', *i. e.* 'from your real
self's resources'. —— **lateribus**: see n. on 14. —— **Aelius**: his *cognomen* was Paetus; he was consul in 198, and censor in 194 B. C. He
was one of the earliest and most famous writers on Roman Law.
His great commentary on the XII tables is often referred to by Cicero,
who several times quotes Ennius' line about him — *egregie cordatus
homo catus Aelius Sextus.* —— **tale**: *sc. dixit.* —— **Coruncanius**: n.
on 15. —— **P. Crassus**: consul in 205 B. C. with the elder Africanus;
pontifex maximus from 212 to his death in 183. He was famous both
as a lawyer (see below, 50; also Liv. 30, 1, 5 *iuris pontifici peritissi-
mus*) and as a statesman (see 61). *Modo* therefore covers a space of
at least 33 years, so that it cannot well be translated by our 'lately';
say rather 'nearer our time'. The amount of time implied by *modo*
and *nuper* depends entirely on the context; for *modo* see Lael. 6 with

note, for *nuper* below, n. on 61, where it is used of Crassus as *modo* is here. —— **praescribebantur**: the meaning is that these lawyers practised in old age as jurisconsults; *i. e.* according to old Roman custom, they gave audience in the early hours of the day to all who chose to consult them about legal difficulties. —— **est provecta**: literally 'was carried forward', *i. e.* 'continued', 'remained'. Some wrongly take the phrase to mean 'made progress', 'increased', a sense which would require the imperfect, *provehebatur*. —— **prudentia**: here, as often, 'legal skill'.

28. orator: emphatic position. —— **senectute**: causal ablative; not 'in age', but 'owing to age'. —— **omnino — sed tamen**: 'no doubt — but still'. *Omnino* (literally, 'altogether') has two almost exactly opposite uses — (1) the affirmative, cf. 9; (2) the concessive, which we have here and in 45. The circumstance which is contrasted with the admitted circumstance is usually introduced by *sed tamen* or *sed* as in 45, but in Lael. 98 by the less emphatic *autem*, while in Lael. 69 there is no introductory particle. —— **canorum ... senectute**: *canorum* implies the combination of power with clearness in a voice. For the mixture of metaphors in *canorum splendescit* edd. quote Soph. Phil. 189 ἀχὼ τηλεφανής; Cic. De Or. 2, 60 *illorum tactu orationem meam quasi colorari*. —— **nescio quo pacto**: literally, 'I know not on what terms'; quite interchangeable with *nescio quo modo*; cf. 82. A. 334, *e*; G. 469, Rem. 2; H. 529, 5, 3). —— **adhuc non**: purposely put for *nondum*, because more emphasis is thus thrown both on the time-word and on the negation. The common view that *nondum* was avoided because it would have implied that Cato *expected* to lose the *canorum* is certainly wrong. —— **et videtis**: 'though you see my years'. The adversative use of *et* for *autem* or *tamen* after the negative is not very uncommon in Cicero, but there are few examples of the usage in the speeches. Cf. Lael. 26 *et quidquid;* so sometimes *que* as above, 13; also Lael. 30 *ut nullo egeat suaque omnia in se posita iudicet.* —— **seni**: Madvig's em. for *senis.* In Leg. 1, 11 allusion is made to the great change which advancing years had wrought in Cicero's own impassioned oratory. He was no doubt thinking of that change when he wrote the words we have here. —— **sermo**: 'style of speaking'; a word of wider meaning than *oratio*, which only denotes public speaking. —— **quietus et remissus**: 'subdued and gentle'. The metaphor in *remissus* (which occurs also in 81) refers to the loosening of a tight-stretched string; cf. *intentum* etc. in 37 with

n. With the whole passage cf. Plin. Ep. 3, 1, 2 *nam iuvenes confusa adhuc quaedam et quasi turbata non indecent ; senibus placida omnia et ordinata conveniunt.* —— **facit audientiam :** 'procures of itself a hearing for it '. In the words *per se ipsa* there is no doubt an allusion to the custom at large meetings in ancient times whereby the *praeco* or κῆρυξ called on the people to listen to the speakers. Cf. Liv. 43, 16, 8 *praeconem audientiam facere iussit.* Note that this is the only classical use of the word *audientia ;* it has not the meaning of our 'audience' either in the sense of a body of listeners, or as used in the expression 'to give audience'. —— **composita et mitis :** 'unimpassioned and smooth '. Cf. Quintil. 6, 2, 9 *affectus igitur hos concitatos, illos mitis atque compositos esse dixerunt.* —— **quam ... nequeas :** 'and if you cannot practise oratory yourself '. Evidently *quam* refers to *oratio* in the widest sense, not to the special style of oratory mentioned in the last sentence. With *si nequeas* cf. *nisi exerceas* in 21 with n. —— **Scipioni et Laelio :** '*a* Scipio and *a* Laelius '; *i. e.* 'young friends such as Scipio and Laelius are to me '. —— **praecipere :** here absolute, = *praecepta dare ;* usually an accusative follows. —— **studiis iuventutis :** 'the zeal of youth '. *Studiis* does not imply here the deference of youth to age; the *studia* meant are the *virtutum studia* of 26.

29. ne ... instruat : *docere* is to impart knowledge, *instituere* (literally 'to ground ' or 'establish ') is to form the intellect and character by means of knowledge, *instruere,* to teach the pupil how he may bring his acquirements to bear in practical life. —— **offici munus :** 'performance of duty '; cf. 35, 72 ; Fam. 6, 14. In scores of passages in Cicero we find *officium et munus,* 'duty and function ', as in 34. —— **Cn. et P. Scipiones :** in Cic. the plural is always used where two men of the same family are mentioned and their names connected by *et.* In other writers the plural is regular, the singular exceptional, as in Sall. Iug. 42, 1 *Ti. et C. Gracchus ;* Liv. 6, 22 *Sp. et L. Papirius.* Even with other nouns the plural is regular; *e. g.* Cic. Phil. 2, 101 *arationes Campana et Leontina,* though a little above we have *mense Aprili atque Maio.* [See Draeger, Hist. Synt. 1², p. 1.] Gnaeus (*not* Cnaeus — see n. on Lael. 3) Cornelius Scipio was consul in 222 B. C. and was sent to Spain at the outbreak of the Second Punic war to command against Hasdrubal. Publius was consul in 218, and after being defeated by Hannibal at the Ticinus, joined his brother in Spain. At first they won important successes, but in 212 they were hemmed in and killed, after a crushing defeat. —— **L. Aemilius:** the father of Macedonicus. He was consul in 219 and defeated the Illyrii; but when consul again in 216 was defeated and killed at Cannae. See 75. For *avi duo* cf. 82. —— **consenuerint ... defecerint:** *coniunctio,* for which see n. on 16. For the mood see A. 313, *a*; G. 608; H. 515, III. and n. 3. —— **etsi:** see n. on 2. —— **senectute:** MSS. and edd. have *senectutis,* but the sense requires the abl.

P. 13. — **30. Cyrus:** the elder. —— **apud Xenophontem:** 'in Xenophon'; so in 79 where see n.; also 31 *apud Homerum.* See Cyropaedia, 8, 7, 6. —— **cum ... esset:** '*though* he was very old', the clause depends on the following words, not on the preceding. —— **negat:** in Latin as in English the present tense is used in quotations from books. —— **Metellum:** was consul in 251 B. C. and won a great victory over the Carthaginians at Panormus (Palermo); consul again in 247. See below, 61. —— **memini ... esse:** for the construction of *memini* with the present or perfect infinitive, see n. on Lael. 2; also A. 288, *b*; G. 277, Rem.; H. 537, I. —— **puer:** the expression is peculiar, being abbreviated from *quod puer vidi* or something of the kind. Quintil. 8, 3, 31 has *memini iuvenis.* In Rep. 1, 23 Cicero says *memini me admodum adulescentulo.* —— **viginti et duos:** the commoner order of the words is *duos et viginti ;* see n. on 13 *centum ... annos.* —— **ei sacerdotio:** 'that sacred college'; *i. e.* the pontifical college consisting of the *pontifex maximus* and the inferior *pontifices.* —— **requireret:** see n. on 13 *quaereretur.* —— **nihil:** n. on 1, l. 1 *quid.* —— **mihi:** dat. for acc. to emphasize the person. —— **id:** 'such a course'; cf. 82 *ut de me ipse aliquid m o r e   s e n u m glorier.*

31. videtisne ut: here *ne* is the equivalent of *nonne,* as it often is in the Latin of Plautus and Terence, and in the colloquial Latin of the classical period. For *ut* after *videtis* see n. on 26. —— **Nestor:** *e. g.* in Iliad 1, 260 *et seq.*; 11, 668 *et seq.* —— **tertiam aetatem:** cf. Iliad 1, 250; Odyssey 3, 245. —— **vera ... se:** 'if he told the truth about himself'. —— **nimis:** 'to any great extent'. *Insolens* does not correspond to our 'insolent'; it is almost the equivalent of *ineptus,* and has no harsher meaning than 'odd', 'strange', 'in bad taste'. —— **melle dulcior:** Homer, Il. 1, 249 τοῦ καὶ ἀπὸ γλώσσης μέλιτος γλυκίων ῥέεν αὐδή. In Or. 32 Cic. says of Xenophon (whom the Greeks called Ἀττικὴ μέλιττα) that his *oratio* was *melle dulcior.* —— **suavitatem:** notice the change from *dulcior,* which seems to be made for the mere sake of variety, since elsewhere (De Or. 3, 161) Cicero writes *dulcitudo orationis.* —— **et tamen :** see n. on 16. —— **dux ille :** Agamemnon; see Iliad 2, 370 *et seq.* —— **nusquam :** *i. e.* nowhere in Homer. —— **Aiacis :** *i. e.* Aiax Telamonius, who was the greatest Greek warrior while Achilles sulked (Iliad 2, 768). The genitive after *similis* is the rule in Cicero, though many examples of the dative are found even with names of persons; see Madv. on Fin. 5, 12.

32. sed : see n. on 26. —— **redeo ad me :** so 45; Lael. 96, Div. 1, 97 *ad nostra iam redeo ;* also below, 67 *sed redeo ad mortem impendentem.* —— **vellem :** see n. on. 26. —— **idem :** A. 238; G. 331, Rem. 2; H. 371, 2. —— **quod Cyrus :** see 30. —— **queo :** the verb *queo* is rarely found without a negative, *possum* being used in positive sentences; cf. hcwever Lael. 71 *queant,* where see n. —— **miles etc. :** see 10 above. —— **fuerim ... depugnavi :** A. 336, *b*; G. 630, Rem. 1; H. 524, 2, 2). *Depugnavi* = 'fought the war out', or ' *to the end*'; cf. 38, *desudans ;* 44 *devicerat.* —— **enervavit :** *enervare* is literally 'to take out the sinews'; cf. the expressions *nervos elidere* (Tusc. 2, 27) and *nervos incidere* (Academ. 1, 35) both of which are used in a secondary or metaphorical sense. —— **curia :** = *senatus.* —— **rostra :** cf. n. on 44 *devicerat.* —— **fieri :** A. 331, *a*; G. 546, Rem. 1; H. 498, I. n. —— **esse :** emphatic, = *vivere ;* see n. on 21. —— **ego vero** etc. : 'I however would rather that my old age should be shorter than that I should be old before my time'. —— **mallem :** see n. on 26 *vellem.*

P. 14. — **nemo cui fuerim :** cf. Plaut. Mercator 2, 2, 17 *quamquam negotium est, numquam sum occupatus amico operam dare.*

33. at : as in 21, where see n. —— **T. Ponti centurionis :** the centurions were generally men of powerful frame; cf. Veget. 2, 14 *centurio elegendus est, qui sit magnis viribus et procera statura ;* Philipp. 8, 26 *centuriones pugnaces et lacertosos ;* Horat. Sat. 1, 6, 72. —— **moderatio :** 'a right application'; literally 'a governing '. —— **tantum ... nitatur :** cf. 27 *quidquid agas agere pro viribus,* also 34 *quantum possumus.* —— **ne :** the affirmative *ne,* often wrongly written *nae* on the absurd assumption that the word passed into Latin from the Greek *vaí,* is in Cicero always and in other writers nearly always followed by a pronoun. For the form of the sentence here cf. Fam. 7, 1, 3 *ne ... nostrum ;* Tusc. 3, 8 *ne ista* etc.; Fin. 3, 11 (almost the same words). —— **per stadium :** 'over the course'; cf. Athenaeus 10, 4, p. 412 E; Lucian, Charon, 8; Quint. 1, 9, 5 *Milo quem vitulum* *assueverat ferre, taurum ferebat.* As to Milo see n. on **27**. For *cum sustineret* a modern would have been inclined to use a participle, which was perhaps avoided here because of the close proximity of another participle, *ingressus.* ——**umeris**: this spelling is better than *humeris*, which is now abandoned by the best scholars. There is no sound corresponding to the *h* in words of the same origin in cognate languages (see Curtius, Greek Etym. 1, 423 of the Eng. Trans.), and although undoubtedly *h* was wrongly attached to some Latin words, there is no evidence to show that this happened to *umerus.* —— **has**: *i. e. Milonis*, corresponding to *Pythagorae.* —— **Pythagorae**: chosen no doubt because tradition made Milo a Pythagorean; see n. on **27**. —— **malis**: *i. e. si optandum sit* (cf. Plaut. Miles 170). For the ellipsis see n. on **26**. —— **denique**: 'in short'. —— **utare**: the second person of the present subjunctive hortative is very rare, excepting when, as here, the command is general. Had the command been addressed to a particular person, Cicero would have written *ne requisieris.* Cf. Madvig, Opusc. 2, 105; Roby, 1596; A. 266, *a, b*; G. 256, 2; H. 484, 4, n. 2. —— **dum adsit, cum absit**: as both *dum* and *cum* evidently have here a temporal sense, the subjunctives seem due to the influence of the other subjunctives *utare* and *requiras.* A. 342; G. 666; H. 529, II. and n. 1, 1). —— **nisi forte**: see n. on **18**. —— **cursus**: for the metaphor cf. n. on **83**; also Fam. 8, 13, 1 (a letter of Coelius) *aetate iam sunt decursa;* pro Quint. 99 *acta aetas decursaque.* For *certus* cf. below, **72** *senectutis certus terminus.* —— **aetatis**: here = *vitae;* see n. on **5**. —— **eaque**: this is a common way of introducing with emphasis a fresh epithet or predicate. Often *idque* (καὶ τοῦτο) occurs, the pronoun being then adverbially used, and not in agreement with the subject. Cf. n. on **65** *illius quidem;* also *neque ea* in **22**. —— **simplex**: life is compared to a race, in which each man has to run once and only once around the course. —— **tempestivitas**: 'seasonableness'; cf. **5** *maturitate tempestiva*, with n. —— **infirmitas**: the context shows that not physical but intellectual weakness is meant; so in Acad. 2, 9 *infirmissimo tempore aetatis;* Fin. 5, 43 *aetas infirma.* —— **ferocitas**: 'exultation', 'high spirit'. —— **iam constantis aetatis**: *i. e.* middle age, the characteristic of which is *stability;* cf. **76** *constans aetas quae media dicitur;* also **60**; Tac. A. 6, 46 *composita aetas.* For *iam* cf. Suet. Galb. 4 *aetate nondum constanti;* pro Caelio 41 *aetas iam corroborata;* Fam. 10, 3, 2 *aetas iam confirmata.* —— **maturitas**: 'ripeness', *i. e.* of intellect or judgment. —— **suo**: G. 295, Rem. 1; H. 449, 2.

34. **audire te arbitror** : 'I think that news reaches you'. ——
hospes : see n. on 28 *orator*. —— **avitus** : there was a strong friendship between the elder Africanus and Masinissa, king of Numidia,
who in 206 B. C. passed over from the Carthaginian alliance to that
of the Romans. He was richly rewarded by Scipio, and remained
loyal to Rome till his death. He lived to welcome the younger Scipio
in Africa during the last Punic war, and to see the utter ruin of Carthage. See Sall. Iug. 5, 4. For the expression *hospes tuus avitus* cf.
Plautus, Miles 135 *paternum suom hospitem*. —— **cum ingressus**
etc. : *i. e.* protracted exercise of one kind did not weary him. ——
cum ... equo : though Cic. says *in equo vehi, esse, sedere* etc. the preposition here is left out because a mere ablative of manner or means
is required to suit the similar ablative *pedibus*. So Div. 2, 140 *equus
in quo vehebar*, 'the horse on which I rode'; but ib. 1, 58 *equo advectus
ad ripam*, 'brought to the bank *by the aid* of a horse'. —— **siccitatem** :
'wiriness', literally 'dryness' or freedom from excessive perspiration,
colds and the like; cf. Tusc. 5, 99 *siccitatem quae consequitur continentiam in victu;* Catull. 23, 12 *corpora sicciora cornu*. —— **regis** : here
= *regia*. —— **officia et munera** : see n. on 29. —— **ne sint** : 'grant
that age has no strength'. This formula of concession for argument's
sake is frequent in Cicero, who often attaches to it *sane*. A. 266, *d*;
G. 610; H. 515, III. —— **senectute** = *senibus:* see n. on 26. ——
legibus et institutis : 'by statute and precedent'. —— **muneribus
eis** etc. : chiefly military service. —— **non modo ... sed ne quidem** :
when a negative follows *non modo* these words have the force of *non
modo non*, a negative being borrowed from the negative in the subse-
quent clause. But often *non modo non* is written; the negative after
modo is then more emphatic, being independent. Here *non modo non
quod non* would have had a harsh sound. A. 149, *e*; G. 484, 3 and
Rem. 1.; H. 552, 2. —— **quod** : adv. acc. (see n. on 1 *quid*). Cf.
Liv. 6, 15 *sed vos id cogendi estis*.

35. **at** : as in 21, where see n. In his reply Cato adopts the same
form as that in which the objection is urged, *at id quidem* etc. So
in 68 *at senex ... at est ...*

P. 15. —— **commune valetudinis** : 'common to weak health', *i. e.*
to all in a weak state of health. *Valetudo* means in itself neither good
nor bad health; the word takes its coloring from the context. ——
filius is qui : a pause must be made at *filius;* the sense is not 'that
son of Africanus who adopted you', but 'the son of Africanus, I mean

the man who adopted you'. —— **quod ni ita fuisset :** 'now if this had not been so'; a phrase like *quod cum ita sit* and *hoc ita dici.* Cf. also 67 *quod ni ita acideret ;* 82 *quod ni ita se haberet.* —— **alterum ... civitatis :** *illud* is put for *ille,* by attraction to *lumen.* Roby, 1068. A. 195, *d ;* G. 202, Rem. 5 ; H. 445, 4. Cf. Fin. 2, 70 *Epicurus, h o c enim vestrum lumen est,* 'Epicurus, for *he* is your shining light'. —— **vitia :** 'defects'. —— **diligentia :** scarcely corresponds to our 'diligence'; it rather implies minute, patient attention; 'painstaking'.

36. habenda ... valetudinis : 'attention must be paid to health'; so *valetudini consulere* (Fam. 16, 4, 3) *operam dare* (De Or. 1, 265) *indulgere* (Fam. 16, 18, 1) *valetudinem curare* often; cf. also Fam. 10, 35, 2 ; Fin. 2, 64. —— **tantum :** restrictive, = 'only so much'; so in 69, and often. —— **potionis :** *cibus et potio* is the regular Latin equivalent for our 'food and drink'; see below, 46; also Tusc. 5, 100; Fin. 1, 37 ; Varro de Re Rust. 1, 1, 5. —— **adhibendum :** *adhibere* has here merely the sense of 'to employ' or 'to use'. Cf. Fin. 2, 64. —— **non :** we should say 'and not' or 'but not'; the Latins, however, are fond of *asyndeton,* called *adversativum,* when two clauses are contrasted. —— **menti ... animo :** properly *mens* is the intellect, strictly so called, *animus* intellect and feeling combined, but the words are often very loosely used. They often occur together in Latin ; Lucretius has even *mens animi.* —— **instilles :** see n. on 21 *exerceas.* —— **et :** 'moreover'. —— **exercitando :** in good Latin the verb *exercitare* is rare except in *exercitatus,* which stands as participle to *exerceo, exercitus* being unused. The word seems to have been chosen here as suiting *exercitationibus* better than *exercendo* would. So in 47 *desideratio* is chosen rather than *desiderium,* to correspond with the neighboring *titillatio.* —— **ait :** *sc. esse ;* the omission with *aio* is rare, though common with *dico, appello* etc.; see n. on 22. —— **comicos :** not 'comic' in our sense, but = *in comoediis,* 'represented in comedy'. So Rosc. Am. 47 *comicum adulescentem,* 'the young man of comedy'. The passage of Caecilius (see n. on 24 *Statius*) is more fully quoted in Lael. 99. —— **credulos :** in almost every Latin comedy there is some old man who is cheated by a cunning slave. —— **somniculosae :** the adj. contains a diminutive noun stem (*somniculo-*). —— **petulantia :** 'waywardness'. —— **non proborum :** Cic. avoids *improborum* as being too harsh; with exactly similar feeling Propertius 3, 20, 52 (ed. Paley) says *nec proba Pasiphae* for *et improba P.* Cf. Off. 3, 36 *error hominum non proborum.* —— **ista :** implying contempt. A. 102, *c ;* G. 291, Rem. ;

H. 450, 1. n. and foot-note 4. —— **deliratio** : 'dotage'; a rare word, used by Cic. only here and in Div. 2, 90.

37. robustos : 'sturdy'; implying that the sons were grown up. —— **tantam** : *sc. quantam habuit ;* only a little more emphatic than *magnam* would have been; see n. on 52. —— **Appius** : see n. on 16. —— **regebat** : the *pater familias* in early Roman times was an almost irresponsible ruler over his children and household. For a full discussion of the *patria potestas* see Coulanges, Ancient City, Bk. II. Ch. 8; Maine, Ancient Law, Ch. 5; Hadley, Introd. to Roman Law, Chapters 5 and 6. —— **et ... senex** : 'though both blind and old'. —— **intentum** : commonly used of *animus*, like the opposite *remissus* (28). —— **tenebat** etc. : the *patria potestas* is often denoted by the word *imperium ;* cf. De Invent. 2, 140 *imperium domesticum.* —— **vigebat** etc. : 'in him ancestral spirit and principles were strong'. While *animus patrius* here evidently means the strong will for which the patrician Claudii were proverbial (as *e. g.* in Rosc. Am. 46 *intellegere qui animus patrius sit in liberos*) it indicates the feeling of a particular father for his children.

P. 16. — **38. ita :** = *ea lege* ' on these conditions, viz. ...', the clause with *si* being an explanation of *ita*. This correspondence of *ita ... si* is common in Cicero; see n. on 12 *ita ... quasi*. Here translate 'age can only be in honor 'if it fights for itself '. —— **se ipsa** : cf. Cic. Acad. 2, 36 *veritas se ipsa defendet ;* see also the n. on 4. —— **si ... est** : 'if it has passed into bondage to nobody'. *Mancipium* is a piece of property ; *emancipare* is to pass a piece of property out of its owner's hands. The word acquired two exactly opposite meanings. When used of a slave, or of a son *in patria potestate,* who was legally subject to many of the same ordinances as a slave, it means 'to set free', unless, as in Fin. 1, 24 *filium in adoptionem D. Silano emancipaverat,* some person is mentioned to whom the original owner makes over his rights. But in Plaut. Bacchid. 1, 1, 90 *mulier, tibi me emancupo* the sense is ' I enslave myself to you ', *i. e.* 'I pass myself out of my own power into yours'. So in the well-known passage of Horace, Epod. 9, 12 (of Antony) *emancipatus feminae* 'enslaved to a woman'; cf. Cic. Phil. 2, 51 *venditum atque emancipatum tribunatum.* —— **senile aliquid ... aliquid adulescentis** : chiasmus. For the sense cf. 33 *ferocitas iuvenum ... senectutis maturitas.* —— **quod qui sequitur** : ' and he who strives after this ', *i. e.* to combine the virtues of age and youth. Cf. Aesch. Sept. 622 γέροντα τὸν νοῦν σάρκα δ' ἡβῶσαν φύει.

—— **mihi ... est in manibus** : 'I have on hand', 'am busy with'. Cf. n. on 22. —— **Originum** : as to Cato's literary labors see Introd. —— **omnia colligo** : referring to the materials Cato was collecting for his 'Origines'. —— **quascunque defendi** : 'as many as I have conducted'. *Defendere causam* here is simply to act as counsel in a case, whether the client be defendant or plaintiff. So in Lael. 96 and often. —— **nunc cum maxime** : 'now more than ever', νῦν μάλιστα. The phrase is elliptic; in full it would be '*cum maxime conficio orationes, nunc conficio*', 'when I most of all compose speeches, I now compose them'; *i. e.* 'the time when I most of all compose is now'. The words *cum maxime* generally follow *tum* or *nunc* and add emphasis to those words, but are sometimes used alone to express the ideas 'then' and 'now' more emphatically than *tum* and *nunc* would. Cf. Ver. 4, 82; Tac. Ann. 4, 27. The orators were in the habit of working over their speeches carefully for publication and preservation. —— **ius augurium** etc.: 'the law pertaining to the augurs and pontifices'; *i. e.* the principles applied by them in the performance of their duties. The pontifices had the general oversight of religious observances. See Dict. of Antiq. —— **civile** : the meaning of *ius civile* varies according to the context. Here it is the secular law as opposed to the sacred law, as in 50; sometimes it is the whole body of Roman law as opposed to the law of other states; often, again, it is the older portion of the Roman law as opposed to the newer or 'equity' portion. —— **commemoro** : 'I say over to myself'. In Cicero *commemoro* is a verb of speaking, and never has the meaning of *recordor* or *memini*. —— **curricula** : see nn. on 33. —— **magno opere** : better so written than in one word *magnopere ;* so *maximo, minimo, nimio opere*. —— **adsum amicis** : 'I act as counsel to my friends'. This legal sense of *adesse* is common. —— **frequens** : literally the word means 'crowded' (connected with *farcire* 'to cram' or 'to crowd together'), hence *frequens senatus* and the like phrases. Then *frequens* comes to be used of actions or events that often recur; *e. g.* Orat. 15 *Demosthenes frequens Platonis auditor ;* De Or. 1, 243 *frequens te audivi*. On the use of the adj. here see A. 191; G. 324, Rem. 6; H. 443. —— **ultro** : 'unasked', 'of my own motion', a reference to the well-known story that, whatever subject was discussed, Cato gave as his opinion '*delenda est Carthago*'. See Introd. —— **tueor** : 'advocate', 'support'. —— **lectulus** : a couch usually stood in the Roman study, on which the student reclined while reading, composing or dictating, or even writing.   Cf. De Or. 3, 17, *in eam exedram venisse in qua Crassus l e c t u l o posito recubuisset, cumquᴇ eum in c o g i t a t i o n e defixum esse sensisset, statim recessisse* ...; Suet. Aug. 78 *lecticula lucubratoria.* —— **ea ipsa cogitantem** : = *de eis ipsis cog.*: so Acad. 2, 127 *cogitantes supera atque caelestia*, and often. —— **acta vita** : 'the life I have led'; cf. 62 *honeste acta superior aetas ;* so Tusc. 1, 109; Fam. 4, 13, 4. —— **viventi** : dative of reference. A. 235; G. 354; H. 384, 4, n. 3. 'As regards one who lives amid these pursuits and tasks'. —— **ita sensim** etc.: *sensim sine sensu* (observe the alliteration) is like *mentes dementis* in 16, where see n. *Sensim* must have meant at one time 'perceptibly', then 'only just perceptibly', then 'gradually' and almost 'imperceptibly'.

39. quod ... dicunt : not strictly logical, being put for *quod careat, ut dicunt.*   In cases like this the verb of saying is usually in the subjunctive. Cf. Roby, 1746; A. 341, Rem.; G. 541, Rem. 2; H. 516, II. 1. The indicative here is more vivid and forcible. —— **munus ... aufert** : to say that a gift robs one of anything is of course an *oxymoron ;* cf. n. on 16 *mentes dementis.* —— **aetatis** : almost = *senectutis :* cf. n. on 45. —— **id quod est** etc.: 'the greatest fault of youth'; *i. e.* the love of pleasure.   In this passage *voluptas* indicates pleasure of a sensual kind, its ordinary sense, *delectatio, oblectatio* etc. being used of the higher pleasures.   In 51, however, we have *voluptates agricolarum.* —— **accipite** : 'hear'; so *dare* often means 'to tell'. With *accipere* in this sense cf. the similar use of ἀποδέχεσθαι. —— **Archytae** : Archytas (the subject of Horace's well-known ode, 1, 28) was a contemporary and friend of Plato, and a follower of the Pythagorean philosophy. He wrote philosophical works, and was also famous as a mathematician and astronomer, besides being the leading statesman and general of the commonwealth of Tarentum.   For another saying of Archytas, cf. Lael. 88. —— **tradita est** : 'was imparted to me', *i. e.,* by word of mouth. —— **cum ... Tarenti** : 'when as a young man I stayed at Tarentum'. For *adulescens* cf. n. on 26 *senes.* —— **nullam ... pestem** etc.: cf. Lael. 34 *pestem ... cupiditatem ;* Off. 2, 9 *consuetudo ... honestatem ab utilitate secernens, qua nulla pernicies maior hominum vitae potuit afferri.* —— **capitaliorem** : 'more deadly'; *caput* was often equivalent to *vita*, so that *capitalis* comes to mean 'affecting the life'.

P. 17.—40. **hinc** etc.: cf. Cic. Hortensius fragm. *quod turpe damnum, quod dedecus est quod non evocetur atque eliciatur voluptate ?* Observe the singular *patriae* followed by the plural *rerum publicarum*; the plural of *patria* is rare. On the significance of this passage see Lecky, Hist. of European Morals, I. p. 211, n. (Am. ed.). —— **cum hostibus** etc.: attributive phrase; cf. Phil. 12, 27 *colloquia cum acerrimis hostibus*. —— **scelus**: this word looks chiefly to the criminal intention, whether it be carried into action or not, *malum*, *facinus* to the completed crime; *flagitium* is sin rather than crime. *Facinus* in sense is often rather narrower and lighter than *scelus*; cf. Verr. 5, 170 *facinus est vincire civem Romanum, scelus verberare, prope parricidium necare*. —— **impelleret**: sc. *homines*; so *nos* is omitted after *iubebat* below. —— **excitari**: 'stirred up'. In 39 and 41 we have the verb *in-citare*; for the difference between the two verbs cf. Qu. Fr. 1, 1, 45 *haec non eo dicuntur, ut te oratio mea dormientem excitasse, sed potius ut currentem incitasse videatur*. —— **homini ... dedisset**: cf. Acad. 1, 7 *nec ullum arbitror maius aut melius a dis datum munus homini*. Notice *homini* 'man', in the same sense as *hominibus*, above. —— **muneri ac dono**: the two words *munus* and *donum* are often found together; the difference in meaning is hardly perceptible. *Donum* implies the fact of giving, *munus* the generosity of the giver. —— **tam ... inimicum**: notice the separation of *tam* from *inimicum*.

41. **libidine**: = ἐπιθυμία; *temperantia* = σωφροσύνη. *Dominari* is a very strong word, 'to tyrannize'; *dominatio* = τυραννίς. For *locum* cf. Lael. 52 *in tyranni vita nullus locus est amicitiae*. —— **consistere**: 'find a foothold'. Cf. Fin. 4, 69 *sapientia pedem ubi poneret non habebat*. —— **fingere animo**: 'to imagine'. —— **tanta ... quanta ... maxima**: 'the greatest that could possibly be enjoyed'. The form of expression is common, *e. g.* Lael. 74 *tanta quanta maxima potest esse distantia*. —— **tam diu dum**: this is not exactly equivalent to the ordinary *tam diu quam*, but there is ellipsis —'so long as this, I mean while etc.'. Cf. Cat. 3, 16 *tam diu, dum urbis moenibus continebatur*; Off. 1, 2 *tam diu ... quoad ...* —— **mente ... ratione... cogitatione**: 'by thought, by reasoning, by imagination'. *Cogitatio* like διάνοια has often the sense of 'imagination'. The close juxtaposition of words nearly synonymous is quite characteristic of Cicero's Latin. —— **quidem**: concessive, as in 32 and often. —— **maior atque longior**: 'very intense and protracted'. Superlatives might have been expected, in view of *quanta percipi posset maxima* above. *Longus* in the sense of 'long-continued' is rare in Ciceronian Latin, excepting when, as in 66 *longa aetate*, it is joined with a word distinctly referring to time.   For the general drift of the passage cf. Cic. Hortensius (fragment) *congruere cum cogitatione magna voluptas corporis non potest ; quis enim, cum utatur voluptate ea qua nulla possit maior esse, attendere animum, inire rationes, cogitare omnino quidquam potest?* —— **animi lumen :** a common metaphor; *e. g.* Cic. Rep. 6, 12 *tu, Africane, ostendas oportebit patriae lumen animi tui.* Cf. 36 *haec ... exstinguuntur ;* also below, 42 *mentis oculos.* —— **C. Pontio :** C. Pontius Herennius, the father of C. Pontius Telesinus who defeated the Romans at the Caudine Forks during the Second Samnite war, in 321 B. C.   The father is several times mentioned by Livy 9, cc. 1 and 3; cf. especially 1, § 2 *C. Pontium, patre longe prudentissimo natum.* —— **Nearchus :** mentioned by Plutarch, Cato 2, as a Pythagorean and friend of Cato. —— **permanserat :** *i. e.* during the siege of Tarentum. —— **interfuisset :** not in accordance with English idiom; cf. n. on 4 *putassent ;* also 44 *devicerat.* —— **Plato** etc.: although Plato made two journeys to Italy and Sicily (or, as some authorities say, three) it is scarcely likely that he was present at Tarentum in the year mentioned, 349 B. C., two years before his death, when he was of advanced age.   The latest date assigned by other authorities for Plato's last visit to the West is 361 B. C. —— **reperio :** *sc. in annalibus ;* so in 15; cf. *videmus* in 26.

42. efficeret : *efficeret, liberet,* and *oporteret* can be properly rendered into English only by the present tense.   Although these verbs express circumstances which *continue,* since the *general* effect of old age is being described, they are thrown into the past to suit the past tense *dicebam* or *dixi* which, though not expressed, is really the principal verb.   Cf. below, 62, 78. —— **consilium :** ' deliberation '.

P. 18. — **ut ita dicam :** this softens the metaphor, as *quasi* or *quasi quidam* often does, and as οἷον, ὥσπερ do in Greek [but not ὡς ἔπος εἰπεῖν, which is often wrongly said to be the equivalent of *ut ita dicam ;* see n. on Lael. 2].   The phrase *mentis* or *animi aciem praestringere* often occurs without anything to soften the metaphor ; *e. g.* Fin. 4, 37. —— **nec habet** etc.: ' and has no relations with virtue '.   The use of *commercium* in the metaphorical sense is common. —— **invitus :** see ref. on 38 *frequens.* —— **feci ut :** a periphrasis not unusual. A. 332, *e ;* G. 557 ; H. 498, II. n. 2. —— **T. Flaminini :** see n. on 1, l. 1. —— **L. Flamininum :** as praetor he commanded the fleet under his brother Titus during the Macedonian war ; in 192 B. C. he was consul.   *Septem annis* denotes seven *complete* years (cf. n. on 19), as

Cato was censor in 184. A reference to Livy 39, 43, 2 will show that Cicero borrows his account of Flamininus' crime from the old annalist Valerius Antias. Livy also quotes (39, 42, 7) an account of the matter given by Cato himself in a speech, which is even more disgraceful to Flamininus. —— **eicerem :** the phrase commonly used is not *eicere*, but *movere, aliquem senatu. Notare* and *nota* (*censoria*) are technically used of degradation or disfranchisement inflicted by the censors. For the spelling see Roby, 144, 2; A. 10, *d*; H. 36, 4 and foot-note 1. —— **fuisset :** for the mood see A. 342; G. 666; H. 529, II. and n. 1, 1); for the tense see Roby, 1491; A. 324, *a*; G. 233, 2; H. 471, 4. —— **cum ... Gallia :** not 'when he was consul in Gaul' but 'when he was in Gaul during his consulship'. *Cum* with the imperfect or pluperfect subjunctive often has a sense differing very little from that of *cum* with the imperfect or pluperfect indicative. No doubt when the usage originally arose, the clause with *cum* was regarded as expressing the *cause* of the action or event denoted by the principal verb ; here the presence of F. in Gaul might be regarded as *a cause* of the crime. It is more than doubtful, however, whether in actual use the subjunctive in these phrases continued to carry with it to Latin readers any idea of cause. See Roby, 1720, Kennedy, 211; also A. 325, 323 and foot-note 1; G. 586 with Rem.; H. 521, II. 2 and foot-note 1. —— **exoratus est :** 'was persuaded'; cf. Liv. 39, 43. —— **securi feriret :** the story was that L. Flamininus himself acted as executioner. —— **eorum qui ... essent :** the subjunctive because of the class-notion, 'of such persons as were'. —— **Tito censore :** *i. e.* in 189 B.C.; see n. on 1. —— **Flacco :** L. Valerius Flaccus was the life-long friend of Cato, and his colleague in the consulship and in the censorship. He entirely favored Cato's political views. See Introd. —— **imperi dedecus :** Flamininus was at the time Roman governor of the district.

43. audivi e : Cic. uses *audire ex, ab*, and *de aliquo*, almost indifferently. —— **porro :** 'in turn'; literally 'farther on', here = 'farther back'; cf. Livy 27, 51. —— **C. Fabricium :** see n. on 15. —— **Cinea :** the famous diplomatist, minister of Pyrrhus. He was a pupil of Demosthenes and himself one of the most famous orators of his time. Cineas was the ambassador who tried to negotiate peace on the occasion mentioned in 16. —— **se sapientem profiteretur :** the omission of *esse* is common in such phrases; *e. g.* Fin. 5, 13 *Strato physicum se voluit.* Epicurus, who is here meant (born 342 B.C., died 270), was blamed for calling himself σοφός or *sapiens*. Others, says Cicero, who had borne the title had waited for the public to confer it on them (Fin. 2, 7). —— **eumque :** 'and yet he'; cf. n. on 13 *vixitque.* —— **faceremus :** for the tense cf. n. on 42 *efficeret ;* also *expeteretur* below. —— **ad ... referenda :** 'ought to be judged by the standard of pleasure', *i. e.* anything which brings pleasure may be regarded as good, and its opposite bad. So in Greek ἐπαναφέρειν τὶ εἴς τι. On the moral teachings of Epicurus consult Zeller, Stoics, Epicureans, and Sceptics, Ch. 19; Ueberweg, History of Philosophy, § 59; Guyan, La morale d'Épicure et ses rapports avec les doctrines contemporaines. —— **Curium ... Coruncanium :** see n. on 15. —— **id ... persuaderetur :** intransitive verbs are used in the passive only impersonally (Roby, 1422; A. 230; G. 199, Rem. 1; H. 301, 1); when so used the dative may follow as in the active (see Madvig, 244, *b*; G. 208; H. 384, 5). A neuter pronoun in the singular sometimes, as here, accompanies the passive, and may be regarded as an adverbial accusative of respect or extent, or as a nominative qualifying the impersonal subject. The former is probably the real construction. Cf. Roby, 1423, and Madvig, 229, *b*, Obs. 1. —— **Samnitibus :** then in alliance with Pyrrhus. —— **vixerat ... cum :** not to be taken literally of living in the same house; the phrase merely indicates close friendship. In Acad. 2, 115 Cic. writes *Diodoto qui mecum vivit tot annos, qui habitat apud me,* clearly showing that the phrases *vivere cum aliquo* and *habitare apud aliquem* are not equivalent. —— **P. Decio :** this is P. Decius Mus, who at the battle of Sentinum in 295 gave his life as a propitiatory offering to the powers of the unseen world, in order to bring victory to the Roman arms. His father had sacrificed himself in the same way at the battle of Veseris (close to Vesuvius) in 340, fought against the Latins and Campanians. —— **devoverat :** Liv. 10, 28, 13 (speech of Decius) *datum hoc nostro generi est ut luendis periculis publicis p i a c u l a simus ; iam ego mecum hostium legiones mactandas T e l l u r i et dis M a n i- b u s dabo.* —— **aliquid** etc.: 'some principle'; in his philosophical works Cicero often confounds the Epicureans by quoting the action of the Decii and others like it, as showing that pleasure is not the end of existence. Cf. especially Fin. 2, 61 *P. Decius cum se devoverat et equo admisso in mediam aciem Latinorum irruebat, aliquid de voluptatibus suis cogitabat ?* Cf. also below, 75. With regard to *natura* see n. on 5. —— **sua sponte :** 'for its own sake'; 'on its own account' Cf. Leg. 1, 45 *vera et falsa sua sponte non aliena iudicantur,* where a few lines later *sua natura* occurs as equivalent to *sua sponte* —— **ex-**

peteretur : em. for *peteretur* in the MSS.   The words *expetere, expetendum* are technically used in Cicero's philosophical works to express the Greek αἱρεῖσθαι, αἱρετόν as applied to the *finis* or τέλος, the supreme aim of moral action.   *Pulchrum* above is a translation of the Greek καλόν, a term constantly applied to the τέλος, particularly by the Stoics.
—— **spreta et contempta :** the first word is much the stronger of the two ; *spernere* is καταφρονεῖν, 'to scorn'; *contemnere* ὀλιγωρεῖσθαι, 'to make light of', 'hold of no account'.   *Contemnere* is often no stronger in sense than *omittere,* 'to pass by, neglect'.   Cf. 65 *contemni, despici.* —— **optimus quisque :** see A. 93, *c* ; G. 305; H. 458, 1.

P. 19. — 44. **cruditate :** 'indigestion'. —— **insomniis :** 'sleeplessness'; the singular *insomnium* occurs only once in prose (Tac. Ann. 11, 4).   *Insomnia, ae* is found only in poetry and late prose. —— **divine :** this word in Cic. often means nothing more than 'splendidly', 'extraordinarily'. —— **escam malorum :** 'an enticement to evil' (*esca* = *ed-ca*, from the root of *edo*).   Plato in the Timaeus 69 D (a dialogue translated into Latin by Cicero, a fragment of whose translation is still preserved) has ἡδονὴν μέγιστον κακοῦ δέλεαρ.   Cf. also Cic. Hortensius fr. 76 (ed. Halm) *voluptates corporis quae vere et graviter a Platone dictae sunt illecebrae esse atque escae malorum.* —— **modicis :** for the sake of variety Cic. chooses this, not *moderatis,* as the opposite of *immoderatis.*   Trans. 'a moderate amount of goodfellowship'. ——
M. F. = *Marci filium.* —— **devicerat :** pluperfect where a modern would incline to use a perfect.   The battle referred to is that of Mylae, fought in 260; its memory was perpetuated by the decking of the *forum* with the *rostra* of the captured ships ; the *columna rostrata* bore a long inscription, a restored version of which still exists. —— **cena :** so best spelt ; some good texts still print *caena,* but *coena* is decidedly wrong, being based on the fiction that the Latin borrowed the Greek word κοινή and turned it into *coena.* —— **cereo funali :** 'the torchlight'; *cereo,* the em. of Mommsen for *crebro ;* the *funale* was a torch composed of withs or twigs twisted into a rope (*funis*) and dipped in pitch or oil. —— **sibi ... sumpserat :** Cic. seems to think that Duillius assumed these honors on his own authority.   This was probably not the case; they were most likely conferred on him by a vote of the *comitia tributa.*   Cf. Liv. epit. 17 *C. Duillius primus omnium Romanorum ducum navalis victoriae duxit triumphum, ob quam causam ei perpetuus quoque honos habitus est, ut revertenti a cena tibicine canente funale praeferretur.*   No other instance is known where these particu

lar distinctions were decreed; the nearest parallel lies in the right
accorded to Paulus Macedonicus and to Pompeius to wear the trium-
phal *toga picta* for life on each occasion of the *ludi*.   It may be con-
jectured that the music and the torch were part of the ceremony on
the evening of a triumph when the *triumphator* was escorted home.
Cf. Florus 1, 18, 10, ed. Halm. —— **nullo exemplo**: 'without any
precedent'. —— **privatus**: any person is *privatus* who is not actually
in office at the moment referred to, whether he has led a public life or
not. —— **licentiae**: a strong word is used to mark the heinousness
of Duillius' supposed offence against ancestral custom.

45. **alios**: *sc. nomino*. —— **primum**: the corresponding *deinde* is
omitted, as often. —— **sodalis**: the *sodalitates* or *sodalitia*, brother-
hoods for the perpetuation of certain rites accompanied with feasting,
were immemorial institutions at Rome.   The clause *sodalitates ... acceptis* must not be taken to mean that Cicero supposed these brother-
hoods to have been first instituted in the time of Cato; it is only
introduced to show that Cato, so far from being averse to good living,
assisted officially in the establishment of new clubs.   Most of the *sodalitates* were closely connected with the *gens;* all members of a *gens*
were *sodales* and met together to keep up the old *sacra*, but in historical times fictitious kinship largely took the place of real kinship, and
feasting became almost the sole raison d'être of these clubs.   [See
Mommsen's treatise *De collegiis et sodaliciis Romanis*.]   The parallel
of the London City Companies readily suggests itself.   The national
sodalitates or priesthoods such as those of the *Sodales Titii, Luperci,
Augustales* etc. were somewhat different. —— **autem**: for the form of
the parenthesis cf. 7. —— **Magnae Matris**: the image of Cybele was
brought to Rome in 204 B. C. from Pessinus in Phrygia.   See Liv. 29,
10.   The *Sacra* are called *Idaea* from Mount Ida in Phrygia, which
was a great centre of the worship of Cybele.   *Acceptis*, sc. *in civitatem;*
the worship of strange gods was in principle illegal at Rome unless
expressly authorized by the State. —— **igitur**: the construction of
the sentence is broken by the introduction of the parenthesis, and a
fresh start is made with *epulabar igitur*.   *Igitur* is often thus used, like
our 'well then', to pick up the broken thread of a sentence.   So often
sed or *ergo*. —— **fervor**: Cf. Hor. Od. 1, 16, 22 *me quoque pectoris
temptavit in dulci iuventa fervor.* —— **aetatis, qua progrediente**:
'belonging to that time of life, but as life advances'.   The word *aetas*
has really two senses here; in the first place it is *bona aetas* or *iuventus*

(cf. 39 where *aetas = senectus*), in the second place *vita* (for which see n. on 5). —— **neque enim** : the *enim* refers to *modice*. —— **coetu ... sermonibus** : for the order of the words see n. on 1 *animi tui.* —— **metiebar** : cf. n. on 43 *referenda.* —— **accubitionem** : a *vox Ciceroniana*, rarely found in other authors. —— **vitae coniunctionem** : 'a common enjoyment of life'. —— **tum ... tum** : here purely temporal, 'sometimes ... sometimes'; often however = 'both ... and'; cf. 7. —— **compotationem** etc.: cf. Epist. ad Fam. 9, 24, 3. *Compotatio =* συμπόσιον; *concenatio =* σύνδειπνον. —— **in eo genere** : see n. on 4. —— **id** : *i. e.* eating and drinking.

46. **tempestivis ... conviviis** : 'even in protracted banquets'. Those banquets which began *early* in order that they might last long were naturally in bad repute, so that the phrase *tempestivum convivium* often has almost the sense of 'a debauch'. Thus in Att. 9, 1, 3 Cicero describes himself as being evil spoken of in *tempestivis conviviis, i. e.* in dissolute society. Cf. pro Arch. 13. The customary dinner hour at Rome was about three o'clock in the afternoon. The word *tempestivus*, which in 5 means 'at the right time', here means 'before the right time'. So in English 'in good time' often means 'too early'. See Becker's Gallus, p. 451 *et seq.* —— **qui pauci** : the substitution of the nominative of the relative for the partitive genitive (*quorum*) is not uncommon. A. 216, *e*; G. 368, Rem. 2; H. 397, 2, n. —— **pauci admodum** : Cic. usually says *admodum pauci* rather than *pauci admodum.* —— **vestra aetate** : = *eis qui sunt vestra aetate.* Cf. n. on 26 *senectus.* —— **sermonis ... sustulit** : notice the indicatives *auxit, sustulit*, the relative clauses being attributive, though they might fairly have been expected here to be causal. G. 627; H. 517, 2. In this passage Cic. imitates Plato, Rep. 328 D. —— **bellum indicere** : common in the metaphorical sense ; *e. g.* De Or. 2, 155 *miror cur philosophiae prope bellum indixeris ;* Hor. Sat. 1, 5, 7 *ventri indico bellum.* —— **cuius est** etc.: *i. e.* nature sanctions a certain amount of pleasure. This is the Peripatetic notion of the *mean*, to which Cicero often gives expression, as below, 77; also in Acad. 1, 39; 2, 139; and in De Off.; so Hor. Sat. 1, 1, 106 *sunt certi denique fines quos ultra citraque nequit consistere rectum ;* cf. Od. 2, 10. —— **non intellego ne** : for the negatives cf. nn. on 24, 27.

P. 20. —— **magisteria** : generally explained as referring to the practice of appointing at each dinner a 'master of the feast', *arbiter bibendi* or συμποσιάρχης. This explanation is not quite correct

Mommsen shows in his work '*de collegiis*' that each one of the *collegia* or *sodalicia* annually appointed a *magister cenarum* whose duty it was to attend to the club-dinners during his year of office and no doubt to preside at them. That some office is meant more important than that of the *arbiter bibendi* appointed for a particular feast is shown by the words *a maioribus instituta*. It is scarcely likely that Cicero was ignorant of the Greek origin of the custom of appointing an *arbiter bibendi*.

—— et is sermo etc.: 'and the kind of talk in which following the fashion of our fathers we engage, beginning at the upper table, as the cup goes round'. The cup circulated from left to right, not, as with us, from right to left. The guests at a Roman dinner reclined on three couches, placed at three tables; two of the couches (*lecti*) were parallel, and the third was at right angles to the other two. The *lectus* at which the cup began to circulate was *summus*, the next *medius*, the last *imus*. For *a summo* cf. *da* (*sc. bibere*) *a summo* in Plaut. Asin. 5, 2, 41. See Becker's Gallus, p. 471 *et seq*. —— sicut...est: 'as we find'; so Off. 1, 32 *ut in fabulis est*, and often. —— in Symposio: 2, 26. —— minuta: see n. on 52. —— rorantia: here with an active sense, 'besprinkling', representing ἐπιψεκάζειν in Xenophon; often however not different in sense from '*roscida*'. —— refrigeratio... hibernus: cf. closely 57 *ubi et seq*. Note the changes of expression in passing from *refrigeratio* to *sol* (*apricatio* would have more exactly corresponded with *refrigeratio*) and from *aestate* to *hibernus* (for *hieme*). —— in Sabinis: 'when with the Sabines', who were celebrated for their simplicity of life. Cato had an estate in the Sabine district. —— convivium vicinorum compleo: 'I make up (*i. e.* to the proper number) a company of my neighbors'. —— quod ... producimus: 'and we continue our companionship to as late an hour as we can, with changing talk'. The phrases *multa nocte* or *de nocte* 'late in the night', *multo die* 'late in the day', are common; cf. also Att. 13, 9, 1 *multus sermo ad multum diem;* Rep. 6, 10 *sermonem in multam noctem produximus*.

47. at: so in 21, where see n. —— quasi titillatio: the *quasi*, as often in Cicero's writings, marks a translation from the Greek. Here the Epicurean word γαργαλισμός is referred to; it is often in Cic. represented by *titillatio;* cf. N. D. 1, 113; Fin. 1, 39; Tusc. 3, 47. —— bene: *sc. dixit*. —— affecto aetate: 'wrought on by age'. Cf. De Or. 1, 200 *in eius infirmissima valetudine affectaque iam aetate.* —— utereturne etc.: 'whether he still took pleasure in love'; *uti = frui*

Cf. Ovid, Met. 4, 259 *dementer amoribus u t i* with Cic. Tusc. 4, 68
venereis voluptatibus f r u i. —— di meliora : *sc. duint ;* this archaic
form usually occurs when the phrase is given in full. The story of
Sophocles is taken by Cicero from Plato (Rep. 329 B) who has
εὐφήμει. —— istinc etc. : cf. the passage in Plato, Rep. 1, 329 C. For
istinc used otherwise than of place cf. *unde* in 12 with n. —— agresti :
'boorish'; *rusticus* denotes simply an ordinary countryman.——
quamquam ... ergo : these words may be scanned as a hexameter
line, but the pause before *ergo* would prevent them from being taken
as a verse. —— hoc non desiderare : 'this absence of regret'; the
words form the subject of *est*. So *hoc non dolere* in Fin. 2, 18. For
the pronoun in agreement with the infinitive treated as noun cf. Persius
1, 9 *istud vivere ;* 1, 122 *hoc ridere meum.* H. 538, 3.

48. si : 'even if', 'granting that'. —— bona aetas : 'the good
time of life ', *i. e.* youth. Tischer qu. Varro de Re Rustica 2, 6, 2 *mares
feminaeque bona aetate* = 'young'. For *bona aetas = homines bona
aetate* cf. n. on 26 *senectus*. —— ut diximus : not expressly, but the
opinion is implied in 44, 45. —— Turpione Ambivio : L. Ambivius
Turpio was the most famous actor of Cato's time, and appeared especially in Terence's plays. In old Latin commonly, occasionally in
the Latin of the best period, and often in Tacitus, the *cognomen* is
placed before the *nomen* when the *praenomen* is not mentioned. Cf.
Att. 11, 12, 1 *Balbo Cornelio*. The usage is more common in Cicero's
writings than in those of his contemporaries. —— prima cavea : 'the
lower tier '. The later Roman theatres consisted of semicircular or
elliptic galleries, with rising tiers of seats; the level space partially
enclosed by the curve was the *orchestra,* which was bounded by the
stage in front. There can be little doubt that Cicero is guilty of
an anachronism here; his words do not suit the circumstances of
Cato's time. Till nearly the end of the Republic the theatres were
rude structures of wood, put up temporarily; it is even doubtful
whether they contained seats for the audience. Cato himself frus-
trated an attempt to establish a permanent theatre. —— propter :
'close by'. The adverbial use of *propter* (rarely, if ever, met with
outside of Cicero) is denied by some scholars, but is well attested by
MSS. here and elsewhere. —— tantum ... est : these words qualify
delectatur.

49. illa : put for *illud,* as in Greek ταῦτα and τάδε are often put
for τοῦτο and τόδε. The words from *animum* to the end of the sen

tence are explanatory of *illa*. —— **quanti**: 'how valuable!' but the word may have exactly the opposite meaning if the context require it; thus in N. D. 1, 55 and Rep. 6, 25 the sense is 'how worthless!' —— **stipendiis**: 'campaigns'. The four words from *libidinis* to *inimicitiarum* are to be taken in pairs, while *cupiditatum* sums them up and is in apposition to all. —— **secum esse**: cf. Tusc. 1, 75; Pers. 4, 52 *tecum habita*. —— **si ... aliquod**: the sense is scarcely different from that of *si ... quod;* the distinction is as slight as that in English between 'if' followed by 'some', and 'if' followed by 'any'. Cf. n. on Lael. 24 *si quando aliquid*. —— **pabulum**: for the metaphorical sense rendered less harsh by *tamquam*, cf. Acad. 2, 127; Tusc. 5, 66 *pastus animorum*. —— **studi**: an explanatory genitive dependent on *pabulum*. —— **otiosa senectute**: 'leisured age'; *otium* in the Latin of Cicero does not imply idleness, but freedom from public business and opportunity for the indulgence of literary and scientific tastes. —— **videbamus**: for the tense cf. Lael. 37 *Gracchum rem publicam vexantem ab amicis derelictum videbamus, i. e.* 'we saw over a considerable period'. See also 50, 79. —— **in studio** etc.: 'busied with the task of almost measuring bit by bit (*di-metiendi*) the heavens and the earth'. For the sense cf. Hor. Od. 1, 28 (of Archytas). —— **Gallum**: consul in 157 B. C., famous as an astronomer and as the first Roman who predicted an eclipse before the battle of Pydna. See Liv. 44, 37.

P. 21. — **describere**: technically used of the drawing of mathematical figures. *Ingredior* often has an infinitive dependent on it even in the best Latin; *e. g.* Cic. Top. 1 *nos maiores res scribere ingressos.*

50. acutis: requiring keenness of intellect. —— **Naevius**: see n. on 20. —— **Truculento ... Pseudolo**: these plays of Plautus (lived from 254 to 184 B. C.) we still possess. The Truculentus is so named from one of the characters, a slave of savage disposition who is wheedled; the Pseudolus from a cheating slave. The latter name is commonly supposed to be a transcription from a Greek word ψεύδυλος, which however nowhere occurs; and as the change from Greek υ to Latin *o* is not found before *l*, Corssen assumes ψεύδ-αλος as the original word. The form *Pseudulus* of the name is probably later than *Pseudolus*. —— **Livium**: Livius Andronicus, the founder of Latin literature (lived from about 285 to 204 B. C.), who translated the Odyssey, also many Greek tragedies. Livius was a Greek captured by Livius Salinator at Tarentum in 275 B. C.; for a time he was the slave of Livius, and, according to custom, took his name wnen set free. For an account of his writings see Cruttwell's Hist. of Roman Literature, Ch. 3; Sellar, Roman Poets of the Rep., Ch. 3. —— **docuisset**: 'had brought on to the stage'. *Docere* (like διδάσκειν in Greek, which has the same use) meant originally to instruct the performers in the play. —— **Centone Tuditanoque consulibus**: *i. e.* in 240 B. C. The use of *que* here is noticeable; when a date is given by reference to the consuls of the year it is usual to insert *et* (not *que* or *atque*, which rarely occur) between the two names, if only the *cognomina* (as here) be given. If the full names be given, then they are put side by side without *et*. Cf. n. on 10. —— **Crassi**: see n. on 27. —— **pontifici et civilis iuris**: the *ius pontificium* regarded mainly the proper modes of conducting religious ceremonial. *Ius civile*, which is often used to denote the whole body of Roman Law, here includes only the secular portion of that Law. Cf. n. on 38. —— **huius P. Scipionis**: 'the present P. Scipio'. So in 14 *hi consules* 'the present consuls'; Rep. 1, 14 *Africanus hic, Pauli filius*, and often. The P. Scipio who is meant here is not Africanus, but Nasica Corculum. —— **flagrantis**: 'all aglow'; so *ardere studio* in Acad. 2, 65. —— **senes**: = *cum senes essent*, so *senem* below. —— **suadae medullam**: 'the essence (lit. marrow) of persuasiveness'. The lines of Ennius are preserved by Cicero, Brut. 58. *Suada* is a translation of πειθώ, which the Greek rhetoricians declared to be the end and aim of oratory. This Cethegus was consul in 204 and in 203 defeated Mago in the N. of Italy. —— **exerceri**: here reflexive in meaning. A. 111, n. 1; G. 209; H. 465. —— **videbamus**: see n. on 49. —— **comparandae**: for the idea of *possibility* which the gerundive sometimes has (but only in negative sentences or interrogative sentences implying a negative answer, and in conditional clauses) see Madvig, 420, Obs.; Roby, 1403. —— **haec quidem**: a short summary of the preceding arguments, preparatory to a transition to a new subject, introduced by *venio nunc ad*. The succession of two clauses both containing *quidem* seems awkward, but occurs in Fin. 5, 80 and elsewhere. —— **honestum sit**: 'does him honor'. —— **ut ante dixi**: in 26, where see the notes. —— **potest esse**: Meissner (n. on 27) says that Cicero's rule is to say *potest esse, debet esse* and the like, not *esse potest* and the like. It is true that *esse* in such cases is very seldom separated from the word on which it depends, but *esse potest* is just as common as *potest esse*; the difference to the sense is one of emphasis only, the *esse* having more emphasis thrown on it in the latter case.

51. **mihi ... videntur :** see Introd. —— **habent rationem cum :** 'they have their reckonings with', 'their dealings with'; a phrase of book-keeping. —— **imperium :** so Verg. Georg. 1, 99 *exercetque frequens telluren atque imperat agris;* ib. 2, 369 *dura exerce imperia et ramos compesce fluentes;* Tac. Germ. 26 *sola terrae seges imperatur.* —— **sed alias ... faenore :** put for *sed semper cum faenore, alias minore, plerumque maiore.* —— **vis ac natura :** ' powers and constitution'. These two words are very often used by Cic. together, as in Fin. 1, 50 *vis ac natura rerum.* —— **gremio :** so Lucret. 1, 250 *pereunt imbres ubi eos pater aether In gremium matris terrai praecipitavit,* imitated by Verg. Georg. 2, 325. —— **mollito ac subacto :** *i. e.* by the plough. *Subigere,* 'subdue', is a technical word of agriculture; so Verg. Georg. 2, 50 *scrobibus subactis;* see also below, 59.

P. 22. — **occaecatum :** 'hidden'. *Caecus* has the sense of 'unseen' as well as that of 'unseeing' or 'blind'. —— **occatio :** Cicero's derivation, as well as Varro's (De Re Rust. 1, 31, 1) from *occidere,* because the earth is cut up, is unsound. *Occa* is *rastrum,* probably from its *sharp* points (root *ak-*); *occatio* therefore is 'harrowing'. —— **vapore :** 'heat'. This word has not in the best Latin the meaning of our 'vapor'. —— **compressu :** a word found only here in Cicero's writings and elsewhere in Latin only in the ablative case, like so many other nouns whose stem ends in *-u.* —— **diffundit et elicit :** 'expands and lures forth'. —— **herbescentem :** this word occurs nowhere else in Latin. —— **nixa :** A. 254, *b* ; G. 403, Rem. 3; H. 425, 1, 1), n. —— **fibris stirpium :** so Tusc. 3, 13 *radicum fibras.* —— **geniculato :** 'knotted'. The verb *geniculo,* from *genu,* scarcely occurs excepting in the passive participle, which is always used, as here, of plants. So Plin. Nat. Hist. 16, 158 *geniculata cetera gracilitas nodisque distincta,* speaking of the *harundo.* —— **spici :** besides *spica,* the forms *spicum* and *spicus* are occasionally found. *Spici* here is explanatory of *frugem.* —— **vallo :** for the metaphor compare N. D. 2, 143 *munitae sunt palpebrae tamquam vallo pilorum ;* Lucr. 2, 537.

52. **quid ego ... commemorem :** this and similar formulae for passing to a new subject are common ; cf. 53 *quid ego ... proferam* etc.; often *nam* precedes the *quid,* as in Lael. 104. The *ego* has a slight emphasis. Cato implies that his own devotion to grape-culture was so well known as not to need description. —— **ortus satus incrementa :** 'origin, cultivation, and growth'. For the omission of the copula see n. on 53. —— **ut :** final, and slightly elliptic ('I say this that etc.') ; so in 6 (where see n.), 24, 56, 59, 82. —— **requietem**: the best MSS. of Cic. sometimes give the other form *requiem*, as in Arch. 13. —— **vim ipsam**: 'the inherent energy'. —— **omnium … terra**: a common periphrasis for 'all plants'; cf. *e. g.* N. D. 2, 120. The Latin has no one word to comprehend all vegetable products. —— **quae … procreet**: 'able to generate'. —— **tantulo**: strictly elliptic, implying *quantulum re vera est*. In such uses *tantus* and *tantulus* differ slightly from *magnus* and *parvus;* they are more emphatic. —— **acini vinaceo**: 'a grape-stone'. —— **minutissimis**: used here for *minimis*. Strictly speaking *minutus* ought to be used of things which are fragments of larger things, *minutus* being really the participle passive of *minuo*. In a well-known passage (Orat. 94) Cic. himself calls attention to the theoretical incorrectness of the use, which, however, is found throughout Latin literature. Cf. 46 *pocula minuta;* also below, 85 *minuti philosophi*. —— **malleoli**: vine-cuttings; so called because a portion of the parent stem was cut away with the new shoot, leaving the cutting in the shape of a mallet. —— **plantae**: 'suckers', shoots springing out of the trunk. —— **sarmenta**: 'scions', shoots cut from branches not from the trunk. —— **viviradices**: 'quicksets', new plants formed by dividing the roots of the mother plant. —— **propagines**: 'layers', new plants formed by rooting a shoot in the earth without severing it from the parent plant; Verg. Georg. 2, 26. —— **eadem**: n. on 4 *eandem*. —— **claviculis**: cf. N. D. 2, 120 *vites sic claviculis*. —— **ars agricolarum**: *agricolae arte freti*, a strong instance of the abstract put for the concrete.

53. eis: *sc. sarmentis*, those which have not been pruned away by the knife. —— **exsistit**: 'springs up'. *Exsistere* in good Latin never has the meaning of our 'exist', *i. e.* 'to be in existence', but always means '*to come into* existence'. —— **articulos**: 'joints'; cf. 51 *culmo geniculato*. The word *tamquam* softens the metaphor in *articuli*, which would properly be used only of the joints in the limbs of animals. —— **gemma**: Cicero took the meaning 'gem' or 'jewel' to be the primary sense of *gemma* and considered that the application to a bud was metaphorical. See the well-known passages, Orat. 81 and De Or. 3, 155. —— **vestita pampinis**: 'arrayed in the young foliage'. —— **fructu … aspectu**: ablatives of respect, like *gustatu* above. —— **capitum iugatio**: 'the linking together of their tops'; *i. e.* the uniting of the tops of the stakes by cross-stakes. So the editors; but Conington on Verg. Georg. 2, 355 seems to take *capita* of the top-foliage

of the vines, an interpetation which is quite possible. Those editors
are certainly wrong who remove the comma after *iugatio* and place it
after *religatio*, as though *et* were omitted between the two words.   In
enumerations of more than two things Cic. either omits the copula
altogether or inserts it before each word after the first; but in enumer-
ating two things *et* cannot be omitted, except where there are several
sets or *pairs* of things.   Cf. n. on 13.——— **religatio** : *i. e.* the tying
down of shoots so as to cause them to take root in the earth.   *Religa-*
tio seems to occur only here.

   P. 23. — **aliorum immissio** : 'the granting of free scope to others'.
Immissio scarcely occurs elsewhere in good Latin.   The metaphor is
from letting loose the reins in driving; cf. Verg. Georg. 2, 364; Plin.
N. H. 16, 141 *cupressus immittitur in perticas asseresque amputatione*
ramorum ; Varro, R. R. 1, 31, 1 *vitis immittitur ad uvas pariendas.*
Some, referring to Columella de Arbor. c. 7, take the word to mean
the setting in the earth of a shoot in order that it may take root before
being separated from the parent stem.   The context, however, is
against this interpretation. ——— **irrigationes** etc.: the plurals denote
more prominently than singulars would the repetition of the actions
expressed by these words. ——— **repastinationes** : 'repeated hoeings'.
The *pastinum* was a kind of pitchfork, used for turning over the ground
round about the vines, particularly when the young plants were being
put in. ——— **multo terra fecundior** : see n. on 3 *parum...auctoritatis.*
   54. **in eo libro** : see Introd. ——— **doctus** : often used of poets, not
only by Cicero buf by most other Latin writers, more particularly by
the elegiac poets ; see also n. on 13. ——— **Hesiodus** : the oldest Greek
poet after Homer.   The poem referred to here is the Ἔργα καὶ Ἡμέραι,
which we still possess, along with the Theogony and the Shield of
Heracles. ——— **cum** : concessive. ——— **saeculis** : 'generations', as in
24. ——— **fuit** : = *vixit.* ——— **Laerten** : the passage referred to is no
doubt the touching scene in Odyss. 24, 226, where Odysseus, after kill-
ing the suitors, finds his unhappy old father toiling in his garden.   In
that passage nothing is said of *manuring.* ——— **lenientem** : see n. on
11 *dividenti.* ——— **colentem** etc.: the introduction of another participle to explain *lenientem* is far from elegant.   *Cultione agri* or something of the kind might have been expected.   The collocation of
appetentem with *occupatum* in 56 is no less awkward. ——— **facit** : n.
on 3 *facimus.* ——— **res rusticae laetae sunt** : 'the farmer's life is
gladdened'. ——— **apium** : this form is oftener found in the best MSS.,

of prose writers at least, than the other form *apum*, which probably was not used by Cic. —— **omnium** : = *omnis generis*. —— **consitiones ... insitiones** : 'planting ... grafting'. On the varieties of grafting and the skill required for it see Verg. Georg. 2, 73 *seq.*

55. possum : see n. on 24. —— **ignoscetis** : 'you will excuse (me)'. —— **provectus sum** : 'I have been carried away'. Cicero often uses *prolabi* in the same sense. —— **in hac ... consumpsit** : Cic. probably never, as later writers did, used *consumere* with a simple ablative. —— **Curius** : see n. on 15. —— **a me** : = *a mea villa ;* cf. n. on 3 *apud quem.* —— **admirari satis non possum** : a favorite form of expression with Cicero ; *e. g.* De Or. 1, 165. —— **disciplinam** : 'morals'; literally 'teaching'.

56. Curio : Plutarch, Cat. 2, says the ambassadors found him cooking a dinner of herbs, and that Curius sent them away with the remark that a man who dined in that way had no need of gold. The present was not brought as a bribe, since the incident took place after the war. Curius had become *patronus* of the Samnites, and they were bringing the customary offering of *clientes ;* see Rep. 3, 40. —— **ne** : here = *num*, a rare use; so Fin. 3, 44; Acad. 2, 116. —— **sed venio ad** : so in 51 *venio nunc ad. Redeo ad* (see n. on 32) might have been expected here. —— **in agris erant** : 'lived on their farms'. For *erant* cf. n. on 21 *sunt.* —— **id est senes** : cf. 19 n. on *senatum.* —— **si quidem** : often written as one word *siquidem* = εἴπερ. —— **aranti** : emphatic position. —— **Cincinnato** : L. Quinctius Cincinnatus is said to have been dictator twice ; in 458 B. C., when he saved the Roman army, which was surrounded by the Aequians, and ended the war in sixteen days from his appointment ; in 439, when Maelius was killed and Cincinnatus was eighty years old. In our passage Cic. seems to assume only one dictatorship. The story of Cincinnatus at the plough is told in Livy 3, 26. —— **factum** : the technical term was *dicere dictatorem*, since he was nominated by the consul on the advice of the senate. —— **cuius** : not in agreement with, but in apposition to, *dictatoris.*

P. 24. — **Maelium** : a rich plebeian, who distributed corn in time of famine and was charged with courting the people in order to make himself a king. Ahala summoned him before the dictator, and because he did not immediately obey, killed him with his own hand. For this, Ahala became one of the heroes of his nation. See Liv. 4, 13. Cicero often mentions him with praise. Cf in Catil. I. 3; p.

Sestio 143, etc. —— **appetentem** : = *quia appetebat ;* so *occupatum = cum occupasset.* —— **viatores** : literally 'travellers', so 'messengers'. They formed a regularly organized corporation at Rome and were in attendance on many of the magistrates. Those officers who had the *fasces* had also lictors, who, however, generally remained in close attendance and were not despatched on distant errands. The statement of Cic. in the text is repeated almost *verbatim* by Plin. N. H. 18, 21. —— **miserabilis** : 'to be pitied'. The word does not quite answer to our 'miserable'. —— **agri cultione** : a rare expression, found elsewhere only in Verr. 3, 226 ; then not again till the 'Fathers'. —— **haud scio an nulla** : since *haud scio an* is affirmative in Cicero, not negative as in some later writers, *nulla* must be read here, not *ulla*. Cf. 73 *haud scio an melius Ennius,* 'probably Ennius speaks better'; also 74 *incertum an hoc ipso die,* 'possibly to-day'. Roby, 2256; G. 459, Rem.; H. 529, II. 3, 2), n. 2. —— **quam dixi** : = *de qua dixi,* as in 53. —— **saturitate** : the word is said to occur nowhere else in Latin. —— **quidam** : *i. e.* the authors of the *tertia vituperatio senectutis,* whom Cato refutes in 39, 59. —— **porco ... gallina** : these words are used collectively, as *rosa* often is; so Fin. 2, 65 *potantem in rosa Thorium.* —— **iam** : 'further'. —— **succidiam alteram** : 'a second meat-supply'. The word seems to be connected with *caedo,* and probably originally meant 'slaughter'. In a fragment of Cato preserved by Gellius 13, 24, 12 (in some editions 13, 25, 12) we find *succidias humanas facere.* Varro, R. R. 2, 14 has the word in the sense of 'meat'. —— **conditiora facit** : 'adds a zest to'; cf. *condita* in 10. —— **supervacaneis operis** : 'by the use of spare time'; literally 'by means of toils that are left over', *i. e.* after completing the ordinary work of the farm.

57. ordinibus : cf. 59 *ordines.* —— **brevi praecidam** : 'I will cut the matter short'. For *praecidam* (*sc. rem* or *sermonem*) cf. Acad. 2, 133 *praecide* (*sc. sermonem*) ; for *brevi* (= 'in brief', ἐν βραχεῖ) cf. De Or. 1, 34 *ne plura consecter comprehendam brevi.* —— **usu uberius** : cf. 53 *fructu laetius ... aspectu pulchrius.* —— **ad quem ... retardat** : some have thought that there is zeugma here, supposing *ad* to be suited only to *invitat,* not to *retardat.* That this is not the case is clear from such passages as Caes. B. G. 7, 26, 2 *palus Romanos ad insequendum tardabat* (= *tardos faciebat*) ; Cic. Sull. 49 *nullius amicitia ad pericula propulsanda impedimur.* On *fruendum* see Madvig, 421, *a,* Obs. 2 and 265, Obs. 2; G. 428, Rem. 3, exc.; H. 544, 2, n. 5. —— **in-**

vitat atque allectat: one of the 'doublets' of which Cicero is so fond; cf. Lael. 99 *allectant et invitant*.

58. sibi habeant: *sc. iuvenes;* contemptuous, as in Lael. 18 *sibi habeant sapientiae nomen;* Sull. 26 *sibi haberent honores, sibi imperia* etc.; cf. the formula of Roman divorce, *tu tuas res tibi habeto.* —— **hastas**: in practising, the point was covered by a button, *pila;* cf. Liv. 26, 51 *praepilatis missilibus iaculati sunt.* —— **clavam**: cf. Vegetius de Re Mil. 1, 11 *clavas ligneas pro gladiis tironibus dabant, eoque modo exercebantur ad palos;* Iuv. 6, 246. The *palus* is called *stipes* by Martial 7, 32. —— **pilam ... venationes ... cursus**: all national amusements, well known to readers of Horace; see Becker's Gallus. *Venationes*, em. for *natationes.* —— **talos ... tesseras**: *tali,* 'knucklebones', were oblong, and rounded at the two ends; the sides were numbered 1 and 6 (1 being opposite to 6), 3 and 4. Four *tali* were used at a time and they, like the *tesserae,* were generally thrown from a box, *fritillus.* The *tesserae,* of which three were used at a time, were cubes, with the sides numbered from 1 to 6 in such a way that the numbers on two opposite sides taken together always made 7. A separate name was used by dicers for almost every possible throw of the *tesserae* and *tali.* The two best known are *canis,* when all the dice turned up with the same number uppermost; and *venus,* when they all showed different numbers. The word *alea* was general and applicable to games of chance of every kind. These games, which were forbidden by many ineffectual laws ('*vetita legibus alea*') were held to be permissible for old men; see Mayor on Iuv. 14, 4. —— **id ipsum**: sc. *faciunt;* the omission of *facere* is not uncommon. Roby, 1441; H. 368, 3, n. 1. —— **ut**: em. for ordinary readings *unum* and *utrum.*

59. legite: 'continue to read'. Cf. De Or. 1, 34 *pergite, ut facitis, adulescentes.* In Tusc. 2, 62 it is stated that Africanus was a great reader of Xenophon.

P. 25. —— **libro qui est de**: so in Fat. 1 *libris qui sunt de natura deorum,* and similarly elsewhere; but the periphrasis is often avoided, as in Off. 2, 16 *Dicaearchi liber de interitu hominum.* —— **qui**: *quique* might have been expected, but the words above, *qui ... familiari,* are regarded as parenthetical. —— **Oeconomicus**: Cicero translates from this work c. 4, 20–25. —— **inscribitur**: see n. on 13. —— **regale**: 'worthy of a king'; different from *regium,* which would mean 'actually characteristic of kings'. Yet Cic. sometimes interchanges the words; thus *regalis potestas* in Har. Resp. 54 is the same as *regia*

potestas in Phil. 1, 3. —— **loquitur cum Critobulo** etc.: 'dis-
courses with Critobulus of how Cyrus etc.'. The construction of
loqui with acc. and inf. belongs to colloquial Latin, as does the construction *loqui aliquam rem* for *de aliqua re ;* cf. Att. 1, 5, 6 *mecum
Tadius locutus est te ita scripsisse ;* ib. 9, 13, 1 *mera scelera loquuntur.*
—— **Cyrum minorem :** Cyrus the younger (cf. 79 *Cyrus maior*),
well known from Xenophon's *Anabasis.* As Cyrus never arrived at
the throne (having been killed at Cunaxa in 401 in his attempt to oust
his brother the king with the help of the 10,000 Greeks) *regem* is used
in the sense of 'prince', as in Verr. 4, 61 and elsewhere; βασιλεύς is
used in exactly the same way in a passage of the Oeconomicus which
comes a little before the one Cic. is here rendering (4, 16). —— **Lysander :** the great commander who in 405 B.C. won the battle of
Aegospotamos against the Athenians. —— **Sardis :** acc. pl.; *-is* represents Gk. *-εις.* —— **consaeptum agrum :** 'park'; the phrase is a
translation of Xenophon's παράδεισον; this will account for the omission of *et* before *diligenter consitum.* —— **diligenter :** 'carefully'. ——
proceritates : the plural probably indicates the height of each *kind*
of tree. —— **quincuncem :** thus: . . . . This was the
order of battle in the Roman army during a great part of its history.
The cause for this application of the term is rather difficult to see; it
originally meant five-twelfths of an *uncia ;* possibly it was thus applied because by drawing lines between the points the letter V (five)
might be produced. As regards its application to trees, see Verg.
Georg. 2, 277–284. —— **puram :** so the farmers talk of 'cleaning' the
land. —— **dimensa :** notice the passive use of this participle, originally deponent; cf. n. on 4 *adeptam.* —— **discripta :** 'arranged'; so
discriptio a little farther on. Cf. n. on 5 *descriptae.* —— **ornatum :**
'costume', used by Latin writers of any dress a little unfamiliar. So
in Plaut. Miles 4, 4, 41 (1177 R) *ornatus nauclericus.*

60. **impedit :** *sc. nos ;* with this construction the pronoun is always
omitted. —— **Valerium :** when a young man, in 349 B.C., he engaged
in combat with a Gaul, in sight of the Roman and Gallic armies, and
came off victor by the aid of a raven, *corvus ;* hence the name Cor-
vinus (Liv. 7, 26). His first consulship was in 348, his last in 299;
Cic. has miscalculated. Valerius was also twice dictator and is said
to have held altogether 21 terms of curule offices. —— **perduxisse :**
sc. agri colendi studia. Cf. Lael. 33 *quod — perduxissent.* —— **esset :**

cf. n. on 21. —— **aetate :** here = the vigorous period of life ; cf. *bona aetas* in 48. —— **cursus honorum :** ' official career '. —— **huius :** *ille* and *hic* are not often found in the same sentence referring to the same person. *Eius* would have been more regular here. —— **media :** cf. n. on 33 *constantis aetatis.*

P. 26. — **apex :** ' the crown ', ' the highest glory '. The word meant originally ' knot ', being connected with *ap-tus ap-isci ap-ere* and other words containing the idea of binding fast or grasping. It was properly applied to the olive-twig bound round with wool, which was stuck in the cap worn by the *flamines* and *salii.* It is sometimes employed to translate διάδημα (a word originally of similar meaning), the royal *insigne,* as in Horace, Odes, 3, 21, 20 *regum apices,* with which cf. Odes, 1, 34, 14. The word is scarcely found elsewhere in a metaphorical sense. Our passage is imitated by Ammianus Marcellinus (a great imitator of Cicero) 27, 7, 2 *Rufinus velut apicem honoratae senectutis praetendens.*

61. Metello : see n. on 30. —— **A. Atilio Calatino :** consul in 258 B. c. and again in 254; dictator in 249, censor in 247. Cicero classed him with old heroes like Curius and Fabricius (Planc. 60). His tomb was on the *via Appia* outside the *Porta Capena,* close to the well-known tomb of the Scipios (see Tusc. 1, 13). —— **in quem ... elogium :** ' in whose honor there is the inscription '. With *in quem* = *de quo* cf. the occasional occurrence of κατά τινος in the sense of περί τινος. —— **elogium :** Greek ἐλεγεῖον (so Curtius) : for the representation of ε by *o* cf. *oliva* with ἔλαια, and Plautus' *lopadas* for λέπαδας. But cf. Roby, 929, *d.* —— **hunc** etc.: the inscription (which is quoted by Cicero also in Fin. 2, 116) is strikingly like that on the tomb of *Scipio Barbatus* which has actually come down to us, and thus begins (Ritschl's recension) :

> *honc oino ploirime cosentiont Romai*
> *duonoro optumo fuise viro viroro*

i. e. hunc unum plurimi consentiunt Romae bonorum optimum fuisse virum virorum. Ritschl thus completes the *elogium* of Atilus, by comparison with others still preserved : *dictator* (ending the second line), *Consul, censor, aedilis hic fuit apud vos.* But Cicero's words (*notum ... sepulcro*) seem to imply a longer inscription than one of three lines; the analogy of the Scipionic inscriptions points the same way. The older monumental inscriptions of Rome were written in

the Saturnian metre, which depended partly on accent. **The** normal
line ran thus :

$$\cup \stackrel{\prime}{-} \cup - \cup \stackrel{\prime}{-} \overline{\cup} \mid \stackrel{\prime}{-} \cup - \cup \stackrel{\prime}{-} \overline{\cup}$$

but there were many deviations. —— **unum :** intensifies *primarium*,
'the very first'; cf. the common use of *unus* with a superlative adjective, for which see n. on Lael. 1 *unum* etc. —— **esset consentiens :**
cf. n. on 26 *agens aliquid*. —— **nuper :** like *modo* (see n. on 27) *nuper*
is loosely used, and has its meaning defined by the context. Cf. n. on
Lael. 13. In Plin. Ep. 1, 2, 2 the orator Calvus, a younger contemporary
of Cicero, is said to have existed *nuper*. —— **Lepidum :** *pontifex maxi-*
mus from 180 B. C., consul in 187 and in 175 ; censor in 179 ; he is said to
have been chosen *princeps senatus* by six sets of censors in succession.
He died in 152. —— **Paulo :** see 29 *L. Aemilius* with n. —— **Max-**
imo : see 10 *et seq*. —— **sententia :** *i. e.* a set speech in the senate.
Cf. De Or. 1, 38 *is non accurata orationis copia, sed nutu atque verbo*
libertinos in urbanas tribus transtulit. —— **honorata :** see n. on 22.

62. in omni oratione : 'everywhere throughout my speech'. *Tota*
oratione would have meant 'my speech viewed as a whole'. —— **de-**
fenderet : the tense is accommodated to that of *dixi*, according to
Latin custom ; see n. on 42 *efficeret*. —— **cani :** *sc. capilli ;* the same
ellipsis is found in Ovid. Cf. *calda* (*sc. aqua*), *laurea* (*sc. corona*), *nata-*
lis (*sc. dies*), *Latinae* (*sc. feriae*), etc.; also *cereo* in 44. —— **fructus**
... extremos : 'receives the reward of influence at the last'.

63 appeti : 'to be courted'; *decedi :* 'to take precedence', literally
'that there should be a yielding of the way'. —— **assurgi :** 'the honor
shown by rising'. Cf. Iuv. 13, 54 *credebant grande nefas et morte pi-*
andum si iuvenis vetulo non assurrexerat, where see Mayor's note. ——
deduci reduci : 'the escort from home and the attendance homeward'. The difference between these two words, which has often
been misunderstood, is shown by Val. Max. 2, 1, 9 *iuvenes senatus die*
utique aliquem ex patribus conscriptis ad curiam d e d u c e b a n t, affixi-
que valvis exspectabant donec r e d u c e n d i etiam officio fungerentur.
—— **consuli :** probably refers to private legal consultations as well
as to the deliberations of the senate. —— **ut quaeque optime :** Cic.
often uses *ut quisque* with superlatives, *ita* following ; see n. on Lael.
19. Translate *ut...ita* 'in proportion as...so'. —— **morata :** from
mos. —— **modo :** in 59. —— **memoriae proditum est :** in Verr. 5, 36
Cic. uses *ad memoriam* instead of the dative. The best writers have

memoriae prodere and *prodi*, '*for the recollection of* posterity', *memoria prodi*, '*to be handed down by* tradition'; but not *memoria prodere*. —— **ludis** : *sc. Panathenaicis,* abl. of time. The Panathenaea was the greatest of the Athenian festivals and was celebrated in honor of Athene, patron goddess of the city, once in four years. The story that follows is told in almost the same words by Val. Max. 4, 5, ext. 2.

P. 27. — **qui** : at this point the *oratio obliqua* is broken off, but it is resumed in the next sentence, *dixisse* being dependent on *proditum est.* —— **legati cum essent** : 'being ambassadors'. —— **illi** : 'in his honor'. —— **sessum recepisse** : Val. Max. uses the same phrase; cf. *Fam.* 10, 32, 2 *sessum deducere ;* N. D. 3, 74 *sessum ire.*

64. plausus multiplex : cf. Verg. Aen. 1, 747 *ingeminant plausu.* Cic. generally says *plausus maximus.* —— **facere nolle** : cf. the well-known saying of Demosthenes, Olynth. 3, § 3 πέπεισμαι γὰρ τὰ πλείω τῶν πραγμάτων ὑμᾶς ἐκπεφευγέναι τῷ μὴ βούλεσθαι τὰ δέοντα ποιεῖν, ἢ τῷ μὴ συνιέναι. —— **collegio** : the college or board of augurs to which Cato belonged. In his time there were nine members ; later the number was increased. —— **antecedit** : *sc. alios.* —— **sententiae principatum** : 'precedence in debate'. Meissner quotes Verr. 4, 142 *ut quisque aetate et honore antecedit, ita primus solet sua sponte dicere itaque a ceteris ei conceditur.* —— **honore** : *i. e.* as regards office, past or present. —— **qui ... sunt** : actual praetors or consuls. —— **comparandae** : n. on 50. —— **fabulam aetatis** : cf. 5, 70, 85. The comparison of life to a play, and mankind to the players, is common in all literature ; *e. g.* 'All the world 's a stage, etc.'. When Augustus was on his deathbed he asked his friends *ecquid eis videretur m i m u m v i t a e commode transegisse* (Suet. Aug. 99) ; cf. Gay's epitaph, 'Life 's a jest, etc.'.—— **corruisse** : *i. e.* through fatigue ; cf. *defetigationem* in 85.

65. at : see n. on 21. —— **morum** : cf. 7 *in moribus est culpa, non in aetate.* —— **ea vitia** : *i. e. ea alia vitia.* —— **habent** etc.: cf. Thucyd. 3, 44 ἔχοντές τι συγγνώμης —— **non ... videatur** : 'not well grounded indeed, but such as it may seem possible to allow'. *Ille* is often used with *quidem* in making concessions where the English idiom requires no pronoun. Roby, 2259 ; Madvig, 489, *b* ; Kennedy, 65, n. 2 ; A. 151, *e* ; G. 292, Rem. 4 ; H. 450, 4, n. 2. —— **contemni ... despici** : see n. on 43 *spreta et contempta.*—— **moribus bonis et artibus** : for the order of the words cf. n. on 1 *animi tui.* —— **in vita** : 'in everyday life'

—— **Adelphis** : *Adelphi* = ἀδελφοί, The Brothers; this play of Terence is still extant. —— **diritas** : 'harshness of temper'; but Suet. Tib. 21 has *diritas morum,* and Varro *scena quem senem Latina vidit dirissimum.* Both *dirus* and *diritas* are rare in Cicero; the former word does not once occur in the whole range of the speeches, the latter scarcely excepting here and in Vat. 9; in Tusc. 3, 29 Cic. uses it in translating from Euripides.

P. 28. — **66. sollicitam habere** : 'to keep in trouble'. *Sollicitus* is, literally, 'wholly in motion', from *sollus,* which has the same root with ὅλος, and *citus,;* cf. the rare words *sollifides, solliferreus.* The perfect participle with *habeo* emphasizes the continuance of the effect produced. Zumpt, 634; A. 292, *c* ; G. 230; H. 388, 1, n. —— **nostram aetatem** : cf. n. on 26 *senectus.* —— **esse longe** : more usually *abesse.* —— **O miserum** : ' O, wretched is that old man '. Cicero oftener joins *O* with the accusative than with the nominative: he rarely, if ever, uses the interjection with the vocative in direct address to persons. —— **extinguit animum** : the doctrine of the annihilation of the soul after death was held by many of Cicero's contemporaries, professedly by the Epicureans (*e. g.* Lucretius, De Rerum Nat. 3, 417 *et seq. ;* cf. also Caesar's argument at the trial of the Catilinian conspirators, Sall. Bell. Catil. c. 51, Cic. in Catil. 3, c. 4), practically by the Stoics, who taught that there is a future existence of limited though indefinite length. —— **deducit** : cf. n. on 63. —— **atqui** : see n. on 6. —— **tertium . . . potest** : 'nothing can be found as a third alternative': so in Tusc. 1, 82 *quoniam nihil tertium est.*

67. quid timeam etc.: so Tusc. 1, 25 *quo modo igitur aut cur mortem malum tibi videri dicis ? quae aut beatos nos efficiet, animis manentibus, aut non miseros, sensu carentis ;* ib. 1, 118 *ut aut in aeternam domum remigremus aut omni sensu careamus.* For mood see A. 268; G. 251; H. 486, II. —— **aut non miser . . . aut beatus** : a dilemma, but unsound and not conclusive; for *non miser* is used with reference to annihilation, and the soul may exist after death in a state of unhappiness. —— **futurus sum** : see n. on 6 *futurum est.* —— **quamvis sit** : prose writers of the Republican period use *quamvis* with the subjunctive only; see Roby, 1624, 1627 ; A. 313, *a, g*; G. 608; H. 515, III. and n. 3. —— **cui** : see n. on 38 *viventi* —— **ad vesperum esse victurum** : 'that he will be alive when evening comes', *not* 'that he will live till the evening'. With the prepositions *ad, sub, in* the form *vesper* is generally used, not *vespera.* With this passage cf. Fin. 2, 92

*an id exploratum cuiquam potest esse quo modo sese habiturum sit corpus,
non dico ad annum, sed ad vesperum?* Also cf. the title of one of
Varro's Menippean Satires, *nescis quid vesper serus vehat,* probably a
proverb. —— **aetas illa ... adulescentes :** some suppose that this
sentence was borrowed from Hippocrates. —— **tristius :** '*severioribus
remediis*'. Manutius. So Off. 1, 83 *leviter aegrotantis leniter curant,
gravioribus autem morbis periculosas curationes et ancipites adhibere co-
guntur.* The adverb *tristius,* which has in prose a superlative but no
positive, occurs in Fam. 4, 13, 5. —— **mens ... ratio ... consilium :**
cf. n. on 41. —— **qui ... nulli :** cf. n. on 46 *qui pauci ;* but *nulli* here
almost = *non.* —— **nullae ... fuissent :** *i. e.* the young men would have
brought every country to ruin ; see 20. —— **cum ... cum :** see n. on 4.

68. in filio ... in fratribus : cf. Lael. 9. As to Cato's son cf. 15,
84. —— **tu :** *sc. sensisti.* —— **exspectatis ad :** a rare construction,
perhaps without parallel ; *exspectatis* is an adjective and takes the
construction of *aptus, idoneus* etc., 'of whom hopes were entertained
as regards honor '. —— **fratribus :** the sons of Paulus Macedonicus,
two of them died within seven days (Fam. 4, 6, 1), one just before and
one just after Paulus' great triumph in 167 B. C. —— **idem :** see n. on
4 *eandem.* —— **insipienter :** adversative asyndeton. —— **incerta ...
veris :** chiasmus avoided. With the thought cf. Off. 1, 18. —— **at
... at :** the objection and its answer are both introduced by *at,* as here,
in 35. —— **at ... adulescens :** these words look back to the preceding
sentence, to which they are an answer. —— **ille ... hic :** here *hic* denotes the person who is more important, *ille* the person who is less
important for the matter in hand; the former may therefore be regarded as nearer to the speaker, the latter as more remote. A. 102,
a ; G. 292, Rem. 1 ; H. 450, 2, n.

69. quamquam : see n. on 2 *etsi.* —— **quid est ... diu :** cf. Tusc.
1, 94 *quae vero aetas longa est, aut quid omnino homini longum ? ... quia
ultra nihil habemus, hoc longum dicimus.* For *est* see n. on 72. ——
Tartessiorum ... Gadibus : the whole of the south coast of Spain
bore the name *Tartessus,* but the name is often confined to Gades, the
chief city. —— **fuit : =** *vixit.* —— **scriptum video :** so in Acad. 2,
129 ; Div. 1, 31 ; cf. also N. D. 1, 72 *ut videmus in scriptis ;* Off. 2,
25 *ut scriptum legimus ;* also cf. n. on 26 *videmus.* —— **Arganthonius :** the story is from Herodotus 1, 163.

P. 29. — aliquid extremum : see n. on 5 ; cf. pro Marcello 27.
—— **effluxit :** strongly aoristic in sense 'at once is gone '. —— **tan-**

tum : 'only so much'. —— **consecutus sis** : 'you may have obtained '.   The subjunctive is here used in the indefinite second person
to give a hypothetical character to the statement of the verb.   The indicative might have been expected; the expression almost = *consecuti
sumus, consecutus aliquis est.*   Roby, 1546;   G. 252, Rem. 3;   H. 486,
III. —— **virtute et recte factis** : the same opinion is enforced in
Tusc. 1, 109. —— **quid sequatur** : 'the future '; cf. Lucr. 1, 459 *trans-
actum quid sit in aevo, Tum quae res instet, quid porro deinde sequatur.*
—— **quod ... contentus** : this passage with the whole context resem-
bles Lucretius 3, 931–977 ; cf. especially 938 *cur non ut plenus vitae
conviva recedis ;* 960 *satur ac plenus discedere rerum.*   Cf. also Hor.
Sat. 1, 1, 117–118.

70. ut placeat : 'in order to secure approval'. —— **peragenda** :
cf. n. on 50 *comparandae.* —— **plaudite** : the Latin plays nearly always ended with this word, addressed by the actor to the audience;
cf. Hor. A. P. 153 *si plausoris eges aulaea manentis et usque Sessuri
donec cantor 'vos plaudite' dicat.* —— **breve tempus** etc. : one of the
poets has said that 'in small measures lives may perfect be '.   Cf. also
Tusc. 1, 109 *nemo parum diu vixit qui virtutis perfectae perfecto functus
est munere ;* Seneca, Ep. 77 *quo modo fabula, sic vita : non quam diu,
sed quam bene acta sit refert.* —— **processerit** : probably the subject
is *sapiens,* in which case *aetate* must also be supplied from *aetatis ;* the
subject may however be *aetas.* —— **ostendit** : 'gives promise of'; cf.
Fam. 9, 8, 1 *etsi munus* (gladiatorial show) *flagitare quamvis quis
ostenderit, ne populus quidem solet nisi concitatus.*   With the whole
passage cf. pro Cael. 76.

71. ut ... dixi : in 9, 60, 62. —— **secundum naturam** : = κατὰ φύσιν,
a Stoic phrase ; cf. n. on 5 *naturam optimam ducem.* —— **senibus** :
dative of reference ; *emori* stands as subject to an implied *est.* ——
contingit : see n. on 8. —— **exstinguitur** : there is the same contrast
between *opprimere* and *exstinguere* in Lael. 78. —— **quasi ... evelluntur** : it is rare to find in Cic. or the other prose writers of the best
period a verb in the indicative mood immediately dependent on *quasi,*
in the sense of *sicut* or *quem ad modum.*   When two things are compared by *quasi ... ita,* the indicative verb is nearly always put in the
second clause, and may be supplied in the clause with *quasi ;* very
rarely are there two different verbs for the two clauses.   Cf. however
Plautus, Stich. 539 *fuit olim, quasi nunc ego sum senex ;* Lucr. 3, 492
agens animam spumat quasi ... fervescunt undae. —— **si ... si** : for the

more usual *si ... sin.* ——— **accedam** : see A. 342; G. 666; H. 529, II.
——— **in portum** : speaking of death, Cic. says in Tusc. 1, 118 *portum
potius paratum nobis et perfugium putemus: quo utinam velis passis per-
vehi liceat! Sin reflantibus ventis reiciemur tamen eodem paulo tardius
referamur necesse est;* cf. also ib. 1, 107.

P. 30. — 72. **munus offici** : see n. on 29. ——— **tueri** : 'uphold'.
——— **possit ;** subject indefinite. ——— **ex quo fit** etc.: the argument
seems to be that youth knows how long it has to last and is therefore
less spirited than age, which knows not when it will end. ——— **animosior ... fortior** : Horace, Odes 2, 10, 21 *rebus angustis animosus
atque fortis appare ;* the two words are joined also in Cic. Mil. 92 : *animosus,* 'spirited'. ——— **hoc illud est** etc.: 'this is the meaning of the
answer made by Solon etc'. Cf. Div. 1, 122 *hoc nimirum illud est
quod de Socrate accepimus,* also the Greek phrase ἢ τοῦτ' ἐκεῖνο. *Est* =
valet as in 69. ——— **Pisistratus** : the despot of Athens, who seized the
power in 560 B.C. Plutarch, who tells the story, 'An Seni Sit Gerenda Respublica' c. 21, makes Solon speak to the friends of Pisistratus, not to P. himself. ——— **quaerenti** : see n. on 11 *dividenti.* ———
audaciter : Quintil. 1, 6, 17 condemns those who used *audaciter* for
audacter, which latter form, he says, had been used by 'all orators'.
Yet the form *audaciter* is pretty well attested by MSS. here and elsewhere in Cicero. [See Neue, Formenlehre, 1² 662.] For the two
forms cf. *difficiliter, difficulter. Audaciter* is of importance as showing
that *c* before *i* must have been pronounced just like *c* in any other position, not as in modern Italian. ——— **certis sensibus** : Acad. 2, 19
integris incorruptisque sensibus. ——— **ipsa ... quae** : see n. on 26. H.
569, I. 2. ——— **coagmentavit** : Cic. is fond of such metaphors; cf.
Orat. 77 *verba verbis quasi coagmentari ;* Phil. 7, 21 *docebo ne coagmentari quidem pacem posse* ('that no patched-up peace can be made').
——— **conglutinavit** : a still more favorite metaphor than *coagmentare.*
Cic. has *conglutinare rem* (Or. 1, 188); *amicitias* (Lael. 32 and Att. 7,
8, 1); *voluntates* (Fam. 11, 27, 2); *concordiam* (Att. 1, 17, 10); in Phil.
3, 28 Cic. says of Antony that he is *totus ex vitiis conglutinatus.* ———
iam : 'further'; so below. ——— **conglutinatio** : the noun occurs only
here and Orat. 78 *c. verborum.* ——— **reliquum** : not infrequently, as
here, used substantively with an adjective modifier. ——— **sine causa** :
'without sufficient reason'.

73. vetat Pythagoras etc.: the passage is from Plato, Phaedo
61 A–62 C. Plato makes Socrates there profess to quote Philolaus,

the Pythagorean; Cic. therefore refers the doctrine to Pythagoras.
Cf. Tusc. 1, 74; Rep. 6, 15. The Stoics held the same view about
suicide, which they authorized in extreme cases, but much less freely
than is commonly supposed; cf. Sen. Ep. 117, 22 *nihil mihi videtur
turpius quam optare mortem.* See Zeller, Stoics, Epicureans, and
Sceptics, Ch. 12, c (2); cf. also Lecky, Hist. of European Morals, I.
p. 228 *et seq.* (Am. ed.) —— **imperatoris ... praesidio :** here Cic.
seems to understand Plato's φρουρᾷ as referring to warfare; in Tusc.
and Rep. he understands it of a prison. —— **sapientis :** Solon was one
of the 'Seven Sages of Greece'. —— **elogium :** the distich is preserved by Plutarch, and runs thus: μηδέ μοι ἄκλαυστος θάνατος μόλοι,
ἀλλὰ φίλοισι Καλλείποιμι θανὼν ἄλγεα καὶ στοναχάς. Cic. thus translates it in Tusc. 1, 117 *Mors mea ne careat lacrimis, linquamus amicis
Maerorem, ut celebrent funera cum gemitu.* The epitaph of Ennius is
also quoted there and is declared to be better than that of Solon (cf.
Tusc. 1, 34). —— **volt se esse carum :** 'he wishes to make out that
he is beloved'; *volt esse carus* would have had quite a different sense.
Cf. Fin. 5, 13 *Strato physicum se volt,* with Madvig's n. —— **haud
scio an :** see n. on 56. —— **faxit :** the subject is *quisquam* understood
from *nemo.* For the form see A. 142, 128, *e,* 3; G. 191, 5; H. 240, 4.
The end of the epitaph is omitted here as in Tusc. 1, 117, but is given
in Tusc. 1, 34 *cur? volito vivos per ora virum.* Notice the alliteration.

74. isque : cf. n. on 13 *vixitque.* —— **aut optandus aut nullus :**
cf. 66 *aut neglegenda ... aut optanda ; nullus* almost = *non* as in 67, but
only in the Letters does Cic. (imitating Plautus and the other dramatists) attach *nullus* in this sense to the name of a particular person;
e. g. Att. 11, 24, 4 *Philotimus nullus venit.* —— **sed ... esse :** 'but we
must con this lesson from our youth up'. For the passive sense of
meditatum cf. n. on 4 *adeptam.* In Tusc. 1, 74 Cic., imitating Plato,
says *tota philosophorum vita commentatio mortis est.* So Seneca, *tota
vita discendum est mori.* —— **sine qua ... nemo potest :** these words
bring the position of Cicero with regard to death wonderfully near
that of Lucretius : the latter argues that for peace of mind one must
believe '*nullum esse sensum post mortem*'; the former's lesson is '*aut
nullum esse sensum aut optandum*'. —— **timens :** = *si quis timet ;* the
subject of *poterit* is the indefinite *quis* involved in *timens.* A. 310, *a* ;
G. 670; H. 549, 2. —— **qui :** = *quo modo,* as in 4. —— **animo consistere :** so in pro Quint. 77; also *mente consistere* in Phil. 2, 68; Div.

2, 149; Q. Fr. 2, 3, 2 *neque mente neque lingua neque ore consistere.*
The word is, literally, 'to stand firm', 'to get a firm foothold'.

P. 31. — **75. L. Brutum :** fell in single combat with Aruns, son
of the exiled Tarquin; see Liv. 2, 6. The accusatives *Brutum* etc.
are not the objects of *recorder* but the subjects of infinitives to be supplied from *profectas.* —— **duos Decios :** see n. on 43. —— **cursum
equorum :** the word *equos* would have been sufficient; but this kind
of pleonasm is common in Latin ; see n. on Lael. 30 *causae diligendi.*
—— **Atilius :** *i. e.* Regulus, whose story is too well known to need
recounting. There are many contradictions and improbabilities about
it. —— **Scipiones :** see n. on 29. In Paradoxa 1, 12 Cic. says of
them *Carthaginiensium adventum corporibus suis intercludendum puta-
verunt.* —— **Poenis :** on the dat. see A. 235, *a* ; H. 384, 4, n. 2. ——
Paulum : n. on 29 *L. Aemilius.* —— **collegae :** M. Terentius Varro.
There is no reason to suppose that he was a worse general than many
other Romans who met Hannibal and were beaten ; the early historians, being all aristocrats, fixed the disgrace of Cannae on the democratic consul. Varro's contemporaries were more just to him. Far
from reproaching him, the Senate commended his spirit, and several
times afterwards entrusted him with important business. —— **Marcellum :** the captor of Syracuse in 212 B. C. He fell into an ambush
in 208 and was killed ; Hannibal buried him with military honors. ——
cuius interitum : abstract for concrete = *quem, post interitum.* ——
crudelissimus hostis : this, the traditional Roman view of Hannibal,
is the reverse of the truth, so far as extant testimony goes. See
Mommsen, Hist. of Rome, Bk. III. Ch. 4 ; Ihne, Hist. of Rome, Bk.
IV. —— **sed ... arbitrarentur :** these words are almost exactly repeated in Tusc. 1, 89 and 101. —— **rustici :** cf. Arch. 24 *nostri illi
fortes viri sed rustici ac milites ;* also above, 24.

76. omnino : see n. on 9. —— **num igitur** etc.: cf. 33 *nisi forte
et seq.* —— **constans :** cf. n. on 33. —— **ne ... quidem :** see n. on 27.
—— **satietas vitae :** cf. 85 *senectus autem et seq.,* and *satietas vivendi*
in pro Marc. 27 ; also Tusc. 1, 109 *vita acta perficiat ut satis superque
vixisse videamur.*

77. cernere : of the mind also in 82. With the context cf. Div. 1,
63 *animus appropinquante morte multo est divinior ; facilius evenit appropinquante morte ut animi futura augurentur.* —— **vestros patres :** n.
on 15. The elder Laelius was prominent both as general and as statesman. He commanded the fleet which co-operated with Scipio Afri-

canus in Spain and afterwards served with honor in Africa. He was an intimate friend of Cato. See Liv. 26, 42 *et seq.* —— **tuque** : so in Lael. 100 *C. Fanni et tu, Q. Muci ;* but above, 4 and 9 simply *Scipio et Laeli.* —— **quae est sola vita** : cf. n. on *vitam nullam* in 7. —— **nam dum sumus** etc.: the whole of this doctrine is Platonic; cf. Lael. 13. —— **munere necessitatis et ... opere** : 'function and task allotted us by fate'.

P. 32. — **immortalis** : Cicero rarely mentions the gods without this epithet. —— **sparsisse** : Horace calls the soul *divinae particulam aurae.* —— **tuerentur** : rule, or guard, or care for. Most editors wrongly take *tuerentur* to be for *intuerentur,* 'to look upon', and regard it as an intentional archaism. But cf. Rep. 6, 15 (where no archaism can be intended): *homines sunt hac lege generati, qui tuerentur illum globum quae terra vocatur ;* also *tuentur* below in 82. —— **contemplantes imitarentur** : perhaps more Stoic than Platonic; the Stoics laid great stress on the ethical value of a contemplation and imitation of the order of the universe. Cf. N. D. 2, 37 *ipse homo ortus est ad mundum contemplandum et imitandum ;* Sen. Dial. 8, 5, 1 *Natura nos ad utrumque genuit, et contemplationi rerum et actioni.* —— **modo** : here *modus* seems to be the Platonic τὸ μέτριον, or perhaps a reminiscence of the Aristotelian doctrine of the mean (n. on 46). Translate 'in moderation and consistency of life'; and cf. Off. 1, 93 *rerum modus* 'moderation in all things'. For *constantia* see n. on 4. —— **ita** : cf. n. on 16 *et tamen sic.*

78. Pythagoran : see n. to 23. No ancient philosopher held more firmly than Pythagoras to belief in the immortality of the soul ; it formed a part of his doctrine of Metempsychosis. He was also noted for his numerical speculations in Astronomy and Music. With him is said to have originated the doctrine of the 'harmony of the spheres'. —— **qui essent** : 'inasmuch as they were'. Cicero often tries to make out a connection between Pythagoras and the early Romans; cf. Tusc. 4, 2 ; also Liv. 1, 18. —— **ex universa mente** : the world-soul. Diog. Laert. 8 gives as Pythagorean the doctrine ψυχὴν εἶναι ἀπόσπασμα τοῦ αἰθέρος καὶ ἀθάνατον. Similar doctrines occur in Plato and the Stoics; cf. Div. 1, 110 *a qua* (*i. e. a natura deorum*) *ut doctissimis sapientissimisque placuit, haustos animos et libatos habemus ;* Tusc. 5, 38 *humanus animus decerptus ex mente divina ;* Sen. Dial. 12, 6, 7. —— **haberemus** : imperfect where the English requires the present. A. 287, *d* ; H. 495, V. —— **Socrates** : in Plato's Phaedo.

—— **immortalitate animorum** : this is commoner than *immortalitas animi*, for 'the immortality of the soul'; so Lael. 14; Tusc. 1, 80 *aeternitas animorum*. —— **disseruisset** : subjunctive because involving the statements of some other person than the speaker. A. 341, *c*; G. 630; H. 528, 1. —— **is qui esset** etc.: 'a man great enough to have been declared wisest'. See n. on Lael. 7 *Apollinis...iudicatum*. —— **sic** : cf. *ita* above. —— **celeritas animorum** : the ancients pictured to themselves the mind as a substance capable of exceedingly rapid movement; cf. Tusc. 1, 43 *nulla est celeritas quae possit cum animi celeritate contendere*. —— **tantae scientiae** : as the plural of *scientia* is almost unknown in classical Latin, recent editors take *scientiae* here as genitive, 'so many arts requiring so much knowledge'. In favor of this interpretation are such passages as Acad. 2, 146 *artem sine scientia esse non posse;* Fin. 5, 26 *ut omnes artes in aliqua scientia versentur*. Yet in De Or. 1, 61 *physica ista et mathematica et quae paulo ante ceterarum artium propria posuisti, scientiae sunt eorum qui illa profitentur* it is very awkward to take *scientiae* as genitive. —— **cumque semper** etc.: this argument is copied very closely from Plato's Phaedrus, 245 C. —— **principium motus** : ἀρχὴ κινήσεως in Plato. —— **se ipse** : cf. n. on 4 *a se ipsi*. —— **cum simplex** etc.: from Plato's Phaedo, 78—80. The general drift of the argument is this: material things decay because they are compounded of parts that fall asunder; there is nothing to show that the soul is so compounded; therefore no reason to believe that it will so decay. Notice the imperfects *esset... haberet...posset* accommodated to the tense of *persuasi* above, although the other subjunctives in the sentence are not; cf. n. on 42 *efficeret*.

—— **neque...dissimile** : in modern phraseology the whole of this clause would be briefly expressed thus, — 'and was homogeneous'. —— **posset** : *quod si* = 'whereas if', the subject of *posset* being *animus*, and *dividi* being understood. —— **magno argumento** : ἱκανὸν τεκμήριον in Pl. Phaed. 72 A. Belief in the immortality of the soul naturally follows the acceptance of the doctrine of pre-existence. —— **homines scire** etc.: See Plato, Phaedo, 72 E—73 B. The notion that the souls of men existed before the bodies with which they are connected has been held in all ages and has often found expression in literature. The English poets have not infrequently alluded to it. See Wordsworth's Ode on the Intimations of Immortality from the Recollections of Early Childhood, 'Our birth is but a sleep and a forgetting' etc.; also, in Tennyson's Two Voices the passage beginning, —

'Yet how should I for certain hold,
Because my memory is so cold,
That I first was in human mould'?

reminisci et recordari: a double translation of Plato's ἀναμιμνήσκε-
σθαι, quite in Cicero's fashion; the former word implies a momentary
act, the latter one of some duration. —— **haec Platonis fere**: 'so far
Plato'.

79. apud Xenophontem: Cyropaedia, 8, 7, 17; for *apud* cf. 30;
when Cic. says that a passage is 'in' a certain author (not naming the
book) he uses *apud*, not *in*. —— **maior**: 'the elder'; cf. 59 *Cyrum
minorem*. —— **nolite arbitrari**: a common periphrasis.   A. 269, *a*,
2; G. 264, II.; H. 489, I. —— **dum eram**: the imperfect with *dum*
is not common; see Roby, 1458, *c*; A. 276, *e*, n.; G. 572, 571; H. 519,
I., 467, 4 with n.

P. 33. — 80. nec... teneremus: the souls of the dead continue
to exert an influence on the living, or else their fame would not
remain; a weak argument. —— **mihi... potuit**: cf. 82 *nemo...per-
suadebit*. —— **vivere... emori**: adversative asyndeton. —— **insipientem**: in Xen. ἄφρων, *i. e.* without power of thinking. —— **sed**:
'but rather that...' —— **hominis natura**: a periphrasis for *homo*;
cf. Fin. 5, 33 *intellegant, si quando naturam hominis dicam, hominem
dicere me; nihil enim hoc differt*. —— **nihil... somnum**: poets and
artists from Homer (Il. 16, 682) onwards have pictured death as
sleep's brother.   Cf. Lessing, How the Ancients Represented Death.

81. atqui: see n. on 6. —— **dormientium animi** etc.: see Div. 1,
60 where a passage of similar import is translated from Plato's Republic IX; ib. 115. —— **remissi et liberi**: cf. Div. 1, 113 *animus so-
lutus ac vacuus;* De Or. 2, 193 *animo leni ac remisso*. —— **corporis**: the
singular, though *animi* precedes; so in Lael. 13; Tusc. 2, 12, etc. ——
pulchritudinem: κόσμον; Cic. translates it by *ornatus* in Acad. 2,
119 where *hic ornatus* corresponds to *hic mundus* a little earlier. ——
tuentur: see n. on 77 *tuerentur*. —— **servabitis**: future for imper-
ative.   A. 269, *f*; G. 265, 1; H. 487, 4.

82. Cyrus etc.: see n. on 78. —— **si placet**: cf. n. on 6 *nisi molestum est*. —— **nostra**: = *Romana* = *domestica* in 12. —— **nemo** etc.:
this line of argument is often repeated in Cic.; see Tusc. 1, 32 *et seq.;*
Arch. 29. —— **duos avos... patruum**: see nn. on 29. —— **multos**:
sc. alios. —— **esse conatos**: loosely put for *fuisse conaturos*, as below,
suscepturum fuisse.   So in the direct narration we might have, though

exceptionally, *non conabantur nisi cernerent* for *non conati essent nisi vidissent.* —— **cernerent**: see n. on 13 *quaereretur.* —— **ut ... glorier**: in Arch. 30 Cic. makes the same reflections in almost the same words about his own achievements. —— **aliquid**: see n. on 1 *quid.*

P. 34. — **si isdem** etc.: cf. Arch. 29 *si nihil animus praesentiret ... dimicaret.* —— **aetatem**: = *vitam.* —— **traducere**: cf. Tusc. 3, 25 *volumus hoc quod datum est vitae tranquille placideque traducere.* —— **nescio quo modo**: A. 210, *f*, Rem.; G. 469, Rem. 2; H. 529, 5, 3). —— **erigens se**: Acad. 2, 127 *erigimur, elatiores fieri videmur.* —— **haud ... niteretur**: in Cicero's speeches *haud* scarcely occurs except before adverbs and the verb *scio ;* in the philosophical writings and in the Letters before many other verbs. —— **immortalitatis gloriam**: so Balb. 16 *sempiterni nominis gloriam.* Cf. also Arch. 26 *trahimur omnes studio laudis et optimus quisque maxime gloria ducitur.*

83. non videre: either *non videre* or *non item* was to be expected, as Cicero does not often end sentences or clauses with *non.* —— **colui et dilexi**: so 26 *coluntur et diliguntur.* —— **videndi**: Cic. for the most part avoids the genitive plural of the gerundive in agreement with a noun, and uses the gerund as here. Meissner notes that Latin has no verb with the sense 'to see again', which a modern would use here. —— **conscripsi**: in the *Origines.* —— **quo**: = *ad quos ;* see n. on 12 *fore unde.* — **Pelian**: a mistake of Cicero's. It was not Pelias but his half-brother Aeson, father of Iason, whom Medea made young again by cutting him to pieces and boiling him in her enchanted cauldron. She, however, induced the daughters of Pelias to try the same experiment with their father; the issue, of course, was very different. Plautus, Pseud. 3, 2, 80 seems to make the same mistake. —— **si quis deus**: the present subjunctive is noticeable; strictly, an impossible condition should require the past tense, but in vivid passages an impossible condition is momentarily treated as possible. So Cic. generally says *si reviviscat aliquis*, not *revivisceret.* —— **decurso spatio**: 'when I have run my race'. See n. on 14. Lucretius 3, 1042 oddly has *decurso lumine vitae.* —— **ad carceres a calce**: *carceres* were the barriers behind which the horses and cars stood waiting for the race; *calx* (γραμμή), literally 'a chalked line', was what we should call 'the winning post'. Cf. Lael. 101; Tusc. 1, 15 *nunc video calcem ad quam cum sit decursum, nihil sit praeterea extimescendum.*

84. habeat: concessive. A. 266, *c*; G. 257; H. 484, 3. —— **multi et ei docti**: as Nägelsbach, Stilistik § 25, 5, remarks, Cic. always uses this phrase and not *multi docti*. One of the books Cic. has in view is no doubt that of Hegesias, a Cyrenaic philosopher, mentioned in Tusc. 1, 84. —— **commorandi ... divorsorium** : 'a hostelry wherein to sojourn'. The idea has been expressed in literature in a thousand ways. Cf. Lucr. 3, 938 *cur non ut plenus vitae c o n v i v a recedis ;* Hor. Sat. 1, 1, 118 *vita cedat uti conviva satur.* Cicero often insists that heaven is the *vera aeternaque domus* of the soul (cf. Tusc. 1, 118). Cf. Epist. to the Hebrews, 13, 14 'Here have we no continuing city, but we seek one to come'. —— **concilium coetumque** : so in Rep. 6, 13 *concilia coetusque hominum quae civitates vocantur.* The words here seem to imply that the real *civitas* is above ; what seems to men a *civitas* is merely a disorganized crowd.

P. 35. — **Catonem meum** : see 15, 68 ; so Cicero in his letters often calls his own son *meus Cicero.* —— **nemo vir** : see n. on 21 *quemquam senem.* —— **quod contra** : = ὃ τοὐναντίον, 'whereas on the contrary'; cf. n. on Lael. 90 where, as well as here, many of the editors make the mistake of taking *quod* to be the accusative governed by *contra* out of place. —— **meum** : *sc. corpus cremari.* —— **quo** : put for *ad quae,* as often. —— **visus sum** : 'people thought I bore up bravely'. —— **non quo ... sed** : a relative clause parallel with a categorically affirmative clause. The usage is not uncommon, though Cic. often has *non quo ... sed quia.* For mood of *ferrem* see A. 341, *d*, Rem. ; G. 541, Rem. 1.; H. 516, II. 2.

85. **dixisti** : in 4. —— **qui** : here = *cum ego,* 'since I ...'. —— **extorqueri volo** : n. on 2 *levari volo.* —— **minuti philosophi** : for the word *minutus* cf. n. on 46; Cic. has *minuti philosophi* in Acad. 2, 75; Div. 1, 62; in Fin. 1, 61 *minuti et angusti (homines)* ; in Brut. 265 *m. imperatores ;* cf. Suet. Aug. 83 *m. pueri.* —— **sentiam** : future indicative. —— **peractio** : the noun is said to occur only here in Cic.; cf. however 64 *peragere ;* 70. —— **haec ... dicerem** : the same words occur at the end of the Laelius; for *habeo quod dicam* Cic. often says *habeo dicere,* as in Balb. 34.

A Latin Grammar

By Professor CHARLES E. BENNETT, Cornell University. 12mo, cloth, 265 pages. Price, 80 cents.

THE purpose of this book is to present the essential facts of Latin Grammar in a simple and direct manner, and within the smallest compass consistent with high scholarly standards. While especially adapted to the needs of secondary schools, it has also been prepared with a view to the larger demands of the college and university. By omitting rare forms and rare syntactical usages of the ante- and post-classical Latinity, and by relegating to an Appendix for Teachers the discussion of the moot points of historical grammar, the compass of the book has been limited to 250 pages, exclusive of Indexes. The experience of teachers in the German schools has shown that books of this scope meet the exacting demands of the entire gymnasial course. It is believed that a real service may be rendered the study of Latin in America by offering such a Grammar to our teachers and students.

The Appendix for Teachers contains a discussion of the Evidences for Pronunciation, Hidden Quantity, History of Sound Changes, Origin of Inflectional Forms, Historical Syntax, Prosody, etc, and is bound up with the Grammar in a special Teachers' Edition.

Professor John C. Rolfe, *University of Michigan:* Our school grammars have been increasing in bulk with each new edition, until they have come to contain a great deal of matter which is of value only to advanced students. The idea of publishing a grammar which shall contain within the briefest possible compass the essential principles, and of relegating the rest to an appendix for the use of teachers and advanced students, seems to me a thoroughly good one. I have had occasion to test Professor Bennett's book, and am convinced that it contains everything necessary for the purpose for which it is intended. Brevity is not its only merit. In some respects — for instance, in the treatment of the dative case, in the recognition of the ablative of attendant circumstance, in the chapter on Latin style, and in not a few minor details — it appears to me more satisfactory than most of its predecessors. The typography and arrangement make it particularly handy as a reference book. On the whole, I am inclined to regard it as the best school grammar which has yet appeared in America.

Selections From Tacitus

Embracing the more striking portions of his different works. With Notes, Introduction, and a collection of his Aphorisms. By J. T. CHAMPLIN. Fifth edition. 16mo, 272 pages. Price $1.10.

THE design of this book is to give a comprehensive view of the writings of Tacitus in a comparatively small space. For this purpose, portions have been taken from all his works except the Germania, but not without due regard to unity in the main parts. All biographical and historical information which seemed to be required has been introduced into the notes. The Introduction contains a translation of Dr. Draeger's excellent essay on the peculiarities of the language and style of Tacitus.

Selected Fables of Phædrus

With Indicated Quantities. Edited for reading at sight by Professor JOSEPH H. DRAKE, University of Michigan. 16mo, paper, 68 pages. Price, 30 cents.

Thirteen Satires of Juvenal

With Notes by Rev. A. J. MACLEANE, with additions by Rev. SAMUEL HART, Trinity College, Hartford. 16mo, cloth, 262 pages. Price, $1.10.

THE text is that of Long's version of Macleane's, with three Satires omitted. The notes are abridged by omitting quotations, and discussions as to readings and interpretations.

The Satires of Persius

With Notes, based on those of Macleane and Conington, by the Rev. SAMUEL HART. 16mo, cloth, 91 pages. Price, 75 cents.

Scipio's Dream

Edited, with Notes, by Rev. SAMUEL HART. Price, 20 cents.

Pliny's Letters

Selections from the letters of the younger Pliny. Edited, with Notes and Index, by GEO. O. HOLBROOKE. 16mo, cloth, 216 pages. Price, $1.00.

Selected Orations and Letters of Cicero

With Introduction, Notes, and Vocabulary by Professor FRANCIS W. KELSEY. 12mo, half leather, 518 pages. Illustrated. Price, $1.25.

THE Orations given in this edition are the four against Catiline, those for the Manilian Law, Archias, Marcellus, and the fourth oration against Antony. These are edited with a view to showing their value as examples of oratory, rather than as offering mere material for grammatical drill. The student's attention is directed to the occasion and circumstances of their delivery, as well as to the motive and method of presenting the matter contained in them. Modes of legal procedure, the Constitution and form of government in Cicero's time, and the whole environment of the orator, are brought into clear view, and made a reality to the student.

The Letters are selected with reference to the light they shed on Cicero as a man rather than as a politician. They afford pleasant glimpses of his private life, and help to make real the pupil's conception of the times in which he lived. As material for short exercises for sight translation or rapid reading they will be found of special value.

A Table of Idioms and Phrases presents in form convenient for use, constructions that deserve special attention.

Lincoln Owen, *Principal of the Rice Training-School, Boston:* Kelsey's Cicero is a model in the art of text-book making. It cannot fail to be a success for editor, publisher, and user. I count the teachers and the pupils of the present generation fortunate in having such admirable "instruments of education" as Professor Kelsey is preparing for us.

Professor J. W. Stearns, *University of Wisconsin:* Kelsey's Cicero commends itself more than any words of mine can commend it. It is a teacher's book, up to modern times, both in text and annotations, and admirably printed.

Miss Ellen F. Snow, *High School, Keene, N.H.:* I have now used it in my classes for five weeks in connection with . . . in the hands of a part of the class. Kelsey has the preference every time. It gives a body to the ideas, and tells the scholars things that they want to know in a way suited to them. I have been waiting long enough to test it, and I like it better every week.

Cæsar's Gallic War

Edited, with Introduction, Notes, Vocabulary, Table of Idioms, and twenty full-page Illustrations, by Professor FRANCIS W. KELSEY, University of Michigan. 12mo, half leather, 506 pages. Price, $1.25.

THROUGHOUT the book every effort has been made, by way of illustration and comment, to render the study of Cæsar attractive and useful, a means of culture as well as of discipline. That the result has been to produce the best-equipped edition of the Gallic War is generally conceded.

The Introduction, besides giving a full review of Cæsar's life and character, furnishes also a concise and logical account of the Roman art of war in Cæsar's time. The Illustrations consist of six full-page colored plates, of a double-page map of Gaul, and of fourteen full-page maps and plans.

The text is clear, accurate, and uniform in its orthography, and is conveniently divided by brief English summaries.

The Notes are apt and sensible, with full references to the Grammars of Bennett, Allen and Greenough, and Harkness.

The Table of Idioms and Phrases, found in no other edition, will enable a teacher to drill his class on those constructions which are most perplexing to beginners.

The Vocabulary, like the Notes, is intended to give the pupil only such help as he needs, and such knowledge as he can digest.

Charles S. Chapin, *Principal High School, Fitchburg, Mass.:* I consider Kelsey's Cæsar, both for teacher and pupil, the most admirable edition in the field, combining in one volume text, notes, dictionary of antiquities, maps, and all the instruments for successful study of the Commentaries.

O. D. Robinson, *Principal High School, Albany, N.Y.:* As a text-book it seems to me if not absolutely perfect, to approach as near perfection as any book I have ever examined. The Introduction and colored plates are invaluable as aids to a clear understanding of the text, and are superior to anything of the kind elsewhere. The maps, notes, vocabulary, and table of idioms, are unsurpassed in any text-book of Cæsar now in use.

Professor H. W. Johnston, *Indiana University:* I have no hesitation in saying that it is the best and handsomest edition of the most important school author that has appeared from the American press.

Cicero's Cato Major (de Senectute) and Laelius (de Amicitia)

With Introduction and Notes by JAMES S. REID. American Edition. Revised by Professor FRANCIS W. KELSEY, University of Michigan. 16mo, cloth. Price, in one volume, $1.20. Separately, 70 cents each.

Cicero's Cato Major

Text only, with indicated quantities. Paper. Price, 25 cents.

Lucretius de Rerum Natura

Books I. to VI. With an Introduction and Notes to Books I., II., and V., by Professor FRANCIS W. KELSEY. 12mo, cloth, 442 pages. Price, $1.75.

THIS Edition gives the text entire for literary reasons ; but the first, third, and fifth books are chosen for comment because they contain the gist of the poet's doctrine and a greater number of fine passages than the others.

Fifty Topics in Roman Antiquities

By Professor FRANCIS W. KELSEY. 12mo, paper, 101 pages. Price, 50 cents.

THESE "Topics with References" are printed for convenience in assigning work in Roman Antiquities to university Latin students.

Outline of Greek and Roman Mythology

By Professor FRANCIS W. KELSEY. 12mo, paper, 40 pages. Price, 20 cents.

THIS is a brief but systematic outline of the Greek and Roman Mythology, with a list of reference books.

Topical Outline of Latin Literature

By Professor FRANCIS W. KELSEY. 12mo, paper, 47 pages. Price, 30 cents.

Selections from Viri Romæ

With Notes, Exercises, and a Vocabulary by Professor JOHN C. ROLFE, University of Michigan. 16mo, cloth, 301 pages. Price, 75 cents.

URBIS ROMÆ VIRI ILLUSTRES is a compilation from Cicero, Livy, Valerius Maximus, and other Roman writers. It is admirably adapted to help the pupil over the difficult transition from the introductory Latin book to Cæsar or Nepos.

The advantage in its use lies in the fact that it is full of variety and interest, and that it gives the pupil a sketch of Roman history from Romulus to Augustus in an attractive form, together with many allusions to the customs of Roman life.

In the present edition the quantities of all the long vowels, including "hidden quantities," are marked; exercises for translation of English into Latin, based on the text, are given.

Thirty-nine pages of the book have been prepared for reading at sight. The other selections are annotated with grammatical and explanatory notes.

Isaac B. Burgess, *The Morgan Park Academy, University of Chicago:* After considerable class-room use, I take pleasure in commending the edition of Viri Romæ by Professor John C. Rolfe. The notes and vocabulary show care and accuracy. The marking of all long vowels is very valuable in elementary work. The hints for translation into Latin admirably cover a good deal of ground in a little space, and the exercises for translation from English into Latin save a teacher much work.

L. C. Hull, *Lawrenceville School, New Jersey:* Rolfe's edition of Viri Romæ is an excellent book; attractive, scholarly, and able to stand the test of class-room use. I have been compelled to let the management of the class that is using the book pass into the hands of another teacher; so that I have missed most of the pleasure that has come from its adoption here. But I can vouch for its excellence.

George H. Browne, *Cambridge, Mass.:* Every time I have looked over Rolfe's Viri Romæ I have admired the aim and method of its editor more and more, and cannot commend too highly the success he seems to me to have attained. After using, I expect to make the same report.

Professor J. H. Dillard, *Tulane University, New Orleans, La.:* It gives in excellent form, with judicious notes and timely suggestions, correct material for easy work in reading Latin. I should like to commend also the careful marking of the long vowels.

The Lives of Cornelius Nepos

With Notes, Exercises, and Vocabulary by Professor JOHN C. ROLFE, University of Michigan. 12mo, cloth, 387 pages. Price, $1.10.

IN general the same plan is followed as in the Selections from Viri Romæ.

In the text, as well as elsewhere throughout the book, the quantity of all the long vowels is marked, including "hidden quantities."

The notes are designed to enable the pupil to understand the writer's meaning, and to get a clear idea of the events and personages referred to. Instruction in syntax is given mainly by the Exercises for Translation into Latin. These exercises have been prepared both for oral and for written work, and are based on the text.

The book is provided with a full vocabulary, in which special attention is given to the definition of proper names, and with maps, including all the places mentioned by Nepos.

Charles C. Ramsay, *Principal of High School, Fall River, Mass.:* It would be difficult to say too much in praise of Professor Rolfe's " The Lives of Cornelius Nepos." The Introduction, Notes, and Vocabulary are unusually well done, and will render the study of the lives interesting and delightful. The publishers, moreover, deserve a share of the praise for the very attractive form in which the book is issued. The typography is clear, and the paper is good.

Walter A. Edwards, *Principal of High School, Rockford, Ill.:* I am delighted with your Rolfe's edition of Nepos, both as to its typographical appearance and as to the educational value of the work. Taking it altogether it is a most attractive text-book. I am not clear in my mind whether we are ready to drop Cæsar yet and turn to some such work as this, which would certainly have the advantage of greater interest, and perhaps a greater practical value. There are some points of value which we should be sorry to lose . . . but I am open to conviction, and Professor Rolfe's book goes a long way toward convincing me.

Professor Leon J. Richardson, *University of California:* As a Latin department we are encouraging the reading of Nepos in the California High Schools. For this purpose your book commends itself very highly.

Professor F. G. Axtell, *Chaffey College, Ontario, Calif.:* The Nepos is the best edition I have seen.

Easy Latin Lessons

By Professor Thomas B. Lindsay, Boston University, and George W. Rollins, Boston Latin School. 12mo, half leather, 382 pages. Price, $1.00.

THIS book aims to present the essentials of Latin Grammar in a clear and simple form. It does not attempt to teach the whole grammar in the first year. The lessons are short and easy, and each is complete in itself. In every instance the exercises consist of complete sentences, not of detached words or phrases. Connected Latin for reading has been introduced as early as possible, and has been continued throughout the book.

The vocabularies are brief, introducing not more than ten new words for each lesson. The Appendix contains a complete view of all the forms of inflection.

The number of words introduced in the lessons besides proper names, is about 900; in the reading exercises 550 more are used. This is believed to be a golden mean between the books that contain only 600 words and those containing more than 2,000.

F. A. Alabaster, *Department of Latin, Nebraska Wesleyan University:* In contrast with the book I had been using for the four years previous to the introduction of Lindsay and Rollins's, I would say one of its strong points is the definiteness in regard to the length of each lesson. Then, too, the very judiciously selected vocabulary in each lesson, which is neither too short to fairly equip the student when the book is mastered, nor too long (a common error), so as to discourage and dishearten him. The selection and arrangement of sentences is also gratifying, illustrating as they do the use of constructions that are constantly introduced. The grammatical introduction is, to my mind, a very fitting and necessary part of a beginning book in Latin, though a departure from the ordinary. It is devoted chiefly to a discussion of the various parts of speech, and forms a connecting link to the student as he passes from the study of English to that of Latin.

Carroll Lewis Maxcy, *Troy Academy, Troy, N.Y.:* My class is doing admirably in the new book. It is a great improvement.

Frank P. Brent, *Onancock Academy, Virginia:* The book is admirably graded, and clearly presents just those things that should be learned by a pupil during the first year in Latin. We are using it with marked success.

Livy, Books I., XXI., and XXII.

With Introduction and Notes by Professor JOHN H. WESTCOTT, College of New Jersey, Princeton. 12mo, cloth, 426 pages. Price, $1.25.

AN attempt has been made in this volume to present in simple and convenient form the assistance needed by young students making their first acquaintance with Livy.

The editor's experience in the class-room has led him to annotate the text copiously. On the other hand, that fulness of illustration which apparently aims to supersede the function of the teacher has been carefully avoided.

Dr. Cecil F. P. Bancroft, *Principal of Phillips Academy, Andover, Mass.:* I have been using Westcott's Livy this term and last, and it seems to me an excellent book.

Professor Charles E. Bennett, *Cornell University, Ithaca, N.Y.:* It seems to me an excellent book. I examined part of the notes, and found them exceedingly fresh and scholarly. They call attention to the right things, and in the right way. This edition is superior to any similar edition with which I am acquainted.

Professor Samuel Hart, *Trinity College, Hartford, Conn.:* I am greatly pleased with Professor Westcott's Livy. It is admirably annotated, and cannot but be of great and real service.

Professor James H. Dillard, *Tulane University, New Orleans, La.:* I should like to say that Westcott's Livy is the most satisfactory text-book that I know of. Other works may put on a greater show of learning; but when one comes to every-day class-room use, the editing of this text is found to be exceptionally satisfactory.

Professor W. B. Owen, *Lafayette College, Easton, Pa.:* I take great pleasure in expressing my gratification. The text is a delight to the eye, and the notes are clear and judicious, well suited to the wants of students at the stage when Livy is usually read.

Professor Edgar J. Shumway, *New Brunswick, N. J.:* The clear yet concise introduction, and full, clearly expressed notes, together with typographic excellence of the book, render the edition one of great value.

Livy, Book I.

Text, with Indicated Quantities, by Professor JOHN C. ROLFE, University of Michigan. 12mo, paper, 82 pages. Price, 25 cents.

Latin Selections

Specimens of the Latin Language and Literature, from the Earliest Times to the End of the Classical Period. Edited by EDMUND H. SMITH ; revised by Professor WILLARD K. CLEMENT, University of Idaho. 12mo, cloth, 446 pages. Price, $1.50.

BEGINNING with the Song of the Arval Brothers, and fragments from the Laws of the Kings and of the Twelve Tables, these Selections illustrate Latin Literature down to the time of Boethius. More than 130 authors are represented, and no name of any reputation is wanting. No such condensed and complete view of Latin literature can be found in any other publication.

The text of this revised edition has everywhere been carefully compared with that of a standard critical edition, and may be considered as authoritative.

Professor Tracy Peck, *Yale College :* The plan seems to me to be carried out with excellent judgment and taste. This work certainly gives, in suc-cinct and attractive form, a clear view of Roman literature throughout its best periods.

Fifty Stories from Aulus Gellius

Edited for reading at sight by Professor JOHN H. WESTCOTT, Col-lege of New Jersey, Princeton. 16mo, paper, 81 pages. Price, 30 cents.

THIS is a collection of interesting stories, which form excel-lent material for sight-reading. The Notes, which are quite full, are at the bottom of the page.

One Hundred and Twenty Epigrams of Martial

Edited by Professor JOHN H. WESTCOTT. 16mo, paper, 81 pages. Price, 30 cents.

THIS selection is intended for rapid reading, or even for sight-reading with students of sufficient ability. For the sake of convenience and rapidity in reading, the notes have been placed on the pages with the text.